YALE
SOPHOMORE

YALE SOPHOMORE

*An Epic Novel
of Youthful Ambition,
Fulfillment and Despair*

Robert Leland Johnson

To order additional copies of this book, contact:
Xlibris Corporation
1-888-795-4274
www.Xlibris.com
Orders@Xlibris.com
17925

FOR

(1). Justin W. Brierly—my college counselor at East High School, Denver, Colorado, and my rainmaker in the practice of law—a boon companion to Jack Kerouac—"Denver D. Doll" in *On the Road*; clerk to Judge Benjamin Barr Lindsey of the Denver Juvenile Court in 1927 when they went to a hill in North Denver and burned all the juvenile court records; psychologist to the Quiz Kids in Hollywood; appointed by Winston Churchill to head the evacuation of the children from London during World War II—a man of energy and imagination who had a vision of the potential of youth.

(2). My paternal ancestors Colonel Edmund Scarborough II (1618-1671) and his seventeen year old Swedish mistress Anne Toft (1643-1687) of Accomack County, Virginia—graduate of Caius College, Cambridge University; physician; lawyer; Commander In Chief of the Shore Militia; Commissioner (justice) of the County Court; Surveyor General of the State of Virginia; Sheriff; Speaker of the House of Burgesses; owner of a fleet of ships docked in Boston Harbor, Massachusetts; operator of a tanning and shoe manufacturing establishment and a salt-making works (from ocean water); planter; land developer; father of Accomack County, Virginia—best remembered for his great wealth and fiery temper, he was called "The Persecutor" by the Quakers and Puritans; "The Conjurer" by the Indians and "King" Scarborough by the denizens, but still managing to be a political gadfly for no taxation without representation in the Northampton Protest of 1652, which he drafted as a Royalist during the Commonwealth. He had three daughters by Anne Toft and built her plantation house on the eastern side of the county and called it Gargaphia (in classical literature the bower where Diana and her nymphs

7

disported). His wife Mary and he lived at his plantation on the western side of the county at Occohannock House (later Hedra Cottage) in Scarborough Neck just above Occohannock Creek, at present-day Davis Wharf. Their elder son Charles Scarborough was one of the nine founding trustees of the College of William and Mary in 1693. His elder brother Sir Charles Scarborough was the private physician to King Charles II (king of England 1660-1685). His younger sister Hannah married Colonel John Wise and their granddaughter Naomi Anderson married Francis Makemie, the father of organized Presbyterianism in America. After his death, Anne Toft (described as a woman of rare charm and power) married Colonel Daniel Jenifer (a Catholic). Their son Daniel of St. Thomas Jenifer's grandson by the same name was a signer (Maryland) of the Federal Constitution in 1787. The Scarborough family and the name are of Viking origin—in 966 A.D. a harelipped, invading Norseman called Thorgils Skardi set up the fort called Skardaborg ("Skardi" means "harelipped" and "borg" mean "fortress") and this became the present-day town of Scarborough, North Yorkshire, England. His grave marker in Scarborough Neck reads: HEREABOUTS LIES EDMUND SCARBOROUGH, 1618-1671, SURVEYOR GENERAL OF VIRGINIA, VA. CONSERV. COM. 1947. DuPuytren's Contracture in the little finger is a genetic characteristic of the descendants of these Norse Vikings and I carry this gene in my right little finger. Indeed, Colonel Edmund Scarborough II is more myself than I am—originally said of Heathcliff by Catherine in *Wuthering Heights*, by Emily Brontë—a lonely copy of which was placed by my mother on the coffee table at home in New Orleans, Louisiana, during the few months before I left to go to Denver, Colorado, to spend the summer with my father—she urged me to read it—I never did until years later as a young lawyer—then I understood why.

ABOUT THE AUTHOR

Robert Leland Johnson has had a long and legendary career in Denver, Colorado, as a trial lawyer, author, lecturer and political gadfly. He was a lecturer for several years in child development at the University of Colorado. He has authored twenty-three books, some of which are: *The Newspaper Accounts of B.F. Wright, Esq., and Others of Louisa County, Iowa; The American Heritage of James Norman Hall—Woodshed Poet of Iowa and Co-author of Mutiny on the Bounty; Super Babies; Super Kids & Their Parents; Trial Handbook for Colorado Torts Lawyers; Matrimonial Practice in Colorado; Mechanic's Liens for Colorado; The Ancestry of Anthony Morris Johnson (Volumes 1-13)*. He is a member of the National Society of the Sons of the American Revolution, having served as Vice-President General and National Trustee; and the National Society of the Sons of American Colonists, having served as National Chancellor. He is a direct descendant of Sir Edward Cooke (Coke) (1551/52—1634)—first Lord Chief Justice of England—best known for his statement "A man's home is his castle" (vide *The Lion and the Throne*, by Elizabeth Drinker Bowen; and *I, Roger Williams*, by Mary Lee Settle). As a member of Parliament his drafting the Petition of Right, which provided for no taxation without representation, set the stage for the American Revolution, for though the provision provided that only Parliament and not the King, could assess taxes, the colonists interpreted this as meaning that there should be no tax in the colonies unless imposed by their legislatures and the word was in reference to any tax imposed by the British: It is against the natural rights of an Englishman, and therefore according to Lord Coke, null and void. Robert Leland Johnson also descends from many early Quakers in Philadelphia, including Arthur Cooke (first Chief Justice of the Provincial Court of Pennsylvania—the Supreme

Court); Anthony Morris, second Chief Justice of same; and John Simcocke, third Chief Justice of same. Arthur Cooke as presiding justice and Anthony Morris sat on the case of Keith, Boss, Bradford and Budd in 1692 in the County Court of Quarter Sessions (the lower criminal court), which held for the first time that issues of both fact and law should be determined by the jury and that truth is a defense. Andrew Hamilton of Philadelphia later used this precedent in the New York trial of Peter Zengler. He shares a common ancestor—Puritan William Tilton (1586/87—1652) of Lynn, Massachusetts, with George Eastman (founder of Eastman Kodak Company; benefactor and founder of the Massachusetts Institute of Technology). A map collage entitled *When MIT was 'Boston Tech'* by Anthony Morris Johnson celebrates this relationship and is housed in the Institute Archives and Special Collections. When he was a student at Yale College, he had no knowledge of his ancestry except that his great-grandfather B. F. Wright, Esq., had been a trial lawyer who gave political and patriotic speeches from tree stumps in Wapello, Iowa—coming as a young hayseed from East High School in Denver, Colorado to this majestic and awe-inspiring school. In later years, as a young trial attorney, it was with a sense of emulation that he read the obituary of B.F. Wright, Esq., in the Wapello Republican, Wapello, Iowa—where he was described by another lawyer as "the keenest and most perfect trial lawyer in Louisa County." This set the alpha male bar high— but it was always the self-confidence and strong ego which Yale inspired that took him over the top. Justin W. Brierly, college counselor at East High School, told him that Yale was looking for a good middle-class boy who would come back to Denver. This is the story of those magnificent days with the same timeless challenges and rewards and pain that every contemporary college student experiences as life renews itself. Pervaded by the energy and imagination of youth, this is where the egg was hatched and his wry sense of humor was born.

PREFACE

There sat in my office until now a manuscript that I wrote while a sophomore student at Yale College in 1952-53—which is now the following saga. It is universal in context in the sense that it examines subjectively the inner feelings and observations of youth trying to find the path to life—timeless in its scope, written by the hand of gifted youth before the frosts of many winters subdued and crushed many a wild ambition common to all. Its exposition is similar to that of Françoise Sagan in *Bonjour Tristesse*—except its milieu is Yale College as a sophomore in 1952-53 rather than on the Mediterranean in the early teens—diary form. It has a beginning but no ending. And one would think that to add an ending would detract from its universality—as it stands anything could have happened after it ends in mid-year—good, bad or indifferent. So it is not my biography. Perhaps the closest thing to an ending is this Preface.

There is no way that I could ever write this again—I do not recognize this youth as my predecessor in life—but I see him in other youth of today with whom I have contact in various capacities.

The events are real, but all names are fictitious. It was originally written with the wild ambition that it would be worthy of publication but has been kept under wraps until now—certainly I would not have wanted my clients to know that I too was young and vulnerable—since they all want and need strength. Now I am semi-retired from the law and no longer will take trial work. But more importantly it has been kept under wraps until I could test it against the backdrop of raising my only son with a clean slate that was devoted only to him. He has had an exciting life—born in Denver to a middle-age well-known trial attorney, he had the environment to be the beneficiary of the enrichment and stimulation that would give him "the good life." He attended the International School in Denver, a Montessori school here, a year in the Black Forest of Germany—all before six years old. And then he went to Cannes, France, for four years where his native language became French. When he went to England to attend Wellesley House (Broadstairs, Kent, England) he had to be given special tuition in English. He was presented by the headmaster of Wellesley House to Winchester College (Kingsgate House)—the most academic secondary school in all England and probably the whole world—where he was accepted and did the traditional five years, completing his A-levels, before matriculating at MIT as a freshman. In June, 2001, he graduated from MIT with a double major in computer science and literature. He has been accepted to enter graduate school at MIT next year in the Media Lab and in the meantime is doing very complicated things that I do not understand in the computer field and making oodles of money inspite of the hit that the tech field has taken within the last year. He speaks with an English accent, currently rooms with a Wellesley grad that he roomed with in Paris when he did some of his junior year at the Sorbonne as she was also doing. This last week he was in Rochester, N. Y., doing something very complicated for NexPress (a Kodak subsidiary) and driving back to Cambridge for the weekends. Like everyone else our lives have been permanently changed since the tragedy of 9/11. That day I arrived in the office about noon and my first call was from my wife in D.C. telling me she was home safely. "And why would you not be home safely?" "Haven't you heard—the Trade Towers are down and we are under attack here?" When I checked her e-mail that was sent three hours before then—it advised me that "We are under attack. If worst comes to worst my will and benefit papers are in my credenza underneath the computer." I am glad I did not see that e-mail when it came in. She is with the FDIC in an office across from the White House—their mail room has been closed and is being checked for anthrax. This is all very chilling but no more chilling than when I was a senior at East High School in Denver, Colorado, and had to register for the draft because of the Korean Conflict that has just broken out. In those days if one took the deferment test and passed it, then one was deferred. Not many passed it, but the problem was that it was taken in September of the freshman year at Yale and one did not get the results for a couple months. So everyone joined the Air Force ROTC. I did pass it for whatever good it did. So the life we faced then is made even more timeless by these recent events.

Justine W. Bierly, my college counselor at East High School, on notification by telegram from Yale of the largest scholarship ever awarded, remarked casually to me: There is something about you—you are different and that is good—remember that anyone who does anything has enemies and those who talk about him, so get ready—you have great expectations! He then added: Always use your full name and when you shake hands do so firmly. Dean Norman S. Buck would later write that I had set an all-round record never before achieved at Yale. This is the story of those timeless events. I have never been able to figure out what it means to be a Yale man. But I know that I am a better person for having gone to Yale. When asked as a student where I went to school, I would answer very softly: Yale.

Probably I should have asked William E. Barrett (author of *Lilies of the Field*) to have reviewed this manuscript when the opportunity presented itself many years ago as I represented him before the IRS on the evaluation of his manuscripts that he had given to Colorado Women's College. He mentioned at the time that his agent was Harold Ober who was also the agent for the writer of *Light in August*—what was his name?—Faulkner. Anyway, they are all dead and that was a long time ago as can judged by the fact that this is no longer a tax deductible type donation. So we move on to a younger generation—energetic and vigorous—with the timelessness of this manuscript from which young men and women universally can draw the strength that will help them to so enjoy, endure and conquer life that "life can be beautiful" will become for them a byword. "La vie n'est qu'une bataille continuelle" and this is one of them—the search to find one's own identity.

Robert Leland Johnson
rlelandjohnson@aol.com
November 1, 2001
Denver, Colorado

From left to right: Bill Hecht (Class of '61; CEO of the MIT Alumni Association), Anthony Morris Johnson, Robert Leland Johnson. Friday afternoon, October 15, 1999. Reception for Parent Connectors in the M.I.T. Faculty Club of the Alfred P. Sloan, Jr. Building (E52), east of Massachusetts Avenue and facing south on Memorial Drive. On Saturday night after Anthony Morris Johnson had driven Robert Leland Johnson to his bed and breakfast at 13 Lopez Street, Cambridge, Massachusetts, the latter (clad in the same attire as in the above photo) walked north up Massachusetts Avenue to Harvard Square, past Harvard Yard to the law school and then crossed over to the west side of Massachusetts Avenue and walked up north to Shepard Street and went west on it just before it hits Garden Street to the Radcliffe Quad (now used as a dormitory for Harvard students). As he walked back east through the Quad on the southern end, a party was going on with music emanating from one of the dorms. There was some milling around on the veranda and two males were sitting on its parapet as one spied him and intoned in a loud, friendly voice: "That man goes to Yale." Robert Leland Johnson did an eyes-right with a pointed finger and extended right arm and exclaimed: "That's very good!

How did you know that?" With Harvard wisdom the young man replied: "I know." So this is what we look like!

Robert Leland Johnson (right) during the summer of 1952 in the mountains of the Massif Central just west of St. Etienne, France, with Riquet DeGaulmyn (left), one of the members of the French family he stayed with under the auspices of The International Experiment in Living. The swimming suit is an official Yale blue issued to him as a member of the Yale Freshman Swimming Team. Coach of the team was Phil Moriarty, also Red Cross Instructor in a life saving class taken by him. Coach Moriarty used to make him do the same practice exercises over and over again when the others taking the course had to do them only once. At the end of the course Coach Moriarty told him he had failed and would have to take it over again next time. Robert Leland Johnson, however, checked the Red Cross records and they not only showed that he passed everything but was in fact rated "excellent" on all items. Later Coach Moriarty told him: "Johnson, you will never do anything unless someone is pushing you." In any event, he turned an untrained swimmer (dog paddle at best) into a fine competitive swimmer of the crawl. This same statement would be echoed three years later by Dean Clifford W. Mills of the Westminister Law School (shortly thereafter merged into the University of Denver College of Law) to him as a freshman: "Johnson, before you graduate you will call me a bastard many times; but some day you will thank me." This summer set the stage for another exciting year at Yale College, including special permission to carry a six course load instead of the traditional five course load. After living in Bingham Hall (Charles W. Bingham Hall) on the Old Campus for the freshman year, now residence changed to Saybrook College, one of the choice residential colleges, where the Master was Basil D. Henning (a history professor and co-author with Thomas C. Mendenhall and Archibald S. Foord of the Department of History of Yale University and with the collaboration of Gordon S. Craig of Princeton University and Leonard Krieger of Yale University, of *THE QUEST FOR A PRINCIPLE AUTHORITY IN EUROPE 1715=PRESENT—Select Problems in Historical Interpretation*, Henry Holt and Company, New York, 1948). Youth was in full bloom. The full flush of youth—with all its ambition, energy and imagination— was pervasive. The words of Harry Combs, president of the Colorado Yale Alumni Association (then owner of Combs Aircraft and later author of *Kill Devil Hill*, a study of the Wright brothers) still sounded: "You are a leader. Do not put yourself forward. They (your classmates) will do it." Yale College Dean of Admissions Donald K. Walker once remarked to him: "It is the man that makes the school, not the school that makes the man."

Then come kiss me, Sweet-and-Twenty,
Youth's a stuff will not endure.
—Shakespeare, Twelfth Night, II, 3

Robert Leland Johnson, disembarking in Montreal, Canada, from the ship Arosa Kulm on which he returned from France in late August, 1952, after spending the summer under the auspices of The International Experiment in Living out of Putney, Vermont (now in Brattleboro, Vermont) in Saint-Etienne, living with the French family DeGaulmyn and ending the trip by touring with the group of American and French students from the several families involved, on bicycle through the Loire Valley, Normandy, and then on to Paris for a few days at a dormitory of the University of Paris (Sorbonne) on the right bank (north of the Seine River) (classes are held on the left bank)—one faces the direction of the flow of the river, which in this case was to the Atlantic Ocean to get the right and left bank correct; carrying his portable typewriter—a staple item, but today it would be a laptop computer—and an

Army surplus backpack. From there, he and a friend Lou Henshaw hitchhiked to Boston, Massachusetts (first trip there ever), and to Amherst College where the friend was an undergraduate, after which Robert Leland Johnson continued to Yale College in New Haven, Connecticut, to begin his sophomore year. The freshman year at Yale had seen him garner many honors: Allis Chalmers Scholarship in first semester (given by an anonymous donor to whom he had to write a letter of thanks for this stipend additional to his regular full room and board scholarship that also carried a stipend for pocket money); Dean's Honor List; second in Advanced French class—though he protested to his college counselor that he had not had French for two years before that in New Orleans, Louisiana, and did not think he could handle it; passed the United States Deferment Test (given nationally to college students for deferment from service in the military during the Korean Conflict— only a small percentage of students passed it); cadet in the U. S. Air Force ROTC; placed in September 1951, in the very select Advanced English Literature class taught by Cleanth Brooks (co-author of *Understanding Poetry* with Robert Penn Warren, who wrote *All the King's Men*); Freshman Swimming Team; French Club (activities included acting in plays, etc.); worked first year in the kitchen at the Yale Freshman Commons (served the salad with Roquefort dressing; after dinner handled the dishes, glasses and silverware that came through the automatic dishwasher loaded by another student Karl Caton Kopp, now a minister of the Christian Science Church in Denver, Colorado, and in spare moments held on to the side of the unit to practice the Charleston); elected to Chi Phi Fraternity; appointed College Aide (a position of honor and trust) to the Master of Saybrook College (duties to commence in September 1952) and also selected as a Saybrook Scholar to study in a small seminar of other residents of high academic achievement in Saybrook (Saybrook College is one of the twelve residential colleges that students are assigned to after having spent the freshman year on the Old Campus). Social activities included trips to Vassar College and Smith College; organized a dating service for Yalies and Vassar girls (now referred to as women); Yale Freshman

Prom with a Mt. Holyoke freshman—unfortunately, the photograph of the two—one in a rented tux and the other in a strapless gown—kept in a scrapbook, mysteriously disappeared ten years later when dating another freshman—now his wife Pamela Gay Johnson, whom he took to the Greek Week Prom at the University of Denver; attended services every Sunday in Battell Chapel on the Old Campus—Norman S. Buck, Dean of Freshman and Master of Branford College, delivered the sermon sometimes; attended activities at another church also and remember square-dancing there; first few weeks as a freshman attended the dances at the local YWCA—the townies (mostly Italian ladies) on one side of the gym would dance with the Yalies, but the ones on the other side of the room would not; learned to do the Viennese Waltz in France. Other activities included participating in the Yale Community Services Project—painting and rehabilitating homes of the economically disadvantaged; worked various odd jobs on referral from the Yale Employment Office—babysitting, janitorial in Yale Divinity School and putting up the graduation bleachers; also worked in Mory's of The Whiffenpoof Song fame (popularized in 1936 by the Yalie crooner Rudy Vallee), making BLT's (bacon, lettuce and tomato sandwiches); sold miniature footballs that played Boola, Boola, a Yale drinking song, and other items for a student organization, going from room to room in the various residential colleges; attended first Broadway play at the Shubert Theatre in New Haven—*Gigi* with Leslie Caron—at the invitation of the Dean of Admissions; saw the movie *A Streetcar Named Desire* with Marlon Brando when visited by father Ira James Johnson in the fall of 1951. If I could give one year of my entire life to enrich the life of a young person, I would select my freshman year and the summer following it. They do not come any better.

A COLLEGE SOPHOMORE
STARTS A DIARY

October 4, 1952 . . . Dear friends, the idea of writing a diary for publication has long possessed me. I do not merely have reference to a chronicle of events as they happen from day to day and are recorded in the college files. But rather the idea has been to incorporate my personal reactions into this so-called chronicle of events, giving the anxieties and the joys that a college student experiences. Perhaps through such a book other college students will be better able to cope with the problems for which I have had no one to guide me. I remember many situations that arose in my freshman year that would have been much easier to solve if there had been some means by which they could have been compared to what had happened to previous freshmen. And to really understand a person's reactions to given situations, it is almost imperative to know something of that person's background. Thus that you may fully appreciate what will follow as this year wears away, let me tell you something of our family history and myself. My name is Alexis Evelyn and I go to Yale.

I am by natural endowment very athletic, but try hard to downplay that because I want to win the game by my intelligence, though the college counselor at East High School in Denver, Colorado, said that they were looking for "brawn, not brain." My eyes are hazel (blue with a sprinkle of brown around the pupil). I am five feet, ten inches tall, ruddy complexion, blond hair and very Nordic looking. My mother is a brunette with brown eyes and an olive complexion, five feet even in height, ninety-five pounds, is called Dolly because of her small size—has a very come-hither look and once had an offer to go into the movies but my grandmother refused to let her because she thought the atmosphere was immoral. Her shortness in height comes from her Presbyterian trial lawyer grandfather who was five feet four and one half inches tall, with auburn hair; and served as a Second Lieutenant in the 19th Iowa Infantry, Company G, during the Civil War (for my mother) or the War Between the States (for my father). My father has dark brown hair, gray eyes, ruddy complexion and stands five feet six inches tall. They all wondered where this big dumb Swede came from—actually, my paternal Irish great-grandmother (Methodist) had Swedish and Norse blood in her veins from a line way back in colonial Virginia. My mother is a mixture of English, French, Irish, Scotch, and Welch. My father is a mixture of English, Irish, Norse and Swedish. My mother was raised a Catholic by her ex-Jesuit—priest stepfather (he owned a chain of meat markets in Denver but lost his shirt during the Great Depression of 1929 after having invested heavily on margin in the stock market). She was excommunicated on her divorce from my father. She is now Episcopalian. I am Methodist, though I was baptized in a Baptist church when I was in New Orleans, because I found in reading Methodist doctrine that it permitted baptism by immersion. So I educated the minister on this point and was baptized by the Methodist minister in a Baptist church. "One must have chaos within to give birth to a dancing star," so wrote Nietzsche. This then is my dancing star.

My family is not one strewn with intellectuals or college people. Neither my father nor my mother had the opportunity to go to college. Neither one of them had finished high school when they were betrothed. Dad was from a small farm in Oklahoma, mother from a poor family of Denver, Colorado. As the oldest son of a typically large farming family, Dad assumed his responsibilities at an early age. As he reached high school age the farm began to demand more time than could be taken from his studies without ill effect. He was finally obliged to quit school and take up full-time work on the farm. In spite of this disappointment, however, he managed to continue his studies in the evening when all the chores were done. He also became interested in physical culture at about the age of sixteen. They did not have enough money to purchase elaborate gymnastic equipment. Instead he had to use two jute sacks filled with sand, which were fastened to each other by means of a bar. With this apparatus he so developed himself over a period of years, that a certain national magazine published his picture in recognition of a perfect and manly physique. This was not the limit of his adolescent development, however, for he began to wax restless and wanted to leave home. Thus when he was seventeen, Dad set out to explore the outside world. Lacking the resignation that it takes for such an undertaking, he soon returned and once again assumed his responsibilities in the family circle. But the family was not happy, and it was not long before his parents were separated. Added to his already overburdened shoulders, were the paternal chores left by his father. At nineteen, the time had finally come to shuck off the family burden and begin to make a place for himself in the world. The young children were now old enough to take care of themselves with the occasional attention of their faithful mother. So with no high school education, no money, and no friends on the outside, Dad went to Denver, Colorado to enlist in the U.S. Army.

He was nineteen on enlisting. Four years later, he was a private with an MOS as a cook—a top-notch chef and a master of his trade. This was when my mother first entered into the picture. Again I must tell you of that horrible cancer that strikes at the family and has as its goal the destruction of the children. This detestable thing is divorce. But it need not be divorce. It can be the breaking up of a home by other means such as infidelity and the resulting murder of the culprit who has broken the nuptial contract. This is what had happened in my mother's family. She had but one brother and had never known her father. There could hardly be a greater blight to a child's emotional stability and essential happiness than a neurotic mother and a perfidious father. Her mother went through years of mental agony trying to compete with a certain strumpet that held the apple of discord over the hearth. All manner of possible attempts had been made to end this unlawful relationship—pleading, begging, crying, arguing, and threatening. But nothing was of any avail. That was until this perfidious man came home one morning fully inebriated and wishing to have a divorce. He charged into the small home that sheltered a wife, a twelve-year-old son, and a newly born daughter. In an imperious voice, he demanded a divorce. When in her great love for this man, she tried to plead; he turned and began to leave the home forever. Heartbroken and temporarily demented in her desire to retain the unloving procreator of this family, my grandmother ran to the front door and fired the revolver that trembled in her agonized hands as he walked down the sidewalk that led to the street. She had gone to the Denver Athletic Club the night before and peeked through the keyhole of the room in which he was staying and saw him with his paramour. He was a railroad conductor. This is what I remember her saying to me. The Denver Post had a somewhat different version. He had been out all night with his paramour and returned in the morning; she would not let him in the locked door and he was in the process of leaving with his back to her as he walked down the front sidewalk to the street, when she fired—all according to The Denver Post account. She wrote poetry (iambic pentameter) and during her recitation to me of these events, recited in her wistful yeoman's fashion, the first stanza of the anonymous poem *Frankie and Johnny*:

> Frankie and Johnny were lovers, O lordy how they could love,
> Swore to be true to each other, true as the stars above;
> He was her man, but he done her wrong.

The young mother was acquitted, thanks to the many friends they gained from the nation as the newspapers spread the story written by Gene Fowler of The Denver Post under the byline of Eugene Fowler. He later became a very famous author. The young son stood bravely on the witness stand and claimed that the revolver went off when he tried to wrest it from his mother who was threatening to kill herself. Finally the young coquette that had introduced this trouble in the first place, rose to the witness stand. While rivulets of repentant tears rolled down her cheeks, the dishonoring confessions that emanated from her mouth filled the courtroom. Silence seized the spectators and pity rolled from their eyes. For days the trial carried on. Judge Benjamin Barr Lindsey of the Denver Juvenile Court was called by the prosecution to rebut the story of the young son, since he had confided the truth to the said judge. But Judge Lindsey refused to testify and was held in contempt. The contempt was appealed eventually to the United States Supreme Court (Lindsey v. People, 66 Colo 343, 181 P 531, 16 ALR 1250, 255 US 560, 41 SCt 321, 65 LEd 785) by Edward P. Costigan, later a United States Senator from Colorado. A "Costigan Democrat" fit within the crusader mould of compassion. The State had no mercy. It waged it case against an innocent as if one of the Capone men were on trial. But public opinion demanded justice. She was acquitted. But the publicity was unthinkable and my mother was kept out of public school until she was nine years old. Upton Sinclair proposed that newsboys all over the country contribute a penny apiece to pay the fine of "the Judge who would not snitch." An anonymous poet wrote in the *Brooklyn Eagle:*

There's loyalty when kids combine
More strong than that of men is;
And boys will pay Ben Lindsey's fine
With fifty thousand pennies.

The judge but scorned the latest sign
Of hatred and of grudges;
And stands erect, although the fine
Is backed by other judges.

He wouldn't "snitch upon a kid"
Whose words were confidential;
His mood is pride in what he did
And never penitential.

All Denver loves a curveless spine;
Hate smothered in her den is;
And boys will pay Ben Lindsey's fine
With fifty thousand pennies.

Acquitted did I say? Yes, she was acquitted. But before the wounds of the trial had begun to heal, she was placed into an infernal hell that no court could equal in punishment. There were two children to support—one was twelve-years old and the other was but a nursling. The lad quit school and the mother went to work making hats—a trade she had learned before marriage. One marriage followed another. There would be times of poverty and times of plenty. God, how I admire that woman!

In the meantime my mother was being raised and her personality was being shaped by these events. Her mother's character had been greatly embittered through the years as the fight to sustain a daughter waxed and waned in difficulty. It is a piteous sight to see my mother as she expounds on the father that is only a phantom. "If he is in heaven he is surely watching me and guiding me. I know that he was a just man." You can just see that empty spot in her heart that an affectionate father should have supplied. But there was no affectionate father to fill it with joy and thus the cause had its effect. She developed into a shy retiring individual, eager to acquire the affection that lacked. My grandmother married an ex-Jesuit priest who owned a string of meat markets in Denver— he liked to take her to the theater to show her off, according to my grandmother. During Prohibition, they had a sideline— bootlegging of wine. In their fancy Park Hill home there was a basement library that had a secret sliding door consisting of book shelves with books and it was here that they stored the wine. Their customers were the elite of Denver—judges, lawyers, doctors, bankers, politicians and businessmen. The authorities raided them and took the bottles of wine. Their lawyer paid the janitor at the old County Jail to pour out the wine and refill with water. When it came to trial, the case had to be dismissed and the headlines in the Denver Post read: WINE TURNS TO WATER. When the stock market crashed in 1929, he had to take bankruptcy because he had invested heavily on margin in the stock market. The only thing that was not in the bankruptcy was a large home in Aurora, just east of Denver, which was in my grandmother's name. She also kept there her big white stallion that she used to ride into

Denver, which drew a lot of attention to this farm girl from Columbus City, Iowa. This house in Aurora is where I was raised for the first six and one-half years of my life, until my grandmother sold it and built the house where she now lives. He and his brother also owned the Loop Market, a landmark of downtown Denver. It occupied a half block and was leased to many individual vendors of different kinds of food. The other half of the block was the site of the Loop, where the streetcars looped around to start their journey again. Morris Rutland, Esq., handled the bankruptcy for him. He was and is now the law partner of my college counselor Justin W. Brierly at East High School—selected as his partner because he was the brightest in the class, so Justin W. Brierly (a Columbia College graduate) has related to me.

To create a life more miserable than it already was, my mother had to be the victim of a mountain automobile accident. For two weeks she lay unconscious at the Denver General Hospital. And as her mother one day was making her way through the crowd to catch a streetcar to the hospital, she fell and had her legs crushed by the streetcar. Soon they were both lying bed by bed. Yes, and it was during the Great Depression. After recovering mother tried to go back to school, where she was head girl, but found she could not follow the studies and lost her dreams of being class valedictorian a few months hence.

In 1932 my parents were married, only a year or so after the above tragedy. The next year I was born. Three years later there followed another son. A private does not make much now. But during depression the situation was even worse. Twenty-seven dollars was what my father received as a monthly allowance. He could have advanced but cherished the idea of some day leaving the Army and entering the law profession. That day never came. Still his officer friends persisted in trying to persuade him to take the examinations necessary to become an officer. But each time he refused. My mother would grow irritable at this attitude and to this day holds it against him. These were the incipient stages of a certain friction that began to develop between them. To give added impetus to this alienation of affection, my grandmother threw more wood on the fire. Through the hardships and deprivations of the years, she had developed a rather resentful and jealous attitude toward those in the world who were happy. Once again mother tried to salvage the situation. But Dad was too obstinate. When Mother pleaded for him to find another place to live, he retorted with the economic argument that a private's pay did not allow for such a move. To that mother riposted with a catechism as to why he did not try to become an officer and thereby be in a position to afford more luxury. The whole argument came to an impasse. Peace would be made again and a semblance of happiness would dominate the demesne for a while. Then all hell would break loose and the fiery battles would commence again, everyone contributing their part as vehemently as the other.

After six and one half years in the home that my grandmother received when her next to last husband went bankrupt, we built a home in the newer part of east Denver. This was when I was six. There was hardly anything in which Dad took more pride than in that house. To design a house, see it built, and then plant the lawn and shrubbery, is to endear it to one's heart forever. This coupled with the pleasant memories that filled his mind of the things done and said there perhaps outweighed the memory that it was also there that his wife divorced him. It was only three years after we had been there that my mother filed for divorce and received her grant when dad was too depressed to even appear before the court.

Well the memories come to my mind of that time during which Mother was amorously involved with a man for whom I hold no respect. He was about five feet six inches tall, wore spectacles, had a long cespitose material that shaded his round pate from the sun. His ruddy diabolic face was brought into focus by two ophthalmitic projections that were rooted half way between the bottom and the top of his head. And from that tainted orifice that hung just below two large nostrils, flowed such seductive words that my mother found herself under his charming inundation. Such naïveté as she evinced was incredible. She believed this lecher as though he were some deity. And if he were, indeed, he could have been no worse than Satan. For about two years before the divorce this courtship

went on. Oh, how I despise that man! How it hurts me to talk of
him.

How would you react if at the age of nine, your mother asks
you if you would like to have another father? It was in a bank,
which I do not now remember, that Mother asked me this question.
We were in line, waiting to cash a check for this man and I
happened to notice his name on the check. It did not seem like a
very significant occurrence at that time. But you see it is. For that
incident, among many other incidents, has stayed with me. I try
to forget them but find it impossible. What could I have said? No
matter what would have been my response, Mother would not
have changed her mind. The next scene that flashes into my mind
as I review this panorama is that of his visits to the house when
Dad was not there. The wheedling and the cajoling that he used
then so contrasted with his later treatment of my brother and
myself. He gave me a baseball at first. Then came other presents,
such as a five-dollar camera.

My mother and this man were married out of state one evening.
They did not tell us about it. But from this time on I began to
develop an intuition that very seldom failed. The new father brought
his adopted child over to the house that evening. The child, or
more properly the boy of ten (one year and three months older
than myself), was the son of one of his sisters by her first marriage.
She had been married twice. The boy, who was later to became my
stepbrother, stayed with us all night while Mother and this
villainous scoundrel trekked off to get married.

In the ensuing weeks, we saw more and more of the boy and
his uncle. He was bigger than I—a little jealous and therefore
rather domineering. To start our relations off on good footing and
to let us know who would be boss, the "man" put us in a boxing
match. Of course, the bigger lad won. That in itself was not too
difficult to endure, since our incipient relations did look like they
would be good. But as we moved to Reno, Nevada, three months
later, the boy was dispatched to his mother in California where he
also had a brother. We lived in Nevada for a few months. Meanwhile
our new brother was sent to live with my grandmother. Though it

is hard to express sympathy between two young lads of the same age, I certainly felt like telling him that he was getting a rotten deal. I was impeded only by the fear that he might not have received my sympathy very well.

It was mortal agony to be forced to move around all the time as I saw my old friends pass into oblivion. New friends were hard to make in the period of only a few months. Finally we made our peripatetic way to Palm Springs, California, where the "man" had a job as PX manager. Mother seemed to think that he was just looking for better positions in moving constantly. The truth is that he was held in mortal fear of my father. And the farther away he could get from Denver, Colorado, the safer he would be. I thank God that Dad had done no mortal harm to him, though there was many an occasion when such an act would have seemed like heavenly bliss. To protect himself from any bodily assault the "man" carried a gas gun with him. While in Denver, there were many nights when he ridiculously and heroically sauntered outside with a monkey wrench to see what the commotion was. He usually found his new Pontiac slightly damaged but never was able to catch anyone. I learned later that several of the soldiers on the base had offered to tar and feather him. And I know that the only thing that kept Dad from wreaking mortal revenge was the horror that filled his mind when the thought of the position such an act would place his children in.

In California, the other brother now joined us. Happy at first he began to pilfer the valuables that lay around the house. Some psychologists try to explain the disease of kleptomania by saying that it is caused by a sex frustration or by a lack of affection. Certainly, this latter was true of him. For in spite of all the high pretensions that Mother made to the contrary, she never did manifest the same affection for him that she did for us. He knew that and felt it to the quick. The initial jealousies developed into everlasting jealousies. Gradually, my new father began to grow more and more resentful of me as he came to distinguish between the affection that Mother showed for me and for the new brother. Also my resemblance to my real father began to be so noticeable that there was not a day that passed when somebody did not make some remark about it. This constant remembrance of my father created more antagonism. The only way that this new guardian could air his distaste for me was in flaying me ten times harder and longer that either of the other two boys. I shall never forget the glass belt he used for these floggings. He would have me remove my trousers and would then commence as if one could bring a child up right by beating him all the time. The livid marks that were left on my body attested to the strength and vigor that he put into these lickings.

One of the most brutal beatings that I ever received was after he had retrieved me from my first attempt to leave home. As a child, I was wont to scratch mosquito bites and other such sores that were present on my body. One night the three of us youngsters had been to a ball game. In the midst of the ball game I began to scratch, being essentially of a nervous temperament, until several of the sores on my face were raw. Knowing that my parents would have no mercy on me for such an act but would both flog me and deny my allowance for a month, I decided to run away. I was about ten years old at this time. It is difficult for a youth to leave home, however, even if he has the determination. The show is still fresh in my mind that was showing at one of the theaters that evening. It told of army life centered around a canteen . . . how appropriate for the first night away from home. Always we had been connected with the Army, no matter whether we were with our true father or with this bastard father. That was the first show that I saw. The next show I did not get to see all the way through, for down the theater aisle pranced old faithful. With a stern and bitter hand he pulled me from my seat, and the movie that incidentally I had been enjoying, and immediately began for home. At home he tried to break my spirit. But there was little more that they could have done to me, so I thought. The flogging process began its mechanical and sadistic cruelty. He wanted to know why I had fled home. The simple answer, of course, was that no one will take a licking if he can avoid it. But the answer was not as clear cut as that. The real reason was more profound. He knew it, too.

He knew the events that had occurred during the last few years which were already beginning to blight my social personality and to diminish my happiness to nil. All he could do now was to beat me and then beat me some more. And he did, until I thought he would never stop. When he did stop it was not through pity but because he was fatigued.

For two years we stayed in Palm Springs, California. Though there was much fun to be had in the swimming pools and playing in the desert, all the joy was taken out of it by the increasing hardships of discipline that were being inaugurated. At one time the discipline became so ridiculous that we were required to use only the back door of the house and to remove our shoes as we entered.

As our stay in Palm Springs reached an end, our parents made renewed efforts to stamp out any trace of my father's influence. They attempted to adopt us. Made us use the new father's name in classrooms to see how it felt to be called by an accountant's name rather than by a sergeant's name. One evening as we rounded the corner in the automobile, the "man" asked if my brother and I would mind calling him daddy. What could we do but concede him the victory? This night always impressed me as a real crisis in my life. And it seems ideally appropriate that we were turning a corner when the question was posed.

From Palm Springs, we went to Tennessee, then to Texas, and finally returned to Denver. The family unity did grow. But it tended in two directions. Mother, my younger brother, and myself formed one clique and the boy and his uncle formed the other clique. But why should I retell all these incidents, for they are nothing but repetition. There was never anything new that happened. The same unhappy events, the same unhappy people, dominated the scene. That is, everything was the same until I attempted to commit suicide (my mother's interpretation—not mine; I was just trying to survive). Of course, it was not a real attempt at suicide but rather a childish strategy to gain the affection of my mother who seemed to be becoming more and more alienated from me as the days passed on. This was probably a fallacious conclusion, but I was in survivor mode, living by my young wits. Nevertheless at that time it seemed real enough. And it served its immediate purpose, which was to keep her from abandoning me to my father in a very unfriendly way. I simply jumped from the moving car from the back right side of the vehicle, head first, to the gravel shoulder as she drove me to his home, cut my chin slightly and she relented. She apparently thought this was the answer to normal teenager moodiness. The whole thing had arisen because on this 4th of July the family was going to go on a picnic and I did not want to go, but wanted to stay home and have my own space and play with the dog. Her "giving me back to my father" was done once again when she did it for the final time in the summer of 1949, and though she begged me to come back, I refused and went out on my own at the age of sixteen years, after spending the summer with my father. But this first event had far reaching consequences that I had not envisioned. Immediately, my father, who had been returned just recently from overseas duty, began court litigation against my mother and her husband. Oddly enough my first reaction was one of resentment when my father attempted this. Before he had gone overseas, he married a very fine young schoolteacher from Indiana. Indeed, she would have been a good mother. But no woman can substitute for a real mother. My impression was that he was trying to excluded Mother from the scene and replace her with this new woman. For this reason and the fact that I could not bear leaving my mother, his litigation failed and he did not gain custody of us children. Shortly afterwards, we left for New Orleans, Louisiana, where we spent two years of even more growing hatred.

With the feeling of loneliness that began to creep over me I craved some kind of affection. We started going to church. Soon I saw the potency of the Christian religion and began at the early age of fifteen to embrace it wholeheartedly. Soon I became rabid about the faith. This lasted for two years. In the meantime conditions at home were growing worse. The stepbrother had run away and joined the Marines and my relations with the rest of the family were anything but harmonious. One time I grew angry at my brother and threw him in the garbage pail. Apparently, my parents did not regard the act as droll as I did, for they summoned the police and attempted to put me in reform school. I thought that was rather insufficient grounds to jail a youngster on. But as has been said before were we not of one mind. Through a certain glibness, I managed to avoid that time the fate which my stepbrother had already been subjected to on account of purloining. The next time I grew angry at my brother, however, the situation grew more tense. He secured a monkey wrench and swore to cudgel my brains to a pulp. And you may be sure that at that moment the idea did not seem as ludicrous as it perhaps does now in the perspective of time. The police were summoned and went through small fisticuffs in order to secure me. However, their big obese bodies glided very gracefully over my back without the slightest ill effect on me. When they realized the futility of the undertaking, they humbly apologized that they could not mal-handle a minor. Even now my heart and soul is saturated with hate for this man who had started this misery only seven years ago. And after the policemen had decamped from the spot of their recent gymnastic workout, I took it upon myself to liberate a tirade against this repugnant stepfather. I accused him of having stolen my mother and having wreaked an unearthly unhappiness on me. His smutty face curled up in a smile and he retained his reticence for a few moments. Then he uttered the words, which, though intended to curse me even further, were actually the starting point of a hard but happy road that has led to one of the best colleges in the country. He ordered me to leave the house and go to my father in Denver. He was generous enough to give me to the end of the school year—two months. During those two months little was said, but his looks reminded me of his instructions: "If you can't get along with your dad, and I wager you wont, don't come back here." In June I left for Denver.

At the station a radiant father met a radiant but mentally saddened boy. Dad had no idea of the melancholy that now possessed me. And I dared not tell him for fear of ruining the summer for both of us. But part of the pressure that resulted in my being there was from his writing the Methodist minister about me, which resulted in a visit to my mother—he never gave up. So I carefully guarded the harsh words that my stepfather had given me, dreading with greater fear than I had ever known the end of the summer. Would I go back home? No, I could not. But the homesickness and the nostalgia that filled my heart was overwhelming. Yet I could not really stay with Dad either, since he had a new family—a new wife and a new daughter. Though they had invited me, I could not make myself come to realize that such an offer was true and that they really did want me. At the end of the summer my attitude changed. I had decided to go out on my own. And no one could stop me. My stepmother pleaded with me to stay with them or go back home. Now that I reflect on her efforts I thank God that my father was fortunate enough to find such an understanding woman for a wife. Despite the invitations something inside me said that happiness would be found only through leaving all this past behind. This has been my objective since that time four years ago when I moved into an apartment in east Denver and secured a job as a laundry attendant.

For two years I studied and worked, trying to open up a new future. My grades rose from very poor to excellent. Finally, when graduation came I found myself with an all-expense-paid scholarship to one of the Ivy League schools. It seems indeed like a dream and as you can see was worked hard for. Those two years were not easy. Sometimes I would stay up till 3:00 in the morning. I saw little of either my father or other relatives who were living in this same city. There were times when I did not even have enough money to pay streetcar fare. My job paid 55¢ an hour. My room and board cost $50.00 a monthly. To aid me Dad gave an additional $25.00 a month. This meant I had to live on perhaps one or two dollars a week. To save money, I employed every possible means. I remember well that it was possible to get to the Denver Public Library on one fare, if one would transfer to a line running perpendicular to the one he was on, ride a block on the other streetcar, get a transfer, and finally return home on the original line.

I hope dear friends that this brief biography has not bored you excessively. Now you should be able to better realize why my reactions are as they are in the experiences and the situations that follow.

October 11, 1952 . . . A week has passed since I last wrote you. It has not been a week replete with resounding events. It was one of those college weeks that just passes, though something did happen that had the potentiality of bringing me a small bonanza. During the Air Force drill periods, which are in session three times a week, there is a small ten minute intermission about 3:00 o'clock. There is no place near the field where the students can obtain beverages. So it occurred to me that if someone were to take the trouble to install a Coke machine in one of the neighboring buildings, he would be very remuneratively rewarded. It was necessary to clear the project through the head of football, since the drilling is done on the football field, the head of the student agencies, and the drilling captain. The three all were of one accord in granting me permission to complete such a project. One of the representatives of the Coke factory was very enthusiastic and offered to aid me in any possible way that he could. There remained only one hurdle to cross. It seemed like a rather insignificant point. I never thought that any opposition to the plan would arise. But when I went to the Army commander, who is in charge of the armory where the coke would have to be stored, he obstinately refused to allow the use of Army space for a monetary investment of a student. He presented the typical martinet attitude. Of course, my expectations were crushed. But there was something more that ebbed up in my heart. It was something that emanated from the feeling one develops for a person or an institution that holds them back or subjugated them. For me perhaps the feeling is an empathetic one. Since the time when my mother first began to inculcate in me the stymied position she thought Dad was in by being a career soldier, my hatred of the Army has grown and grown. Indeed, it has been the Army that has lulled Dad into a state of inertia.

Whatever Mother may say, though, she deserves a goodly portion of the blame for seeking a divorce on the grounds of lack of initiative. At least, that is what she tried to make me believe. In reality, she applied for the divorce on grounds of cruelty to my brother and myself. Dad had not committed adultery. He was a faithful husband, though my grandmother would frequently make false accusations to Mother about him. At one time Dad was accused of giving a certain wench a ride to work every morning. I rather doubt the veracity of that statement, though there is no question that my stepfather gave Mother a ride every morning. Mother would stand on the corner of the block in front of the Hangar Bar. And soon Lothario would drive up in his sybaritic Pontiac to convey the credulous woman to work, where she worked for him in the Post Exchange as an accountant—he had paid her tuition to the Barnes School of Business, where she received this training. He had only gone to the seventh grade—later was admitted to the University of Denver and did his accounting there—and Mother considered his natural gifts incomparable. I considered them great too. But our difference arose as to where his natural gifts were located—in the mind or in the belly where all men's filth, connivance, and desipience originate. He too hated the Army and despised my father, looking down upon his low rank, though Mother once told me that they had been best friends. All the time we were made to feel that our father was not a worthy man because he was a "noncom." Why did not they tell us that the noncoms are the backbone of the Army, Navy and Marines, that they are the foremen in a machine that is large and complicated? Instead they had to disgrace him and instill a feeling of inferiority in us.

Now you can see how I developed a certain distaste for the officers. Their efforts to turn me against Dad, culminated in creating an intense hatred for the ones they were acclaiming. As I said before, though, Dad was a man of officer quality and therefore he drew no small number of his friends from the officer circles. And since his second wife was a college woman (Indiana University at Bloomington), their prestige was to a certain extent bolstered. Nevertheless, in the presence of officers I felt no small sense of inferiority. Among the officers and their children I felt inferior, and yet among the "noncoms" and their children I could not help from feeling a little superior. Indeed, the sense of inferiority more than overbalanced the sense of superiority. It was only natural that I should develop some feelings of superiority in order to make my humble place in life bearable. Between the two feelings, though, there were times of relative stability and happiness. The memories come back very vividly of a year romance that I had with a sergeant's daughter. Her family and mine were very close and had arranged for us to meet during one weekend that was spent with Dad. I was twelve as was she. The first romance that one has is generally a very chivalrous one. And I was no exception. My castles in the air began to multiply. Every sixpence that came my way was used to purchase this girl a few things that might please her.

There was one grand occasion—the first dance that I had ever attended—for which all my money was spent. The item that pleased her the most was the nine dollar orchid, for which I earned the money working as a scrub-boy in my stepfather's office. For one year we enjoyed each other's company. But as young courtships with no base soon flicker out of their own accord, so did ours. It was at this time that the court litigation against my stepfather began as a result of his harsh treatment. As you know from last week, this period commences a state of unhappiness and confusion. Mother used every possible means to explain why I began to grow despondent. She even attributed it to the termination of my petty and insignificant romance with this girl. I often wonder if she was ever cognizant of the real trauma that introduced this suffering of mind and body. It was the divorce. The effects are not felt at once, but as time went on they became apparent. Mother did begin to suffer, though, to see the enmity grow between her and me and my stepfather's family and my father's family. After the court litigation, every act seemed to be motivated by this newly fired vendetta.

The worry caused me to develop extremely painful headaches, which my stepmother claimed as being imaginary. In all my relations with her there have been only two times that she really ran against my grain. This time was one and the other was when she tried to prevent me from leaving home. This she did, I am sure, in good faith and in none of these actions do I think her motivated by selfish reasons. Mother took me to one doctor after another. No one can say that she was not a good mother. But unless a woman is both a good mother and a faithful wife, the goods of one are cancelled by the evils of the other. No doctor could help us. The headaches continued and money was being spent too rapidly to meet the penurious expenditure rules stipulated by my supposedly prosperous stepfather. Finally, Dad arranged for me to see a psychologist for consultation. It was a Saturday that I had the interview. My brother did not go out to the Army base with me that day. The doctor had a small office in which the desk faced in a northern direction. The door was on the south of the room, just opposite an inconspicuous window over the desk. Behind the desk, seated on a swivel chair, sat a middle-aged amiable psychologist. I took a chair to the right of the desk and he pushed out from the desk with the swivel chair in order to create a more friendly atmosphere. We conversed for a good while. He asked my interests and dislikes. The catechism ended and the result was soon relayed to the court against the defendant. The decision had been that I only needed a "little loving." The phrase struck me repugnantly. Soon I began to detest any minute affection that Mother showed. Her kisses before putting us to bed began to more and more lack in any real meaning. To succor this increasing estrangement, my stepfather's rather inappropriate amorousness began to cause me no little social distress. To describe the affectionate embraces that they would go through in front of us children, would put on paper such disgustingly pornographic literature that you, my friends, would shiver in revolt. But why should I not reveal to you all? If this were to be a dainty storybook, it would lose its purpose.

We were generally five in number at the dinner table. After a fairly substantial meal, supplemented by bread if any hunger remained after the main course, Mother would serve her husband some tea or coffee. She would rise from the table, fetch the coffee or tea urn, and return to my stepfather's chair. Standing beside him and pouring the liquid, she would place her arm around this lecher's neck while his boorish hands reached up her dress to strike her buttocks lightly. Perhaps that is the privilege of a married man. But it is certainly unwarranted in public. And what makes it more odious, is that he carried out his concupiscence in the presence of his supposed children. I do not think that the gestures were made consentaneously. Mother had at certain occasions told me of her desire to desist from some of the habits he had taught her, notably drinking.

To enhance the physical reward of marriage, the varsity lecher had the habit of retiring immediately after dinner, removing his clothes, sprawling out on the bed naked, and whiling away the evening with a murder mystery book. If he was not a neurotic there never was one. And to add the culmination to his sybaritic living, there was always a bottle of whisky at his beck and call. To see him lying there, was to remind one of the debauched Roman civilization. They say that the sons and daughters of ministers usually drink heavily and that the sons and daughters of drunkards imbibe very little. Perhaps the first part of this statement does not have so much truth as the latter. In any event, I attribute my repulsiveness for drink to his poor example. There are many ministers who do not consider an occasional drink as a transgression of the divine law or injurious to the health. There have been many great men throughout the ages who have moderately imbibed. So you see I do not condemn liquor as liquor but the use to which it is put in our society. I remember once reading a book of a great German statesman, great in that he made Germany a powerful nation like no man had ever done before, who said that the greatest good he could do for Germany would be to get rid of her alcoholic beverages and smoking luxury. He pointed out the ills such luxuries produced on the acute mind. Indeed, I do not go that far in declaiming against liquor, though a great many ills have been produced in our society merely as the result of drinking. But my hate for drinking goes perhaps even further than intoxicating drinks. It reaches to coffee and tea. Perhaps it is these two drinks that remind me of the amorous gestures which were enacted at our table every night.

Oh, how can I tell you my feelings? How can I make you believe then what I say is the truth? It is bitter to tell you these things, yet sweet to think that there is someone to listen. How can you know the sharp pains that excruciated my heart and every vestige of hope that I had in the human race, when the recollection of their nights of revelry come to my mind. It was one evening in New Orleans at the time of the Mardi Gras. Everyone is gay, drunk and happy-go-lucky. The children stayed home that night. There were several of our relatives who had come to visit us. There was an aunt who as a relict turned to liquor to drown the sorrows of loneliness. There was a cuckold cousin whose wife had been killed in a car mishap with her paramour. They were a merry bunch, if one likes their kind of gaiety. What happened after they left the house is to some extent conjectural. I know that they went to the Vieux Carré, or Old French Quarter, and imbibed heavily. On returning home they crashed a fire hydrant, denting the car due to the physical state that they were in. My stepfather had great difficulty in keeping his equilibrium as his obese structure thudded into the house. I helped him to bed. Then my cousin staggers in, making apologies for their unseemly conduct. My pity for them was extreme. My heart palpitated with unhappiness as I went to bed, trying to keep the tears from rolling down my cheeks. But that was not the end, nor was it the beginning. This same disgraceful deportment had always been and now was even getting worse.

Once again I have gone off on a tirade about deontological obligations, when it was my original intention to tell you of my experiences this summer. I went to Europe with an international organizational which has its offices in the East. It is particularly appropriate to tell you of the trip this week, since I had rather expected a visit from a girl I met on the boat going overseas. The football team of her school came here to play us today and got miserably trounced. The odds were three to one against us, but we came through. I thought that perhaps she might come up for the game, since her last letter mentioned that she expected to see me soon. But it does not look like she will make it today. So we will postpone this little story until next time.

October 12, 1952 . . . Today is Sunday. We were planning to go to church this morning, but my roommate decided to go mountain climbing. So I will use the time to continue my diary.

Last night after I had finished writing to you, two of the students that I had met this summer while in France dropped in to pay a visit. The girl was in my group, and the boy was in another group that went over and returned on the same boat as we. The boy, let us call him Tim, was rather aloof to the rest of us on the boat. Indeed, he is a very brilliant boy. But his intelligence had seemed to intoxicate. And whereas some people are more likeable when they are slightly inebriated, others are repulsing. He was the latter. His conversation was filled to the brim with sesquipedalians that seemed to remind one of a Sherlock Holmes' story. But underneath all this sham, there was something more to him. We found out that this was just a front. That we could not recognize this at first, only showed our lack of human understanding. His history was a tragic one. I do not know it completely. I do know that his mother had died at an inauspicious time; he was but a young child. Through a chain of events he had developed an inferiority complex. He would not admit it but his behavior could not be interpreted any differently. Sometimes he was really hilarious. One of the fellows who had been in his group told me of one event when they were climbing the Alps in Switzerland. Tim and this other fellow had started early that morning, leaving the others to follow. About mid-day they reached Geneva, where Tim had some family friends who ran a hotel. It was a very luxurious hotel, serving only the upper stratum of society. Any break of etiquette there would have been an unbearable insult to the manager. But since Tim knew the hotel manager personally he did not think it necessary to spruce up before calling on him, even if he was just wearing a red bathing suit, a sailor's cap, and a ragged nondescript shirt—plus mountain climbing shoes. He dismounted from the bicycle, rushed into the hotel, and demanded the manager. The clerk at the desk was rather nonplused and shocked, but there was nothing she could do but to call the manager. The manager, feeling no small amount of chagrin and hoping that none of his high-class patrons would spy him, he tactfully, but with great celerity, sped the boy on his way. Tim did receive an invitation to dinner that evening, though.

The girl he was with was in my group. She had been fairly popular with most of the group and was finally chosen to represent the group at an annual meeting, which is held in one of the eastern states each year by the organization that sponsored us. Alison, that is as good a name as any, represents perhaps the typical college girl—rather dignified, though at sometimes very friendly, moderate social drinker, fond of men, and having her share of pulchritude. As most of the girls in our group and the other group with which we had contact, I had the feeling that they were on the voyage more to find a permanent copemate rather than learn a good deal of French. Perhaps they also had the last in mind, but it was definitely in the background. Alison's closest friend, Mae, and I were on very friendly terms at the beginning of the voyage. She had promised to take me back home from Quebec when we returned. But as the summer withered away, I became to realize more and more that our tastes were too different to allow any romance to develop between us. Coupled with this was the fact that I had not made this voyage in order to find a girl friend but rather to learn something of France. It seemed quite clear to me that if I were to have a girl friend in France it should be a French one. As the French say it "J'ai eu de la chance," because right next door to my French family there was a girl of my own age. And though her ideals and tastes were naturally different from mine because of the differences in the two cultures, we did have a very harmonious relationship. After a while I began to avoid any deliberate contact with her, because my French brother had told me he liked her very much. And it was not my desire to cause any antagonism in this family, which showed me so much care and hospitality. As a result the American girls found themselves being pushed into the background by the more romantic splendor attached to having a French girl friend. Mae was good-natured about the situation throughout the whole trip, though she sometimes, actually rather frequently, employed what coy means she could muster to throw consternation into my soul. After having promised to convey me in her car from Quebec to my destination, she apparently forgot about the matter. At least that was the impression she gave me when at the close of the camping trip, we were all discussing plans to return home. By this time she had asked another fellow if he would like to go as far as she was going in the car. Of course, he accepted. When I then asked if there would still be room for me, she made a grimace that was intended to reveal surprise and at the same time admonish me for not paying more attention to her throughout the trip. Finally, we arranged the plans so that I could go with Alison. This did not materialize either though, since she received a telegram on the boat saying that her parents would be unable to drive to Quebec. So the other fellow and I hitchhiked to our destination. What fun we had!

We were both clad in shorts, wore heavy woolen stockings, and carried heavy haversacks on our backs. We were nondescript creatures. Peopled stared at us. At Troy the people even marked our arrival by verbal recognition. The first night we spent on the outskirts of Quebec sleeping "à la belle étoile." The next night we spent in an army base a few miles from Montreal. One of the girls in our group had promised to meet us at Montreal at 3:00 P.M. Saturday afternoon. But we missed our connections and were obliged to return home on foot. We had been mulling that plan over the night before, however, so that the blow was not unhappily received. While the ship was legally scheduled to land in Montreal, those passengers would wished to, could disembark at Quebec. That is why, when we reached Montreal, we were able to bum a gorge from the skipper of this student ship. The crew was extremely hospitable. They filled our pockets with food, which lasted us for another day, and shared liberally what there was on the table for supper. One Italian sailor gave my buddy a whole bottle of wine. We were once again beginning to gain some confidence in the human race.

Did I say we were once again gaining confidence in the human race? I surely do not want you to think that I am a cynic. But the truth was that the summer, in spite of being a very pleasant vacation and education, so brought out the foibles of mankind that our confidence had been somewhat shattered. The instability of the average growing youth, his blindness, his naïvety, his helplessness, and his desire to be a man form a vertigo in which we swim, always trying not to drown but to reach to the shore of maturity. We were swimming in that vertigo. Every one in our group was. We were tired. The situation in Europe helped to deepen this sense of frustration. The signs on the walls proclaimed the Americans as fiends of capitalistic wantonness in trade and morals and as being microbe warmongers. What could we do? In our position there was nothing we could do. We tried to think of some way the State Department might be aided by our suggestions. But the situation seemed impossible. We had come to an impasse. The girls had been neglected throughout the summer and were now desperately trying to arrange themselves dates for the coming year. The boys were tired. They could see little charm in the girls now. Or maybe that was just I. Maybe the other fellows were not in the same mental attitude that I was. But I rather think that they were, even though it might be embarrassing to admit it. The last night on the boat there was a party. I frankly was amazed at the number of boys the girls turned up with. During most of the voyage I had introvertly been engrossed in reading French. The girls had been doing other things. It was an amazing feat. And I just about laughed at them so funny did the situation strike me. The girl leader of our group had worked one of the other male leaders into her cunning trap.

The girl leader, Mary, had been left in charge of the group when the official leader left France a week before us to get back to his job in the States. Mary had been to Europe last year and had been chosen by the central organization to assist our leader, who did not know too much French. She was a very ambitious girl. As a matter of fact, she was too ambitious. She considered herself a born leader. If she had any characteristics of leadership they were hidden through her egotism. At times her remarks would become very cutting. She sowed the seeds of discontent in the group. It is she that I blame for a good portion of a diminishing desire on the part of the girls to really learn French. The boys, with the exception of one who had not studied the language very recently, never flinched but always struggled to gain perfection in the language. And we did make great progress. But this was in spite of the discouragement that Mary inflicted on us. She asked me why I wanted to learn French, doubting the recompense of the efforts. She began to speak in English a good portion of the time. Frequently she would purposely begin to speak in English to me and then abruptly stop and repeat these caustic words, "Oh, I forgot! You don't speak English." The boys began to develop an intense hate for her. As for speaking French she considered herself a linguistic prodigy. And though her accent was very good for an American, her vocabulary was extremely limited for having been in France for two summers. And considering that she was a prodigy . . . Enough said.

You can now see the state of mind that we two found ourselves in when we disembarked at Quebec. From Quebec to Montreal, then to Troy, Amherst, and Boston. After leaving my friend at his college, I then continued the trip until reaching my university. We had by that time gained a real cosmorama through a summer in France and then two weeks in Canada. It was during those two weeks that we realized that the foibles of the human race are balanced by many fortes. The farmer in Massachusetts who took some time off from working to show us the difference between a Holstein and Guernsey and then treated us to a substantial meal. Then there was the French Canadian woman who tried to get us a job in order that we might have the wherewithal to purchase a meal. In Montreal, there was the policeman who bought us a beverage. The Canucks were splendid. We are really fortunate to have such friendly neighbors. The French had been extremely friendly. And no one can deny New England hospitality. Truly, we had gained a new more wholesome outlook on life. Our experiences had taught us to appreciate man and have more compassion for his shortcomings and his self-inflicted misery. That man is such a delicate machine, more complicated than the inventions of science, redounds to the credit and genius of his Creator.

In telling you of the summer, I have passed over the most important part; that is, most important for me. When we were going over, I met a certain bright and beautiful girl through my work on the ship's paper. She had a job with a universally known church organization, interdenominational in scope and with the goal of bringing all Christians closer together. She is the first girl that I have ever met who meets all the qualifications that I think a girl must meet to be a good wife. But she not only had the traits necessary for a good wife, she has the tenderness and understanding necessary for a good mother. She is everything that my mother was not. And then again she has some of the characteristics which Mother had and which should lack in no woman. She is no Babbitt. She has the courage of her convictions, be they religious or be they secular. Yet she has such a pleasing personality, that people cannot help from liking her and admiring her. Her unselfishness is commendable. Yet above this all, she has a maturity that gives her freedom from maudlin sentimentality. What she does, she does because it is right and not because it serves her private needs. Other girls that I have met and supposedly fallen in love with have never been able to give me the sense of confidence that she does. When she is in the company of others I feel no jealousy, for I have confidence in her. I know that if I were to marry her there would be no divorce. If a woman has the fortitude to buck harmful social habits, such as drinking, she is not going to let the fever of the age—divorce—take hold of her. Her unconcernedness, a certain nonchalantness, of whether I was near all the time showed to me much more maturity than can be seen in a good many girls of today. But on the other had she seemed to be glad and happy to be with me. She is the first girl for which I have shown any prolonged affection, and yet not been desperately afflicted with maudlin sentiments that say I must be with her all the time. Perhaps this is just an increased maturity on my part. I rather think it is more that this girl has such an exemplary character that there is no possible way one would withhold from placing confidence in her. I may not marry her, since I have many years ahead of me before such bliss will be possible. If I do not marry her, let God provide me with a girl who has her personality, beauty, kindness, maturity, education, and religious conviction.

The nights were many on the boat that we spent square dancing. There was a French professor and his wife to whom we taught the art. The days were filled with hard work, I working with the newspaper and she working with the official staff for recreation and orientation. But the evenings were filled with permeating laughter, that lingers still in my heart. The evening at Le Havre that I left her, will always remain in my mind. For once in my life, I had met someone who could make me happy. She has written me two times since then, though we have been unable to see each other. If only she would have the patience to wait until I have enough money to support a family, I know that what the world has so far deprived me of would be mine for good—the love and joy of a real family bound by ties of true love and not by mere social conventions.

I was really glad to get that visit from Tim and Alison last night. It brought back pleasant memories.

October 13, 1952 . . . A sense of confusion, a feeling of futility, and a certain desperation of loneliness has been gripping me all day. I have had no scholastic disappointments today. There was a test in English and Air Science, but they were relatively simple. This weekend I finished two compositions that seemed to me to have some merit. But still I sense a certain futility. I want to do something—something that will give me security. When I met the head of the French Department and he approved me to tutor the elementary courses in French, it seemed for a moment that perhaps I would be able to progress. Now only two hours afterwards, I feel despondent and worthless.

The head of the French Department introduced me to a girl from Paris. She is very pretty and has the joviality that the French are known for. When I looked at her the summer flashed before me in vivid forms and I thought of the girl who had given me so much happiness on the boat. I did not think of her because of a striking resemblance to this girl that stood before me but because of the differences. The differences in culture, personality, and language seemed to weigh in favor of the French girl. Alice began to wane in importance. And Marguerite shown forth with romantic luster. Would she like to come to the next big weekend? Would she like to be my friend?

As I walked away from the building, the realization came to me that this charm for Marguerite was only evanescent, that she offered a means to build a wall against Alice. But why build a wall against Alice? What had she done? She had not written me for a month. I have a fear that she will not write me and yet I know she will. But if she does not write then my pride shall be crushed. So to have another human to rely on, I have chosen this French girl who does remind me of a nation that holds my profound love and respect.

It seems that the man who thought himself becoming more mature through his relations with his paragon of femininity, is now losing his stability and vacillating between two decisions— whether to await a letter from Alice or try to create a friendship with Marguerite. I do not want this friendship with Marguerite. I want my love and admiration for Alice to be perpetuated. But if she does not write, what am I to do?

October 14, 1952 . . . This morning I began to feel some chagrin that yesterday should have been filled with so much anxiety. That I disbosomed to you these anxieties, now fills me with chagrin. Will you think that I am so fickle that my dislikes and likes and my happiness and my desolation follow each other with no apparent reason. I hope you will not. But you see that is what this college life is. One day a fellow feels buoyant and gay. The world seems to be for him. Then the next day he finds himself in the deep depths of despair, finding that his happiness was only caducous. The littlest things are sufficient sometimes to throw confusion into the mind. The way your friends greet you can cause agony or joy. Words that are said tactlessly by a friend, though they may be intended to no caustic end, can cause the heart to palpitate with temporary hate and revenge.

As I walked to the history lecture today, one of my best friends greeted me. "Why are you wearing that odd Army sweater on a hot day like this?" His statement cut me to the quick. He had not intended the remark to by unfriendly. But it was untactful. If I had enough money to buy another sweater, there would not be any hesitation. As it is my father gave me the sweater when I left home. Indeed, it has some sentimental attachment. But the feeling of resentment only lasted a few moments and once again he became my friend.

Maybe that is what college is for—to teach people the value of tact and how important tact is to live with one's fellow man. It is always the insignificant things in life that in the end have the greatest significance.

I have to go to work now. After that I will go to drill.

October 15, 1952 . . . In the history lecture today, the professor mentioned St. Godric of Finchale. He was the unwanted son of a poor peasant family living in the latter part of the Middle Ages. At the time when he was born, trade was being revived. The Norsemen were no longer engaged in piracy on western Europe, the barbarians were no longer powerful, and the Crusades had opened up the Moslem lands. When his father ordered him to leave home, the young lad had no choice but to render obedience. As a corody for the initial part of the journey from the home, St. Godric's father gave him some food and relics that could be carried on the back. This was all that the lad had—no friends and no place to go. He had no destination, no purpose in life. But as it happens in life that unforeseen windfalls sometimes bless the afflicted, so it was with this young maverick. As he wandered beside the seashore one day, there appeared the flotsam of a rich merchant ship. He was able to secure the treasure of the ship. From town to town he wandered, seeking men to bind together with him, pool their money, and start a mercantile enterprise. In time he rose from a pauper to one of the richest men of the era.

As the history professor droned on, I lost the drift of the lecture. My mind wandered high above in the clouds of imagery. St. Godric had risen from humble origins to be a man more powerful and wealthier than the nobles that had subjugated him and his ancestry. And he had done this in spite of the curse that his family had thrown upon him through lack of love and sympathy. This escalade had not been affected by wiles or cunning deceit that one so often associates with a businessman. Our civilization knows no similar luck. There are no buccaneers who leave their ships stranded on a coast for some observing individual to light upon. But in their place, sails a mightier vessel that equips the poor, yet ambitious, youth with the mental wherewithal to cope successfully with his more wealthy competitors. There by the seashore, I could see this stately ship coming into land. The sea was wild and tempestuous as the men brought her into the haven, where they saw the bifurcating roads and rivers that led to a golden castle of love, happiness, human sympathy, and integrity. They disembarked, leaving the crew on board to return home to bring more men, and there beside them was St. Godric to help fight their way to this castle. The nobles were obdurate. They would not improve the roads nor withdraw the toll charges. But when a goal is noble and man knows that it is noble, then can no one turn him back.

Once inside the castle, we began to seek wives from the virtuous girls of golden heart that ran to greet us. Our families would not be small. They would be large. There would be so many children that gaiety mingled with righteousness would never cease from our lives. But we would not live in the castle forever. Rather would we return to our homelands to make room for the other shipload of youths who were disembarking. With us our families would go and the love, happiness, human sympathy, and integrity that had been taught us by the tribulations of the voyage.

I immediately woke up when the lecture came to an end and the students scampered out to eat lunch. Then I thought of Alice and a feeling of happiness filled my heart.

October 17, 1952 . . . This year my bursary employment consists of helping the master of my residential college. At the end of the freshman year the students chose a college from among the several that comprise the university. Then those students who are interested in executive work are interviewed. From these applicants are chosen from four to six boys who become college aides in their sophomore year. They do general work, helping the master and his secretary whenever possible during the hours that he is assigned to work. In addition to the office work, we each have several stints as librarians during the week. All of our hours are fixed except for the Friday night shift, which we rotate. Tonight is my night and here I am in the stacks typing away a little letter to you.

Today has been a rather inconstant one. From an apex of unconcernedness and freedom from worry, I was plunged into a nadir of despair by a low mark on an examination in French. There was really no mark on the paper. It just read "AB" for "assez bien" or good enough. That is the lowest mark one can get in this particular class. It came as a devastating shock to my morale, or more properly to my ego. From the accent that I acquired in France and an equivalent fluency for speaking, it never even entered my mind that the professor could give a grade lower than excellent. I guess there was some mistake. So confidant had I been, that my knowledge of the play is reflected by my referring to a certain character in Moliere's play as a woman. The horrible truth is that this woman was a man. The professor did not like that. So this afternoon was spent in aggrandizing my mental wealth of French. I even became so ambitious that the inspiration just about welled up in my mind to indite a short treatise on Racine's "Phèdre." However, the welling-up was just not sufficient to uplift me from this disgusting faineance. So I finished the French assignment and went immediately to an English chore in Chaucer.

I arranged a rendezvous with the French girl that so disturbed me a few days ago. There were apparently no sentimental ebullitions this time. As a matter of fact, the whole situation took on a rather ludicrous aspect as I contemplated whether or not it would be possible to interest her personally in me. We were by ourselves.

And though she was very amiable and willing to help my French, the atmosphere was one of restraint. She was unconsciously manifesting the anxieties that most women of Europe have for young Americans. Perhaps this results from the license in morals that existed both between the American soldiers and these foreign women during the last war. However, my intentions were not based on the same interest that the soldiers showed during the war and she therefore had nothing to worry about. We arranged an appointment for next Monday. She will then try to improve my accent.

A few hours ago, two alumni who graduated from this residential college some decades ago made a visit in the library. They were pleasant men, sentimental for the evening, it being a long time since they had last traversed this beloved campus of ours. I was as much of a stranger to them as anyone, but as they left, one of the men bade me to keep up the good work and not to let him down. He told of how the university had grown and how fortunate we are to have such a fine library as this. I agreed and was also tempted to ask him if they had had any coy French girls to add to the spirit of the college. But it seemed that that might have been a "might bit" disrespectful.

October 18, 1952 . . . This is one of those Gotham weekends when everyone abandons his "fade" school routine and goes out to have one heck of a good time at the football game and afterwards at the college dance. I certainly do wish that Al was not the only one in our room who is having a date this weekend. When the history class was joyously terminated this morning after completing a census on the number of cows that a certain thirteenth century cotter kept, I was tempted to extravagate out of this cloistered habitation for men just as far as Alice's nunnery about one hundred and fifty miles from here. But I was rather hesitant, since she has not written for sometime. That is a habit that our college giglets get into when they have so many beaux that some one of them must be "flushed." Is that the situation with you Alice? Gr, gr! You know that I will have to ask someone else to go to the dance with me, if you do not get on the ball. And there are only two weeks. If you have not written me by the end of next week, there is no telling how long it will be before this pauper will strike a bonanza large enough to paint the town red. So let's get rid of this procrastination, gal, and send me a letter. You may be sure that I will not write you before you answer my last letter. And remember that this missal must be delivered before the fatal day of next Sunday.

As yet my roommates have not been formally introduced. They are Al, Dick, and Tom. We all come from different geographical locations and from equally different social strata. Al is the scion of a rich Texas oil magnate. It is he that is now in the process of furnishing our three room suite with such sybaritic items as a cotton-tufted rug that covers that whole living room floor, and a set of drapes that exquisitely conceal the northern wall of the living room. The hearth is adorned with gold-finished andirons and a screen to match. Our small built-in bar is stocked with all the beverage delicacies and appropriate glasses that one could need. There are probably not too many grogshops in town that have much more of a variety than we do. And all this is derived from that wonderful black gold of the earth; namely, oil. At the other extreme, I form the poor member of our dwelling, though there has never been occasion to feel chagrin over it. Dick and Tom are more of the average students from the financial point of view. Dick comes from an average New England family and has a small scholarship plus bursary employment. Tom's father is working with a photographic company at the present, though he has also done considerable teaching and did some work on the atomic bomb.

You might call us all average fellows and two of us fellahs. We have a fair degree of popularity on the campus, since we are fairly active in several activities such as football, swimming, debating, and religious work. Our social or economic standings do not, in other words, affect to any large extent our popularity or happiness. But there are problems in living that we have to face all the time. These are the most difficult ones that exist in the college life. There is nothing more trying than to live with people. That is the crux of the matter. One must know how to live with people or suffer many continued disappointments and much vexation. Those who do not know the secrets of living with people when first coming to college, generally have them well stamped on their minds after four years. If at the end of his college stint, the student has learned these secrets, his conjugal life should be very successful. There are small things that one learns to ignore and forget. This is particularly an accomplishment for the sensitive individual, since it is much harder for him to forget slights. And believe me, there are many things that happen in our daily living that cause moments of unhappiness, though we four fellows do have a wonderfully harmonious relationship with each other. Do not think that I know all these secrets to happiness. That would be far from the truth, but I am learning them.

The first year of college, the students are thrown together without regard to their religion, race, interests, or personalities. The result is that many incompatible types are put in the same room. This is what happened to me last year. We were three all told. There was a Jewish lad from Connecticut and another fellow of Swedish descent that hailed from Massachusetts. The former was the most harassing and noisome individual that I have ever met. And this was not because he happened to be Jewish. It was simply his disgustingly thirteen-year-old attitude in regard to every thing. He had to be saying something all the time or badgering my other roommate and myself in one way or another. Sam was extremely patient with him, though I was so pressed for time that it was impossible to try to pacify his crotchets. To him one was not able to live and enjoy the goods of life, if he did not imbibe heavily. He, however, was by no means a connoisseur. I even doubt that he could distinguish between Pabst and Blue Ribbon. At nights, he would make it impossible to study in the room because of the idiotic babbling that poured from his labial orifice. He was in constant fear, also, that someone might accuse him of study. I worked with a high school comrade of his, who admitted to me that Steve had to study desperately hard in high school in order to maintain a very meager average. When I mentioned to Steve this friend, his immediate reaction was to ask what I had told him about his college study habits. Of course, my antagonistic reply was that Steve was a grinding bel-esprit that only left his studies to eat and sometimes missed that. This rather deflated his gaseous ego. His taunts were never ending that were directed at me. That my future success depended on what grades were achieved in the freshman year, did not impress him at all. It was his idea that social obligation came before everything else. What happened when his popularity started declining and mine starting increasing, is hard to say. But he had not changed when we parted at the end of last year.

The other roommate was a very amiable person. In many ways such as interests, personalities, and abilities we were practically the same. The only real difference in our culture was that of religion. Sam was a Lutheran and I was a Methodist. And though we had a non-sectarian church on the campus, Sam did not attend too regularly. One could not have any higher religious convictions that he, however. But I was looking for someone who would go to church with me. It was a small thing in spite of the fact that from this one hour a week, I drew much inspiration to strive more earnestly with my studies the ensuing week. That is then one thing that became a secret to happiness. For others who have had much love from their family perhaps there is not as much satisfaction in going to church. To me it supplied the missing attention and I wanted someone to go with me. I did not want to be left alone.

In the latter respect, fortune has been with me this year, since Dick seems to derive just about as much satisfaction from going to church as I do. This is what makes one happy—when another individual can enjoy your company through a deep interest in the same things. My other two roommates of this year, and I expect of the two following years, are not as frequent church goers. But aside from that, our personalities are very similar, though each of us have certain idiosyncrasies. Psychologists say that the sophomore year is the slump in the student's career. I am not too inclined to agree with that, though there seems to be ample evidence that this period is perhaps the most formative socially, intellectually, and morally. That is where our idiosyncrasies are most patent. In our attempt to mature, we manifest different reactions to the same situations and thus show ourselves different in small things.

To help you form an opinion of us, let me give some more specific details of our personalities. We are all essentially introverts, quiet and reticent, but eager to make friends with most of the other students. Al is much more quiet and shy than anyone of us. He is, like Dick, a "fils unique" or an only child. This has undoubtedly influenced his reticence to a great degree. Sometimes he is very friendly and other times he can be bitterly far away from one. In the mornings it is necessary to take heed as to what is said to him, as is probably true to a lesser or greater extent with most people. At other times he is generally very close to one. On the other hand, Tom is always cheerful, even in the morning, and willing to do anything he can to add to a harmonious arrangement between us. He is especially careful to guard Al from any social abuses or slights.

One evening this last week, Dick was studying late in the library while Tom, Al and myself went to eat. We were first seated at a table which one of the college aides wanted to use to sell tickets to the football dance. We obligingly moved to another table, where I proceeded to take a seat opposite Al. Immediately Tom rather unpleasantly barked at me to move out of that chair and let him have it. Of course, my inner reaction was one of resentment. I clammed up that evening and went out to work, decided that the only way to gain happiness is to disregard the wishes and considerations of other humans. There is no doubt that the incident was a petty thing. It might have resulted from something that I had said previously in the evening or even a general disagreeable atmosphere that the humid weather had inspired. However petty it might have been it was sufficient to hurt one who is essentially sensitive. If Tom had realized both the pettiness and needlessness of his action and the hurt that it inflicted, surely he would not have perpetrated it. For surely I was not going to put Al to any social or other chagrin. I liked him and will continue to like him as much as Tom. But to explain the situation, let me tell you how we came together.

Dick and I had met at work and had applied for a room together in one of the residential colleges. At that time, however, there was no available double room. I had known Al through the French Club and took an immediate liking to him. When I learned that he was going to be in the same college with another fellow, I immediately suggested to him that the four of us room together. The idea struck him very favorably; and after talking with Tom, he gave his assent. But there has from that time forward been a tendency for Al and Tom to do things together and for Dick and myself to do things together. This is not good and should be broken down. I think that we are all doing the most we can to break down any tendency to form cliques; though there will always remain some vestiges, since Al and Tom are more of the same economic level and have passionate interests in music and sports cars. Dick is also deeply interested in music (is in the college glee club) and thus provides one means of integration. Al, Tom and myself are on the debating team. This offers another close association.

One problem that has been facing us is the pleasure of Jean Nicot and Bacchus. I do not smoke and neither does Dick. On the other hand, Al and Tom have recently taken up the habit, though to a moderate degree. That does not bother me or Dick, as we are thoroughly tolerant of this pleasure and can see little vice in it. Al and Tom are not what one could dub drinkers, though they have the room stocked with many fine drinks. They drink to a moderate extent, cultivating it more recently because of it appropriateness to the college life. I have definitely decided that drinking is not for me. I have tried it several times, was even a little high once. But the inner feeling of dissatisfaction, which I would have in the morning, rather dictates the incompatibility of drinking with my personality. When I drink my heart has an uneasy feeling and my whole way of thinking seems to be flummoxed for the remaining week. I do not condemn those who can drink without damage to their conscience. Those who I do condemn are the ones who make a disgrace of themselves by consumedly imbibing. Dick seems to be of the same opinion. There is no fear, therefore, that Tom and Al's drinking will cause any estrangement of sentiments. They may even quit altogether, and again they may not. As was said before this is a period of development and growth, so that it is difficult to predict the outcome. I think that we have a pretty good bunch of fellows for roommates, just the same.

That which I have been able to definitely decide is that a marriage to be happy must be the union between two people with almost the identical interests and religious beliefs. When one chooses a wife she should fulfill more than one or two qualifications. This was once told me by a lady from Denver, Colorado, who had never been married, though she had loved a man very dearly. He was a priest and therefore unable to complete her happiness. So she remained a celibate throughout her life. But her words shall not go unheeded. Since she first gave me these gnomic words of wisdom three years ago, I have been able to establish some traits that would be necessary for my wife. For others these same qualifications might not be the same, since we all differ. My wife must have a certain degree of religious devotion, cheerfulness, and intelligence. With these must come similar interests in the various phases of our culture. With these qualifications I think a woman will have a great sense of fidelity and maternal love. If there is anything that I do not want to be is an uxorious husband and neither do I want my wife to be effusively unindividualistic. A woman that it too affectionate can become just as offensive as one who is unfaithful.

This then is what college has taught me. And it is worth more than all the knowledge that shall be stored in my cranium when the class of '55 graduates in two and one-half years.

October 19, 1952 . . . Studies were finished rather early this evening. And as I was about to leave the library, my eyes glanced upon a psychological book treating alcoholism. I picked it up and began to read. For an hour my eyes stayed transfixed on this work, so interesting was it. The several authors had dealt with almost every phase that could be properly comprised in the term alcohol. But there was one chapter that interested me more than the others. It was in reading this chapter that I spent this hour. The title was *Alcoholic Mores in our Society.*

The author explains how that there are six distinct classes in our society. They are: (1) upper-upper, (2) lower-upper, (3) upper-middle, (4) lower-middle, (5) upper-lower, and (6) lower-lower. In pointing out the different drinking customs in these different classes, the authors stresses the difficulty people have in moving from one stratum to the other in light of the unsimilar social drinking habits. The upper-upper class admittedly imbibes more than any other class. The intensity of drinking diminishes to the lower middle class, where hardly any drinking is done. But below this latter class the drinking once more picks up until, in the lower-lower class, natural tendencies are given full license. It is as difficult for the individual moving from the lower-lower to the lower middle to adjust himself as it is for the individual moving from the lower-middle to the upper-middle or lower upper.

I tried to analyze myself. Am I moving from the lower-middle to some higher level and unable to make the necessary drinking adjustment? Can I help it if my conscience rebels against drinking? Oh, how many times have I decided to do light social drinking and then reneged! Is a man supposed to subjugate his mind to agony and confusion in order to conform to the consuetudinary practices of a new social level into which he is ascending? The author of this chapter had a rather cogent argument for light social drinking. If one is to be accepted by a group, he must do as they do and have been doing. If he does not the group will boycott him, refusing both friendship among the adults and among the children. It is hard to rise from one's birth, even in America. But I am determined to do it. And in doing it I shall not become a drunkard. The unhappy experiences that occurred with my mother because of drinking shall not happen in my family.

The author cites the lives of several ecclesiastical personages, among whom are Luther and Christ himself. He says that "The son of man came eating and drinking." And though Luther was by no means a drunkard or debauched man, he would drink. In the *Holy Writ*, Timothy is given permission to take some wine for his stomach's sake. Why the custom of drinking exists, I cannot say. Some say there is a certain lulling of the senses that gives a temporary bliss. Whatever the cause for drinking, man has continued the custom through the ages. When Christ preaches against drinking, does he preach for total abstinence. I seem to be able to see the light now. A feeling of comfort is seeping into my senses. When Christ preached against drinking, he was not preaching for total abstinence but rather against the flagrantly evil use to which some people put it. It is when mothers and fathers lose all restraint and through drunkenness cause their children untold misery, that drinking becomes taboo. When liquor is the cause of divorces and separations and unhappiness, it is then that it is cursed and vile. If men can derive some satisfaction from moderately drinking, then let them.

Now it will be easier for me to do what social drinking is necessary. But it shall never become for me a stumbling block in marriage. I will take a small drink at social functions where it is served, though the memory that it brings of my stepfather shall always bring the bitterest execrations. I will try to conquer this feeling of hatred toward this man who brought so much heartache to a young lad. It will be hard. But never, never, no never, will it interfere with the happiness of my family. And of every opportunity that there is to shun it, I shall fully avail myself.

October 22, 1952 . . . Elections for sophomore positions on the student council were held today. It was difficult to choose, so many students are there in our class who are deserving of the position. It is the first time for many years that I have been able to participate in an election with a sense of responsibility and not a sense of spite. On returning from Europe this summer, our group elected two representatives to attend the annual alumni meetings in northern New England. There were only three boys and one of the selections had to be a boy. My best friend, who had been a source of inspiration throughout the whole trip when my spirits were not too high, suddenly became an enemy in my mind. Though my popularity was during the first part of the trip perhaps more stronger than any one of the other boys, the end of the voyage found me rather cynical toward women, a little anti-social, and therefore not too popular. The other choice was a student from one of the small eastern schools, not particularly brilliant, nor did he possess a sparkling personality. He was of a very mediocre type and at times rather insipidly indifferent from the next individual on the street. His command of French had not been strengthened one iota by a summer in Europe. I did like him, though, not even begrudging him after the election had gone his way. Why it went his way is something interesting to note from the psychological standpoint.

My friend and I had been the dominating figures in the group after our official leader had returned to America about two and one-half weeks before us. The girl who was left in charge, tried to retain as much authority as she could. But it was soon evident that what this fellow or myself said, met with the approval of the group in overriding her decisions. At this time, there were four boys. The other lad was not considered in the elections, since his domicile was too far south to permit a mid-year migration to the north to attend the alumni conference. But neither he nor the other hobbledehoy, of whom I spoke, commanded much authority. And toward the end of the two-week stay in Paris, they each departed for a short visit to friends in other parts of Europe. I do not doubt that by the end of the stay in Paris, the girls were becoming a little irritable over the fact that neither my friend nor myself could arouse any amorous affection for the girls. By this time we had grown rather blasé about escorting six girls through the streets of Paris. I only wish that that same opportunity would present itself on campus one of these times. But that was not a college—in the strict sense at least. By the time that we embarked to sail homeward, everyone was feeling rather exhausted and cynical toward the world. Blame it on the low morale of the Europeans or a culture shock. I think it was both. The two boys who had led the group while in France, began to pay less and less attention to the females whom they had cosseted in a fatherly manner while on the Continent. I stayed in bed reading during the whole return voyage. My friend stayed with his brother for the larger portion of the time, though he did eventually devote more time to the group than I. There were also discussion groups concerning the personal and group reactions that resulted from this uniquely encouraging, enlightening, discouraging, and joyous experience abroad. I did not attend them. Call it intellectual snobbishness if you will. Say that I was aloof. I admit it and do not think that these meetings represented any more than an effort on the part of the girl leader to dominate the group with her unleader-like qualities.

The outcome of the elections represented the result of my somnolent and bibliophilic sloth and unsociableness and also the conflict between my friend and me. When the elections were to be made, it entered my mind that if this friend were to be elected he would have surpassed a stage of equality with me. Our now fairly equal degrees of popularity would be quickly changed in his favor. Thus I voted for the other boy. In the first round I was eliminated—something that was expected, though not received with any small blow to egotistic sensibility. On the second time around, my friend was eliminated. One of the girls was then nominated. The ebullient faces that went into that meeting came out crestfallen, looking more cynical than when we left Europe. Every one had entertained the hopes of being nominated and only two could have been and were. The more diffident and socially shy individuals did not want a more projecting personality to win. And the more projecting personalities, both among the girls and among the boys, did not want a social rival to trounce them. Thus the formerly more popular leaders of the group set up a barrier for themselves and the others added to that barrier such reinforcements as were necessary to take the election from the former. I wonder if my friend voted for me. I rather have a feeling that he did. He was somewhat more mature than I, and it is not probable that he let petty jealousies run away with him. It is generally true that every social group has its own particular group psychology. Ours certainly had a rather perplexing one to surmount.

It is with a sense of indifference that I voted today—not indifference in not esteeming the worth of the election. Rather I felt greatly the significance of the election and the names that were put on the ballots represent students who should be able to do much for the college. I chose them, my friends, in spite of the fact that it would be adding to their prestige and not mine if they were elected. There was a sense of comfort that came over me as the ballots were completed, the sort of feeling one always gets when he knows that he has done a thing well. There were not motives of personal selfishness in the elections. Nor was there carelessness in choosing. The men that I chose had the qualifications of being friendly, conscientious, and all-round men.

It feels good to have friends and not to feel that one has to conspire against them in order to maintain a sense of equality with them. I only wish that my ballot on the boat had gone for my friend rather than for the fellow it did. But in the end, what does it really matter who is chosen to the council or who is chosen to attend an alumni meeting? We cannot all do the same thing; and if one man is more qualified than another to lead people, there is no reason that we should begrudge him, for we are all directly responsible to the same Being.

October 23 . . . Alice has not written me. There does not seem to be much hope that she will write before the game in a few weeks for which I intend to have a date. I could write her again, even though there has been no response to my last missive. But there is no woman who can make me bow that low to her crotchets. No, if we are to have the relationship that I hope for, it is for Alice to write. Until then she will not receive a letter from me.

In spite of the fact that Alice's lack of correspondence is slightly annoying, I still think of her as the ideal girl for me. Now that the situation presents itself more objectively, I can see more clearly that she is the girl for me. When we got back from the Continent the world looked rather uninviting under the dark adumbrations of cynicism that seem to cloak it. The boys and girls of our group were permeated with it and I was not by any means immune to this European malady. Alice was the only one of all the people that entered into our sphere, that had the same interests, likes and dislikes, personality, and moral standards that formed a part of me. There was an immediate recrudescence of hope the instant that she entered my thoughts while we traveled through France. When the world seemed dark and dreary, I thought of her and felt comforted.

Back in the States once again, I wrote her a long dissertation on the trip, explaining the difficulties that had occurred. She might have construed the tone of the letter to be indicative of a very unstable lad and not the popular newspaper editor that was so active on the ship going to Europe. From the summer, this experience and others, have taught me that one must never tell a person his entire inner feelings. If one needs someone to whom he can unburden his heart, he cannot turn to a human being. Man is too feeble to sympathize with another. Or if he does sympathize it is more in the way of disdainfulness. One's friend begins to feel himself superior in that he is not experiencing the same afflictions. But when two people are suffering the same afflictions, if is reasonably safe for the two to exchange their inner emotions. When they have recovered, however, there will begin to grow a sense of distrust between the two. What was once told in confidence to a friend for comfort becomes the driving force that converts friendship into enmity, though the enmity need not be everlasting.

This happened to me this summer. After seeing that the girls in our group were in Europe more to capture a male than to learn foreign customs and languages, I temporary came under the influence of what one might term a "woman neurosis." All women were essentially bad, as I saw it. The image of my mother could not be effaced from a comparison between our haughty and caustic girl assistant leader, who made herself repugnant to everyone in the group at one time or another. The other girls were becoming irritable when the French girls began to wield more charm for the boys than the former could muster. Surely, this was to a certain extent imaginary on their part, for they really did always retain their charm. But were we in France to meet American "filles" or were we there to find out what the foreign teenager is like? As I explained to you before, there arose much bitterness and hard feelings because of these amorous complications, which were really not amorous in the true sense but merely the cliquing together of a boy and a French girl with no intent to proceed beyond that point. If one is familiar with the high sense of morals that the French possess, he will have no trouble in realizing how impossible it would have been to create an undesirable situation, even if the American boys had pondered the thought. Most of us, however, were above such actions. Nevertheless, the American girls waxed wroth and soon the charm of the French girls began to pall. The result was that the boys avoided the girls and vice versa. At the dinner table it was interesting to note how the boys and the girls separated like in a high school lunchroom. For me the idea of developing an amorous attachment to any of these girls, either American or French, seemed impossible, as it was and is and will forever be. There began to develop a feeling of fraternity among us, though, that bound us together more as brother and sisters than as lovers. I determined that none of the girls would experience any sentiments from me that would not be proper for a sister and brother relationship. That was my feeling before going on the boat to return. It was at this time that the girls found a new corody of live and fresh men. But I stood by my resolutions. Even if they did try to create a new social atmosphere that would be the same as the one that existed on the boat that left from New York about three months ago, I would not flinch. This might have been egotistic obstinateness on my part. But my feelings were completely unresponsive to the idea of renewing the conflict of vying for the prettiest girl. I had done that on the last voyage and won, two girls to be exact—Alice and another lassie in our group.

I had told my friend Skip of these sentiments. We was in full accord. He too had developed a great dislike for the girl leader that had at first attempted to conquer him by her coquettishly intellectual and snaring conformism to very loose morals. He could not stand her and neither could I. But we admired and felt proud of the other girls in the group. This was in Paris. We would escort the girls through the streets of Paris—to the Place of Pigalle, to the Opéra, to the Opéra Comique and sundry other places. We made a rather informal agreement that the girls would be to us more as sisters rather than possible lovers. Skip did admit, however, that he had been eyeing Mary and Alison as potential candidates for a nuptial union. But Mary had disqualified herself by creating a very antagonistic atmosphere in the group and Alison had gone out with one of the fellows from the Rouen group. You will remember that Alison and Tim were here to visit me a few weeks ago. But the agreement was apparently not consentaneous.

On the boat my friend let me down. Instead of standing by the agreement, he let himself be paired off with Alison in the course of the last evening that we spent on board together. My adamant stand was to a certain extent rather immature and the fact that he could associate with this girl without really feeling any antagonism showed that he was one stage ahead of me. But can one be blamed if circumstances force him to cynicism? I was bitter. And it was then that this new gnome that I am permeated with, began to take it culminating form. I had confessed all my feelings to this friend and he had deserted me. And in knowing fully all my feelings he had either pity or disdain for me. I did not want pity. The situation certainly did not warrant that. Neither did I want to be despised because the women had temporarily lost their charm for me. If I had not revealed my feelings but kept up a front and consorted with these females on a different basis, then my original popularity would have been continued. But I was tired and it really did not make that much difference. Now I can reflect on the situation and laugh at it, knowing at the same time that it was a good experience in living.

That which comes out of this experience as a potent axiom is confirmed by the reaction of Alice to my last letter which disclosed a good deal of my feelings just after leaving the group. The thing to realize is, though, that these feelings were not just shared by me. They were shared by everyone. There was not one person in the group that was not affected with much emotional confusion. It is a part of the growing-up process and we were all growing up, formulating our ideals and principles. We were suffering from culture shock and were emotionally so entwined in our problems that confusion reigned throughout. I had to have someone to confide in. When I did not attempt to impress the girls during the last night, it was with the hope of seeing the girl for whom I really longed. So Alice received a letter from me, which probably surprised her. She did not know how unstable I was.

It would have been much better if I had used some tact. There was no need to tell all my griefs and complaints about the summer. That way she would have still considered me as a man of great possibility. Not only did I tell her of this emotional difficulty. A certain paper had given me the opportunity to write for it on a speculative basis. They rather doubted that the material that I would be gleaning would do them much good. But they were willing to give me a chance. Alice knew about this. She probably began to think lightly of me, however, when the letter revealed the disheartening fact that my articles had been refused. I told her of these things with the thought in mind that if she only valued me for a social stability and an ability to write, that our relation was founded on sand rather than on the solid rock that I had thought previously. Time will reveal the secret of this. But the lesson that comes from these experiences is simple enough. Do not reveal all your feelings to another, especially if they are feelings of despair and confusion unless that friend to whom you reveal these feelings has been tried over and over again. Even then it is necessary to use tact in telling your sorrows. One of the greatest keys to living is the ability to use tact. Some people cannot and never will be able to, because they do not realize its value and worth. It is only human that people do not esteem an unstable person as highly as a stable person. And surely we are all to a certain extent unstable. We change our ideals and ideas from time to time. One cannot even say that this phenomenon is limited to youngsters, for adults are just as wavering. But the adult has learned to use tact. The youngster has not had enough experience to know its value. Thus in telling our sorrows to others it should always be remembered that tact is the golden key to happiness. The most devoted friend will unconsciously consider you more highly if there is tact in you speech, though he might have been ever so sympathetic to your misery expressed in unminced words of desolation. And for this mankind is not to be condemned.

October 25, 1952 . . . It was one year ago today that I last saw Dad. He came to the campus from Indiana to spend the weekend with me. We went to the football game, saw the movie *A Streetcar Named Desire*, and talked over the events of the short part of the freshman school year that had already passed. It was a lonely weekend for me. One would think that a visit from the family would warm the weekend up to a state of joy. For Dad the weekend was the fulfillment of a dream he had always nurtured—visiting a beloved son in college. Instead of feeling joy, however, I was lonely and empty as we walked up the streets together. Dad appeared to me as a man who has already lived through the prime of his life and is gradually losing his chances for success by the attrition worked by deadly time. The thought was always in my mind that he could have been a colonel instead of a warrant officer. I felt chagrin as we walked up the steps to the freshman refectory. But he was beaming with joy. He was proud of his son and not at all socially shy as we passed senators, generals, and rich business men. It gave my heart a bit of radiance to see this man who had suffered so much proudly marching at the side of a son in whom he had placed so much faith. I felt pity for him. Why one should feel pity is hard to say, for he was not the one whose heart was void and lonely, yearning for some comfort and unable to find it.

The weekend was not unlike the day that I left home in Denver. Dad drove me to the rooming house that I had ferreted out for its economy the previous week. I stepped from the car, taking with me all the lares and penates that had accumulated since many years hence. But in the car, at the wheel, there remained something more prized than all the worldly possession that I shall ever have. Dad did not get out. The event was as painfully unpleasant for him as it was for me. We both tried to maintain fronts that would become us as men. And we succeeded. The parting lacked in effusive sentimentality. We were facing the facts, as bitter as they might have been. With a disguised determination, I picked up my baggage and stiffly bore them to my new abode—a cubicle with a bed and a chiffonier. The door opened into a kitchen that was dimly lighted both day and night. In my room there was not enough space to install a desk or a card table on which I might study. It was in this fuliginous atmosphere that I passed a year before going to the miasmal abode of my grandmother. For this room I paid fifty dollars per week. This included all meals except Sunday breakfast and dinner and weekday lunches. For these collations I had to pay extra. For two unsubstantial sandwiches I paid the menstrual sum of five dollars. On Saturdays I worked at a launderette that was only one block distant from my grandmother's home. She would provide me with the necessary victuals. She was no novice when it came to serving delicate but substantial meals. More than once did I guttle myself on her fine food. But why go on with this history? I have already told you my childhood and hebetic biography. It helps to relieve me of this sense of defeatism and hypochondria, though, to be able to speak to someone about these events that still haunt me. Always these past events are present in my mind. There is no way to escape them. They are as a black steel hand that hovers over my destiny, threatening to crush me. It is against these memories that I constantly fight, trying to forget them and forge ahead to a new life. But it is impossible, for there is always some event or some person that will remind me of some phase of this past life.

So it happened today that the anniversary of my father's last visit to the campus recalled to me the unpleasant recollections of the past and threw me into a miserable state of melancholy. Of course, this is not the sole cause, for the attack has been building up since the middle of the week when I wrote about the elections. As the days drew nearer for the final elections, my hope grew that the student body might even put me on the student council. The hope was not great—no more than every one of us probably entertained. But my name was not in the final elections. It was a small blow but enough to start me thinking how unpleasant I must be to others. But this is just imaginary. We cannot all be on the council and in the final analysis I was not keen on securing the position. To this is added the weekend spirit that usually takes hold when I see the other fellows with dates and wish that my funds would allow such frivolity also. Last night I talked to Pete about having a date for the final football game and even promised to get him a date. But as I was getting ready to retire, the problem of finances began to resound with caustic force. The football tickets would cost four dollars a piece. The dance would cost two dollars and if there would be no extra bedrooms in the master's house from four to six more dollars would have to be added. I just do not have that much money to spend on a weekend engagement. Yet the promise has already been given to secure a date for this friend. And I do so want to have a date.

The question of which girl I should have for this weekend is not even clear. Should it be one of the girls in our group from the summer excursion on the Continent or should it be Alice? If it were to be one of the girls from the group, I should choose Jane, merely from the fact that she is the antithesis of Alice. Apparently, Alice has decided not to attend Columbia this year. Last night I decided to call her after some persuasion from Pete and was told that there is no one by that name listed in the graduate school. Is she not writing me from the fear that my response would be unfavorable on hearing the contrary to what had been expected, or did she perhaps meet someone else on the returning boat that is more compatible? There is an age difference of about three years between us. She graduated last June from Vassar College. This might possibly be building a barrier between us. To me the age significance is nil. But since she is by no means seeped in naïveté, Alice might consider it unwise to continue the relation for my sake. If she upholds this age difference as sufficient grounds to prevent our relationship from developing to the happy state that it could, Alice is wrong. But it is not for me to change her mind. That is for her to do, though the temptation is great to phone her at home. I just do not know what to do. Should I call Alice, write Jane, or completely forget the weekend date?

Dad has invited me to come home for Thanksgiving vacation. It was at first hard to decide what course of action should be taken. I really did not want to go home. To go home seems to be going into the past. How can one go visit his father without thinking of his mother? I know that it will be hard to concentrate on school work after returning from the vacation. The same nostalgia that swept me into tears the night that we parted at the rooming house in Denver, will vanquish my spirit for a few days. My departure from home will be no different than that night in Denver. Neither of us will show emotion. But both of us will have the spirit taken out of our souls as the train departs. And though I will not weep the deluge of tears that covered my pillow that night, nevertheless the mind and soul will temporarily lack substance, being empty and saddened by this inevitable event. That is why I am not extremely anxious to see my father. I fear having to go through the agony of homesickness with which those first few days always abound.

The football team is returning. Dick's folks will be here in a few moments.

October 26, 1952 . . . It is amazing how much influence a girl wields on the college atmosphere. She does not have to be near the college to exert her influence. But what she says in her letters and by long-distance telephone can either create a happiness or a slough of despondence. This is what happened to Dick today. He wants to have a date for the next big football game, but the girl that was to get him a date reneged at the last moment. He has exactly one week in which to get another date. He was so cheerful this morning when we went to church with Pete. He talked of hurrying back to the room after church because this girl was supposed to call at 12:15. There was lightness in his gait and certain jollity in his talk. He talked jestingly of taking an offering so that I would be able to have a date for the big game two weeks hence. Then we walked into the room, picked up the message, and sat down. An unusual reticence took hold of Dick and tears could almost be seen to roll from his eyes. I knew how he felt. Often the same thing had happened to me. For the remainder of the day he remained rather chopfallen and irritable. It was as if all society were against him. Time will put things back in kilter. Tomorrow he will be the jolly roommate that I know most of the time.

Pete has finally persuaded me to write Jane for a date. Over the period of this weekend, I changed my mind half a dozen times. Some moments I would think of Alice and decide to get in contact with her. Then it would come to mind how dangerous such a tactic would be if this is the girl that I want to esteem me as a man always. It is not good to be rash or impetuous in any occasion that I have yet confronted. In the case of a romance it is one way to lose the loved one. People are only human and cannot refrain from thinking that one who is too eager to make friends is either emotionally unbalanced or working to no good end. And to let one's friends have confidence in him, a person must show himself as a stable-minded individual. With this idea in mind, then, I wrote a curt invitation to Jane, who was in the other overseas group that accompanied us on the boat.

Jane is not lacking in pulchritude, though she is sometimes very tactless. Through a lack of tact she presented herself as a quite offensive individual this summer. Some remarks that she make manifested great naiveté. And though I do not think that she meant any harm by some of her observations, some of them were quite embarrassing to the person to whom they were directed. I recall one instance when the group was discussing how the unscrupulous behavior that a certain Parisian ruffian displayed toward one of our young females. His action was apparently directed at sullying this girls honor. The young men in the group, myself and Skip, thwarted his efforts. In relating this anecdote to the other group, I was embarrassed no small bit when Jane replied: "You wanted to keep her for yourself? Ha, ha!" First of all I stopped to ponder what she had said, rather suspecting that my auditory sense had failed me. But sure enough she had said that. The potency of the statement was diminished by the fact that it was so potent. It was hard to believe. This was not the last of her faux pas, though, for she seemed to be incapable of conversing without making some blunder. In all other respects the girl is very sociably agreeable—is pretty, intelligent, happy, and kind-hearted. She had mentioned more that once how good it would be to give some money to this organization that they might send more students to Europe on scholarships. Whether she was merely saying this to increase her prestige is difficult to say. I think she was genuinely sincere, though there is ample space to expect that the statements were not inspired solely from altruistic motives. In one of her naive observations, Jane made it clear that she was on the Continent in order to stalk a mate. This she said in unminced words in front of two other boys and three other girls as we sat in a Latin Quarter cafe. But there was not one in the group that did not have his or her faults. I have no doubt that Jane will develop into a very likeable girl once she has learned the value of tact.

October 27, 1952 . . . Last night before going to bed I promised
Dick to have a date for him from town this weekend. It helped to
cheer him up temporarily. But when I told him that it was up to
him to call the girl and make the arrangements for the date, he
balked. Dick wants me to get the date and then let him call the
girl and make the final arrangements. That would be completely
cogent reasoning if I knew the girl. But I do not. This caused him
more anguish, assuming the attitude that the world is against him.
He should not be condemned for this, though. At least I am not
one to do so, since the occasions have not been few when the same
miasmic despondency has made the world just as dark and bleak
for me. After classes I tried to contact some of the girls whose
names had been given me last year at a Christmas party by my
date and some other girls. The only time that the phone was
answered, the rather unexpected riposte was that the girl was taking
her honeymoon now. They were a little gruff in their interrogation.
I asked for this girl, saying that one of her girl friends had referred
her to me. At this time the phone changed hands and a formal
catechism commenced. I supposed they might have suspected that
one of her former suitors was still contending in spite of the
matrimonial status that had just been assumed. The phone calls
were fruitless, however. This evening will be a more convenient
time to call the girls.

Marguerite was very friendly in our hebdomadal interview
today. We both made a record of our conservation. The atmosphere
was more relaxed than the preceding two weeks and I think that it
will be eventually possible to secure a date with her. While
discussing the trip to Europe this summer, she asked if I was on a
Fulbright Scholarship. My response was no, but I think she has
been deluded into thinking that my age corresponds more closely
to hers than it really does. It will take time to develop our
friendship, though, to a point where it will be safe to ask her for an
engagement without having any fear that in so doing I would
embarrass myself. There must be certainty that she will accept
before the offer is proffered. My French professor is a potential
rival and it is necessary to be rather chary until it is known just

what his relations are with Marguerite. The first composition that I turned in, one on "L'Ecole des Femmes", received only an eighty-three. In the course of last weeks conversation I mentioned that to Marguerite. The next French session the professor expounded for one hour on merits and demerits of our works. He also stressed that since we are not children it is not necessary to give nineties to everyone, looking at me while he said it.

October 28, 1952 . . . There is not too much time left to arrange for the big weekend date with Jane two and one half weeks hence. The hotel managers are already beginning to reply in the negative when asked if they have any rooms left for that Saturday evening. I called two hotels this morning. One of them charges six dollars for the night. That is the best hotel that we have. It is located just across from the Freshman Campus. The other hotel is located near the railroad terminal, and though it is half as cheap, the reputation that it has acquired tends to make one ponder for sometime before getting a room there for his girl. In addition to the hotels, the school has a student rooming agency. Rooms can be obtained very cheaply through this organization, which is operated by students who secure overnight rooms in private home of respectable families. Most of the rooms close to the campus are already taken for this weekend, though there are many still available some distance from the campus if the student has an automobile. Tom thinks that he will be able to use his parents' car that evening. If so, we will probably secure rooms in one of the private homes.

There is something that compels me, though, to think that the hotel by the railroad terminal will be best. Tom says he thinks it will be an insult to get Jane a room there. But why did I ask Jane to come if it was not that she is so totally different than Alice. When one lives in an all male college and does not see a decent girl for weeks or months at a time, he can become extremely frustrated. It happens all the time. Sometimes it suffices to merely dance and talk with a date. That is usually what does happen when we have a date down. But when the girl is not here, there is a compelling passion that burns inside one which says he wants to be alone with that girl. At a private home there would be hours that would have to be respected and we would not really be alone. The hotel across from the campus is too expensive. There is nothing unscrupulous in my intentions and yet there is always that feeling that dictates that this date does not really matter. Am I a man now or not?

October 30, 1952 . . . Jane's reply to my invitation to the football game and dance two and one half weeks hence, came today. She apparently has another date for that weekend but invited me to spend the weekend of the 8th or the 22nd. The reply did not come as a shock since I had waited so long before sending the invitation. For a big weekend it is sometimes necessary to ask the girl months in advance especially if she is very popular. In certain respects her declining the invitation came as a relief and at the same time a very minor disappointment. She is the type of girl that one wants to have for the weekend. She is likeable, pleasant, and no prude. On the other hand this gives me an opportunity to ask Marguerite for a date. At this early stage in our acquaintance, an invitation might be hazardous to our relations. It is quite apparent, though, that Marguerite considers me more than a student whom she tutors once a week. That she inquired to see if I went to Europe on a Fulbright Scholarship indicates that a tangible interest has been aroused. I hope that by inviting her to the football game and the dance that my French professor will not become estranged and thus give me a lower mark than is deserved.

If my banking account were more substantially endowed, it would not be hard to accept Jane's invitation to make a one or two day sojourn to her campus. But the question of money is always recurring. Never is it possible to avoid the issue. Money has been the only thing that has made me hesitant to have a date for this big weekend. Today in the history class we were told that the next reading assignment would deal with the arts of the Middle Ages. The most important cathedral or architectural work that will be studied is that of Chartres. I had a chance to see that edifice while in France but money put a damper on such plans.

During the final days in Paris the group made a trip to Chartres on the funds that remained from the summer expenditure. The trip had already been deferred two days because of a virus that I had contracted. There have been few times when my body has suffered as much as it did from the cachexia that resulted from this attack of the grippe. For three days my head burst with an excruciating pain. Violent pains attacked my dyspeptic intestines.

From my febrile lips emanated groans of misery that seemed to allay the pain. All of our bodies had been weakened by the camping trip. Some had already succumbed. One girl fell on a grating during the latter part of the camp. This was enough with the debilitating effects of the camping trip to cause her to fall into a deep state of despondency. The contusion inflicted by the fall temporarily marred her facial features. If the camping trip had not ended only a few days latter, there is no doubt that she would either had to leave the group or suffer a nervous breakdown. The night that she fell was also the one that the boys of the group contracted a rash which we soon found out was the souvenir that flees leave their victim. When we got to Paris, this girl was ready for a good resting period and everyone in the group was so harassed with flees and so dirty and tired that it is no surprise that our resistance should be lowered to the extent that Paris drinking water could cause us so much distress. I was the first one to get sick in Paris and Jane was the second. Many of the others told me later that they had already suffered such an attack while still in St. Etienne.

When the group went to Chartres without me, it was understood that I should be reimbursed for what they would spend on transportation and viands. This in itself offered a grand temptation to remain in Paris even if I had not been sick, for my coffers were just about empty and there were many things to be bought. This was the chance of a lifetime to purchase real French books. They were all over Paris—chiliads and myriads of selections. And there were presents to be bought for the friends at home. Where was the money to come from? I had no other source of income but that which was earned by my own hands. This auspicious time that the grippe took to seize me, provided some money to execute a small portion of the planned purchases. But if I had had enough money, the places that could have been visited and the cadeaux that could have been bought—enough—why say any more—it makes me burn with fury. Someday, though, I will have this money.

October 30, 1952 ... Two years ago when high school commencement exercises were only a few weeks distant, the school's college counselor offered summer jobs to a limited number of outstanding scholars. The manager of the paint factory in which we were to work was on the Denver Board of Education and through this body had met our college counselor. The pay was to be $1.56 per hour, which was no meager sum compared to the 60¢ that I had been receiving from the work in the launderette. This member of the board had given the college counselors in the various schools a certain number of jobs that they could distribute among the scholars at their own discretion.

During my work at the paint factory I made the acquaintance of a lad from one of the other high schools, who was headed for the same university as I. From the beginning of our relations there began to grow between us a certain enmity. Whether the antagonistic feelings were equally shared by both of us is not easy to say. On my part, though, it involves not a small bit of restraint to refrain from blaspheming this pompous gascon. He thought his wit was superb. In effect, it lack substance. His jests usually consisted of saying something very trite and then ignoring those in whom they were intended to arouse laughter. Maybe I am too harsh—perhaps lacking in his finer sensitivity to subtle jokes. But his were so subtle that I have not yet been able to decipher them. He must have some uncanny ability for drollery. His first joke involved a play on the famous phrase "back to the salt mines."

The members of our prospective college had invited us to an outing of the club one Saturday evening and this in turn was to be followed by square dancing in the historic mining town of Central City. Since Jabe and I worked together it was only natural that we should go to the party ensemble. Working in the factory was not a bonding experience, but it was interesting. There were many of the workers who had been disappointed in life—some reacted with an admiration that one could almost construe as their vicariously achieving what I was about to do—some were resentful and fit into the category of white factory trash, who had learned the hard way that nobody is going to give you anything. In any event this is where we worked. His date was inspired with a lethargy that pinned her to his side and made her laugh in convulsions at his wonderful jokes. It seemed that every word which he uttered, contained some subtle and dry wit in it. But the first time he bypassed the subtle wit was in saying that it would soon be necessary to "go back to the salt mines," as school was to reopen in a few weeks. His girl friend thought this was extremely hilarious. And so did Jabe, though he had his head directed toward the sky the whole time like Darwin's camelopard. I thought that he was perhaps getting some inspiration through this posture. Whether the posture inspired poetic fervor or not, Jabe had definitely become an inveterate stargazer, holding his pate high in disdain of the rest of the humble and sordid world. If he deemed his intelligence sufficient to warrant this haughty attitude, I think his justification was woefully lacking in evidence. If he thought that his scholarship to one of the Ivy League schools entitled him to this disdain of the rest of mankind, the thought apparently escaped this superior being that he had not even seen his college yet, let alone gone through four years of tough grinding. But if his facial pulchritude and brawny physique were his reasons, then maybe Jabe had some cogent reasoning. From the ground to the top of his gaunt figure could be measured six feet and an equal amount of inches. Ah, what form, what graceful manliness. And on this rod that stuck up from the ground, there was a sunflower with a small retroussé pistil nose. He wore a perpetual teenager smirk. From this was the source of the jests that had enthralled the audience that evening. Out of his sunflower face came the words that were to charm the world "back to the salt mines" we must go. Ha, ha! I can boast, though, to never having shown any antagonistic spirit toward him. The thought kept pestering me that it was my personality that induced him to act that way. Later I have been convinced to the contrary, finding that he can be sociable if being sociable offers him some material benefit or enhanced prestige. His father is a fireman, which may account in part for his abrasive personality and obvious need to impress others in superficial ways that are transparent to all and it makes one wonder if he feels out of his element here. He is not a well-integrated person. You cannot make a racehorse out of a mule.

Last night as I stood in the art gallery pondering a map of Carcasonne to determine its strategic importance during the Middle Ages, Jade approached the map with another fellow. Though he stopped right in front of me there was no attempt on his part to give a sign of recognition. I broke the silence with a customary greeting to which he replied with an inaudible guttural sound that was hard to distinguish. Through the whole performance never once did he lower his head in a friendly manner but held it completely aloof from my peasant person. Never have I attempted to antagonize this bombastic and pompous skeleton, but he is always saying or doing something which would serve as a model to any lawyer or debater for curt causticity. I left the room without further attempting to converse with him, though my insides were burning with fire to spite him. My ire mounted and mounted. He knew it, too, for his first remarks to this accompanying friend were directed my way. Jabe observed from the map of Carcasonne that the city plan showed an amphitheater. This would be on the history test, since it was when he took the course last year. Jabe's friend was struck with the profundity of this observation since the map did not have a label over the picture of the amphitheater. "How did you know that?" replied the amazed comrade. Jade turned his head, casting a barely perceptible surreptitious glance in my direction. Then when he was sure that I was nearby and listening, he whispered audibly out of the side of his mouth facing me that he had been there himself. My "adieu" could not have been soon enough, tiring at his increasingly dysfunctional fireman approach to life.

It was not long afterwards when the opportunity came to spite this despicable fiend, for as I repaired to the dormitory another Colorado student came up the street towards me. He inquired if I were going to the cocktail party to be given this Saturday evening. Cocktail party! I certainly had heard nothing of a cocktail party. Apparently my dear friend Jabe had forgotten in his peculiarly crude way to write an invitation. There and then my anger mounted to a climax and I decided that if he were going to have a girl at this party it would be up to me to woo her away from him. I have seen him in action with girls before. From these former observations it does not seem that the task will be too difficult, unless the girl likes subtle and terrifically potent dry wit. God must sprinkle the earth with a few nonentities just to make it challenging.

With this decision to bird-dog this unfriendly snob, also came the conviction that he should be removed, either by overt or subtle means, from his position as secretary of the Colorado Club. Jabe was elected through the maneuvering of one of the senior members who took a liking to him. This member suggested Jabe since he had been at all the club meetings. None of us as members of the freshman class were sure enough of ourselves at that time to publicly nominate another candidate from our own class. The result was that Jabe was elected over a junior whom the student who had nominated Jabe thought should not be elected under the existing circumstances. What the circumstances were I have not yet been able to determine. There is a strong possibility that he had reference to the fact that this other nominee was pursuing an engineering course and would not therefore have enough time to fulfill the office of secretary. Nevertheless Jabe was elected and what a joke he is.

Reflecting on this election brings to mind the one that we held on the boat to choose the two representatives for the annual reunion that the organization that sponsored us holds each year at their office territory in the northeastern part of the States. The psychology of a group tends to always vary according to various factors, such as the personality of the group and the leader, the experiences through which they have been together, and the particular environment in which they find themselves at a given time. I remember well how Skip was eliminated from the election. It is not always the most popular man socially that is elected. On the boat it was a compromise between choosing between Skip and myself. Some of the group had grown tired of our direction while in Paris. And most of the group had grown weary from thinking of how much French I had learned and that I refused to talk English.

In another group, the fact that I had talked English all the time might have served to give me more popularity and consequently the nomination. But our male leader could not speak French very well and instilled a shame in the group for endeavoring to speak it. What good will it do you! Imagine a response like that from the leader of the group—this group was especially in France to learn the French language. Now the experience is passed and I hold no ill feelings toward him. But I know now that time will not repeat the same experience. Every time that I hear one doubt the worth of doing a job, the thought comes to mind "Whatsoever thou doest, do well."

November 1, 1952 . . . A letter came through the mail this morning
from my former employer at the Denver launderette where I worked
while finishing the last two years of high school. They were glad,
he and his wife, to receive the fruitcake from France and would like
to hear from me soon. The old launderette is being surpassed by a
more modern building, which will be solely for the processing of
diapers. They were just developing that phase of the business when
I left to come here to school. It was in the process of reading this
letter that the idea struck me that this same business might be a
potential Golconda in Cuba. What the governmental laws are
controlling foreign enterprise in Cuba, I do not know. The idea
inspired me—gave new belief that there is new adventure for the
young man. From a few pennies these brothers, Jack and Bob, had
made a small mint and were forever bringing in more shekels.
Why can I not do the same thing?

The first thing on the agenda was to write to the President of
Cuba. In the letter I told him of my intentions to study at a
university in Santiago this next summer and at the same time of
my intentions of inducing some American business men to finance
the establishment of a launderette. What his response will be, will
be worth waiting for. The project will probably not materialize.
But if it does then I will be on the road to riches and wealth.

At the same time in a more altruistic vein, I wrote several foreign
service voluntary organizations and the government offering my
services in South America without any charge if they would finance
the expenses incurred through eating and lodging.

The whole afternoon has been spent in writing to these different
people. It was originally to be used in studying so that it would be
possible to attend the Colorado Club cocktail party this evening.
Now it will be necessary to study instead of bird-dogging Jabe—
assuming he has a date—highly unlikely. He has the reputation of
being a faggot, which, however, may be more descriptive than actual.
I do not particularly want to bother him now, anyway. What
difference does it make if he persists in being unfriendly?
Throughout the whole of one's life there are disagreeable people
who must be avoided. And that is the best thing that one can

do—avoid them or give them the cold shoulder, both effective tools of leadership if used properly. It does no good to intentionally spite them. That only increases the existing enmity and makes people think lowly of the one who counterattacks. Life is hard but the struggles once passed seem as balm to the one who has past them. Please do not think that I am doing too much philosophizing. But what I say here has proven true in every case that has confronted me. Something is wrong with him. If a more draconian approach is called for, the "stare treatment" works wonders with this omega wimp type—start at the feet and slowly, blandly, expressionlessly and deliberately move the eyes up the entire body to the head! We will see how it plays out.

November 2, 1952 . . . The question of drinking has been creeping into my mind inchmeal throughout the whole weekend, though there has been no challenge to my customary teetotaler attitude. I had no date this weekend. And generally it is with a girl that the question most often arises: "Shall I drink or not?" Even though I decided after reading a book on alcohol the other week that I would drink at social affairs, it cannot be thought that the problem is resolved that easily. I decided in words but my conscience says a categorical no. Between the time that the resolve to drink was made and the present there has been no occasion at which it could be definitively proven that I would indulge without detriment to my conscience. But this weekend changed things. Dick had a date and so did Al. It was their having a date that tried me inwardly and has made me decide what path to follow the next time that social drinking must be indulged in.

Dick is by no means a crapulous individual. He is a regular churchgoer. But he is also a well-rounded individual. He likes to have a good time, is a healthy extrovert, and has a penchant for girls. However, he is no Beau Brummell or Lothario with the women. He is not extremely handsome, though his personality is one of the most pleasing that I have had the opportunity to know. For friendliness and amiability he is topped by very few of my acquaintances. Yet the ambitious woman is generally not too keen over him. Last night he had a rather reticent snob for a date. She was to me the typical social climber, a regular Babbitt, willing to temporize always to suit the occasion if it is to her advancement. She reminded me of Mother. Every time that I think of drink I think of Mother and her debauched husband. And at the same time I think of Dad, how that he has always been the antithesis of this despicable man. Dad's wife always comes to mind also, how that she has created a happy home for him through her Christian ways. She has never, to my knowledge, indulged excessively. Yet she has provided a spiritual happiness to Dad that he never knew after this other man robbed our home of a mother. Between those two alternatives my decisions are always vacillating. The decision would not be hard to make if I were not afraid that by commencing to drink my tolerance would lead to the excessive and tristful state that was constantly present in my home life with mother and this other man. I do not want my wife to have to undergo the same unhappiness that struck our family, nor will I tolerate having my children go through the mental agony that has thus resulted from the broken home and the excessive drinking. It is the thought of the future mingled with the past that I cannot bear. Wont society let me forget this unhappy past? To be a member of society do I have to revert to the same things that make me want to forget it? I want to be a member of society. I want to be liked by other people. But my character is essentially that of an introvert that has been afraid of the instability of his family from the age of six and cannot bear the thought that the same tragedy will be reenacted in conjugal life after college. This is why Alice has appealed to my ideals. She does not drink, yet she is liked by practically everyone. I do not drink and am not liked by everyone.

Dick took a glass of ginger ale spiked with whisky and gave it to his girl friend. She said thank you in a rather matter-of-fact way. Then he took a glass for himself. It was not spiked, though he had taken one shot of Bourbon earlier during the evening. In bringing the drink to his lips Dick said: "It is just ginger ale." He was apologizing to this girl for drinking too much. Yet only one shot of Bourbon had soothed his throat. He was apologizing to someone to whom it was not necessary to apologize. If there was anyone to whom he should apologize it was himself, for the fact that one shot of Bourbon rested in his stomach charged his conscience with guilt. It was to himself that this verbal apology was directed. I know how he felt. I have felt the same many times heretofore. But he looked so pitifully ridiculous. It was at this moment that the problem of drinking began to once more flare up into a large conflagration after a period of forty-eight hours. Something that bothers the conscience does not begin with a boom. The process is slow and gradual. But when the apogee of this suffering comes there is no consolation. Afterwards, when the problem has been resolved, there are a few moments of sweet bliss.

After studies were finished this evening, I went to visit one of the faculty members of the college who had recommended me to the heads of the overseas organization with which I traveled this summer. With heeling several organizations connected with the school there had not been much time to visit him before tonight. There were several other students who were present when he ushered me into his living room. He paid little attention to me. Was it that I had slighted him in not paying a visit directly when arriving France? Or was it that I had done something wrong? Or maybe someone of the other students had given him an unfavorable report to him of me? Was it that he was beginning to resent the fact that I do not drink? All these possibilities flashed across my mind. After some time, during which he regarded me rather coldly or not at all, the other students left. For about fifteen minutes before the others left I began to gain a little confidence that he really was not angry at me, at all. When I finally quitted his suite and began to distribute circulars, the thought began to cry with haunting inexorableness that my social ability to mix must be increased. It is volubleness that my personality lacks. Some think I am the strong, silent type and that may be true. I do not mean to be antisocial but there is a great lack of confidence that other people have an interest in what I would say. Toward the end of the evening it could be easily seen that this man received me more warmly when he saw that I had enough courage to introduce articles of conversation on my own. When the others left the room then a feeling of naturalness came over me and I could talk with him more at ease as the pictures that were taken in France this summer were flashed before his face. But the impression that followed me the rest of the evening was that there has to be something done to increase my popularity, or rather my amiability. The first answer to this that presented itself was joining a fraternity. They carry considerable influence and I should be able to make it. The second thing that came to my mind was that it would be necessary to work harder in everything, since it is possible that he is disappointed in my extracurricular or scholastic showing. Why he should be, I have not idea. My grades are high and I have been doing some outside things, such as extra work, debating, intramural swimming, and the French Club.

There was no one here when I opened the door on returning from delivering the circulars. My first move was toward the rum bottle. I took one shot, then another. At this time Tom entered the room. I will get drunk. My head did not begin to twirl on the first shot. That is why I went back for another. Soon a sweet and dulcet alleviation swept into my veins to drown this sorrow. Is this then the reason that people drink? I was determined to find out but John came into the room and I was in no mood to make a fool on myself in his presence. Then I began to write. For a little bit my head was cloggy. But soon the headiness wore away.

Dick then entered the room. He said little. But when he did enter the bedroom where I am typing he said: "Hello, handsome." Whenever he is disturbed, or angry, or unhappy he says this. I did not reply. But it did hurt that even he should be antagonistic this evening.

I am going to quit writing for this evening. I am going to have another drink. It soothes these aches.

November 3, 1952 . . . Marguerite accepted to go to the dance with me on the fifteenth of this month. She really seemed happy that I had been thoughtful enough to think of asking her. A big gleaming smile came across her face with the sentence: "Ça me fera plaisir." Once again it seemed that the wheel of destiny turned in my favor, reinstating this pariah dog once more in the social circle of good fellowship.

One of the items to which our conversation turned this morning was the drinking habits of the average Frenchman. It was I who broached the subject and it was she who followed up with a catechism of my personal drinking habits. "I do not like alcohol too much," was her reply. But wine is a different thing. Frenchmen do not consider wine as real alcohol. Most of the wine that is purchased in France does not exceed nine per cent proof. That means that one has to drink a considerable quantity before inebriation comes. In some families that drink a great deal of wine, whisky is taboo. I remember well the first time that this interesting fact came to my attention. Just before the "grand déjeuner" one day, the extreme length of my hair necessitated a visit to the local tonsorial artist. In the course of the conversation we began to discuss the merits of the various wines. Then out of the blue sky he solemnly declared, "I have never touched a drop of whisky. They drink a lot in America, don't they?"

This does not mean that every Frenchmen cringes in shame when someone finds him indulging in a glass of cognac. But they do consider it more vile to constantly drink of whisky, brandy, or bourbon than to drink of wine. Wine carries no stigma with it. It is the culture of the people to drink wine. The location of the country allows for the growth of the vine and they are not willing to pass by its soothing savor for perhaps a glass of milk or water. The most religious families drink wine. Very seldom is it that one will see a member of the peasants, bourgeoisie, or the aristocracy, in an alcoholic stupor. They are a drinking but temperate people. The working class present another side of France, though, for it is often that one will see a worker sitting at a table with his head crumpled over a bottle of wine or sometimes a glass of some more potent substance. But can one blame them after seeing the hard and unpleasant conditions under which they are forced to live?

Our conversation this morning started by a discussion of the drinking among this working class, how that they earned but little and spent that on drink and some food. During the trip from Paris to St. Etienne this summer there was on board a doctor whose destination was Lyon, where he lived and had finished medical school. He, like many doctors, was under the impression that it would be a great blessing to France if drinking could be outlawed for the working classes. Of course, this road is an impractical one and would only lead to bitter discontent in the mainstay of the French nation. But this morning helped to crystallize these ideas. It is the man who carries something to an extreme that causes others to suffer. The human race is so made that it can only subject itself to so much rigorous discipline. If too much discipline is imposed the individual becomes a slave to his own ideals. Likewise if too much freedom is engaged in the soul becomes blasé to the niceties that this freedom should give to one's relaxation. The man then becomes a slave to his own vices, no longer enjoying them.

In France that is what happened to me. I saw this constant drinking and it brought back memories of my stepfather. This wall against drinking began to strengthen. I know that drink was the root of all evil. But that was only a superficially biased analysis of the problem. As the workers, my stepfather had used intoxicants to an excess, to the point where it was causing others unhappiness. And I was causing others unhappiness in opposing most radically a tradition that formed an integral part of their culture. In the two extremes there must be found a happy medium. The worst evil that I know is that of excess, be it religious or secular.

The weekend that Marguerite will have this date with me, will bring to her memories of France. There will be wine from France and we will drink, though not to excess.

November 4, 1952 . . . This Jamaica rum really is not so bad tasting, after all. I mixed a small quantity of it with a cocktail glass of fruit juice. The resulting concoction has a very delectable tang. On election evening those students who do not have too much homework for the following day succumb to the excitement and take a holiday for a party. Our particular school is pro-Eisenhower, which means that the Republican local headquarters will be filled with anxious undergraduates waiting for a victory. As the election results stand now (11:00 P. M.) the Republican candidate is in the lead.

Since the elections more or less cause all other activity to seem rather unimportant for twenty-four hours, it would not have been too practical to try to sell any beer steins or musical footballs this evening. Instead I returned to the dorm after the studies were completed and found Tom seated in the arm chair with his legs sprawled lackadaisically on the hassock and discussing ancient French music with a student who rooms upstairs. Henry is an ardent Eisenhower supporter, who has campaigned for him with a rabid enthusiasm during the past months. They were both waiting to receive the election returns later in the evening. I walked in the room, giving a usual greeting. They responded likewise. But as I put my books down and returned to the living room, I could see that Tom was in an unusual humor. He talked with Henry, paying little attention to me. It was almost as if he were talking to Henry in order to spite me.

Henry is one of those rare individuals who is not socially popular in a crowd of playboys. He has a manner which is at first rather repulsive and unconducive to good harmonious friendship. There is very little that he says that is not accompanied by his proper chorus of puerile laughter. As we have commensally partaken of the evening meals during the past two months it has been Henry who has always supplied incoherent remarks to the conversation about the Republican party. The last time that we were talking about sex, he volunteered the remark of such sententious pertinence to the conversation that the Republican party had founded some unheard of governmental office in 1922. I was rather impatient and offered the scowling remarked of "Oh." With this I turned my head and ignored him.

It is human nature that they change constantly their feelings toward other people, as they also change their ideas and beliefs from time to time. This evening, for some unknown psychological reason, Tom demonstrated a remarkable degree of amiability for this neighboring student and copemate. I tried to break the barrier—maybe it did not exist other than in my mind. I tried to talk of something interesting, first to Tom. But when it was apparent that he was unusually distant, I tried extreme friendliness on Henry to the deliberate exclusion of Tom. Tom would attempt to say something and I would immediately try to say something else more quickly than he. We were both equally culpable of this deliberate antagonism. Then I decided that this temporary barrier of relations must be devastated. Tom does not yet know that I have begun to indulge, though he did see me finishing the dregs of the glass of rum the other night when I wrote to you. It seems to be always an excess that estranges people. We see too much of a person and we begin to become annoyed with him. We see a religious fanatic and we begin to stray from religion. We see a rabid politician and we begin to think that all politicians are venal and prompted either for this or the desire for glory, to work so hard at deceiving and confusing the people. It is always an excess which causes bitterness and resentment, be it religious, intellectual, political, secular or mercantile.

Tom left the room temporarily to ring the 10:00 P.M. bells. Before he had left, though, our other roommate Al had returned from a brief visit to the Republican headquarters. As he began to mingle into the little social gathering, the atmosphere grew less exacting in uneasiness. The other two comrades stood up and walked around a little in the room. Henry brought a magazine over to show me a joke. I laughed, though with great strain, not that the joke was not droll but merely that my mind was not in a particularly jolly frame of mind. I was thinking that Al did not know my new license in indulgence. It would not have been socially advantageous to come right out and say what reasoning had led me to this decision. Instead, I proceeded to the cupboard to fetch a can of grapefruit juice, in the most suave and nonchalant manner that one could conceive. To the glass of grapefruit juice was then added a shot of rum. The mixture was unexpectedly delightful. Immediately, there was an intangible change in the friendliness and warmth of the atmosphere. The tension had been removed simply by yielding a little to the rigidity that I had formerly subjected myself to.

When Tom returned, the same procedure was purposely followed. He was not in the room for more than three minutes, when I expressed an intense desire to have another drink. As the evening ended, I had devoured three glasses of rum diluted with grapefruit juice, but there was no excess as would be shown in a feeling of headiness. And a certain intangible tension had been extricated to the happiness of all.

Evening of November 4, 1952 . . . Tom quit school today. He had said nothing to me or any of the other roommates about such an unexpected decision. This afternoon, though, a letter came special delivery for Al, telling of Tom's decision. Nothing could have been more unexpected. Last night there was nothing mentioned in this regard. My last remarks to him were when I went in the front room to turn down the radio prior to retiring. We joked for a few moments. "Have to turn the radio down, Tom, going to sleep." "Never mind, go in the bedroom and I'll adjust it. Let me know when it is low enough." "We'll get the, oh, what the heck do you call it between the rooms?" "Huh, get the what?" "Oh, you know. What is the musical terminology for establishing something between two objects with the idea of not letting it exceed either one of these objects?" "God, what in the hell are you talking about?" "You know, it's, it's . . . That's it. It's frequency." A warm smile flashed across his face and we said good night.

Here is Tom's letter:

> Dear Al
>
> I am sorry I did not have the power to speak to you personally before I left. So I am writing this letter to you to inform you that I have decided after some time to resign from (quit) school. You don't know how hard it is for me to tell you this. My reasons have sounded sensible to my parents and the Dean, and I hope they will sound sensible to you. It is that I have no right being at college. I have wasted good time and money there by not having an interest and eagerness to get a college education. I guess then that I am not maturely prepared to get that college education. If I continued much longer, I feel sure that I would be suspended sooner or later. I would rather quit now (and the Dean knows it) to get my service in the armed forces over with and then return to school, by which time I should be eager and ready to get a college education.
>
> I'm on the train now for home. I am picking up the

Olds and driving back to New Haven Thursday or Friday. See you then.

Sincerely,

Tom

P.S. Glad to see Ike won!

Al has not been in all evening. He is not studying in the library because I just came from there.

November 5, 1952 . . . The matinal hours found me in a pessimistic reaction to the whole world. No matter what entered my mind, there was no ease for this confusion and mental harassment. Last night I had tried to the utmost to create a warm atmosphere among my roommates, Henry, and myself. Every time that Tom's initial frigidity as I walked into the room, comes to mind there arises this enervating mental antagonism toward him. I had tried everything. And though the tension of the evening had to some degree been reduced by my drinking some rum, this remembrance of his original attitude could not escape me.

In the Air Science class, I paid little attention to the lecture. The lecture was lost to my hypochondriac ponderings. My heart did not cease to palpitate unnaturally. Alice came into the mental vista of perplexity. She has not written since I unburden my reactions to the summer abroad. From the letter it was easy to see that the girls in the group had caused me no little inner anguish. Maybe she could see a social misfit or just an immature lad who was striving for maturity and at that time had not yet attained it. Maybe she is waiting until I can gain a socially solid equilibrium. But in my thoughts there was something that said that her action was not unique. Is there something in my personality that causes people to lose respect after they have known me for a while? Is everybody else so well balanced that they scorn my confusion? With these thoughts other images flashed across the vista—my stepfather banishing me from his home, my running away from Dad because of a feeling of insecurity, my difficulty with the group this summer, my unpleasant relations with grandmother, the coldness that the professor showed the other night amidst other students.

At the end of the lecture those darting and excruciating thoughts had so pierced my mind that there was nothing left to attack. I began to think of the fables of Fontaine, especially the one about the miller, his son, and an ass. We cannot hope to satisfy the whims and desires of all the world. What if these people had turned against me? Maybe they had not. For a few moments my heart grew cynical. The world is impossible. What can man do to be happy? Whatever he does there is some one or some event that wreaks devastation on his bliss.

There were two letters waiting in the mail box after classes. One was from the Department of State, saying that there was no vacancy for the type of overseas work that had been requested this last week. The other was from my stepmother, with an appendage from Dad. They still want me to come home for Thanksgiving.

November 6, 1952 . . . There has been a noticeable change in the relationship between the roommates that Tom had left behind. Some of these changes are for the better, while others could be dispensed with and not missed.

Al was very friendly this morning. Usually one has to be careful what is said to him if a rather cold reply, or none at all, is not wanted to start the day. However, this change is not something that Tom's departure wrought over night. It is something that has been developing as we begin to know each other better than we did when unusual circumstances found us rooming together. When the freshman office sent out applications for rooms at the end of last year, I had no idea that any of the present roommates would be together with me. True I had known Dick through our bursary work at the refectory, but rooming with him had never entered my mind until two days before the applications were due. Other students had asked me to room with them but at that time my mind was not made up. I thought that there would be ample time to consider such a problem later in the year. The time arrived and though many friends had been made, I had not made any final arrangements to room with someone for this year. Sam had already chosen other roommates and it would have been unbearable to have been subjected to the juvenility of my other roommate Steve, though I did asked him at the last moment when it was clear that there was not much time to get into a room with someone. That evening at the supper table Dick began to talk about the situation, how that he had also neglected to ask someone to room with him. Immediately, I took advantage of the opportunity and asked him, knowing that he was not a boisterous and childish individual like Steve. However, I must admit there were some wonders in my mind as to how compatible we would actually be, for by this time the unfortunate experiences that had been undergone in living with people was beginning to blight my outlook on life and make me think that no one wanted to live with this confused personality tossed by many ideas.

We applied for a double but they were drawn by the luckier ones, or maybe the less fortunate ones. We began to worry. Who should we ask to room with us in the residential college? The problem soon resolved itself, for we met Tom and Al at one of the master's cocktail parties for freshmen. I had met Al once before through the French Club and had immediately taken a liking to him. Tom I did not know previously. Before the party was over the matter had been settled. We would all room together next year in a quadruple.

The remaining part of that year left me very skeptical as to the wisdom of this decision, for both Tom and Al manifested an unfriendly coldness toward me in the few times that we did see each other before that semester drew to a close. One time during examinations I remember meeting them in a nearby store. Their greeting was not the kind that kindles inspiration; and when in that same conversation they learned that I was going to Europe, it seemed like winter in the springtime. We are planning to do that next year. Oh, did you know Al has already been there. Never a smile. Things looked very bleak, even for someone who was going to have the chance of a lifetime in a few days. Even France could not brighten the situation then. But these troubles were soon forgotten and the summer was enjoyed.

During the early days of our living together Tom and Al were inseparable and formed a small clique in the room. Dick and I did likewise. We each put forth great effort to make the other comfortable and happy in his new surroundings. It was not before we recognized that our decision six months ago at the dinner table had not been in vain. But we came practically to an impasse in dealing with Tom and Al. Tom is by nature very warm and devoted to his friends and was put into the position of bolstering the influence of the less voluble Al. Gradually and unconsciously, though, the barrier began to crumble. Tom kept up his defending friendliness to Al but at the same time began to extend this same warmness to his other roommates. It was not many weeks, therefore, until he more or less served as a liaison man between the others. Only the last few weeks now has it been that Al also has begun to break through the barrier. And now that Tom is leaving the whole system of liaison has been demolished so that he has to act on his own initiative. He also begins to try the aggressive and finds that his roommates are not made of a non-ignescent material that cannot respond with sympathetic scintillations of happiness and friendliness when a human strikes upon it. It makes my heart glad to have a roommate take an interest in me.

This evening's collation was somewhat disconcerting. I had gone to the gymnasium to exercise this afternoon, leaving a note to Al and Dick to let them know that I would be in the dining hall lounge about 6:00 P.M. If they could make it, I would meet them there at that time. Nobody was there. That in itself was not given second thought, since they could both have had other things to do at that particular hour. I sat down to eat with some friends who live across the hall. They were just about finished and soon left. It was only a few minutes, though, before I was joined by Bill, the comrade who is planning to go with me on that double date to Smith two weeks hence. He sat down on my left where one of the fellows that had just left was sitting. In the fuliginous lighting that the candles offered (every Thursday we have candle lighting to vary the monotony of eating under incandescent lighting), it was difficult to see far in the refectory; but surely it was possible to see one table down to the left. Between Bill and me about four places to the left and on the other side of the table sat Dick. Never a word of greeting same from him until Henry came to talk to me, starting rather boisterously and with much gesticulation. Then Dick laconically asked Henry what he was doing and began to imitate him. I looked over with astonishment to see that he was seated so near me. "How long have you been there?" "What?" "How in the heck did you get there?" "I climbed under the table." I felt a little chagrined and angered at him but said nothing further.

After dinner I returned to the library and began to read a short history of Haiti while comfortably seated in an arm chair. In a few moments I was interrupted as Dick made inquiry into what reading matter was presently occupying my interest. I intended to answer him rather coldly but the way in which he asked indicated that he was not trying to be antagonistic. I replied in a convivial manner but still decided to write you in anger about him. But as I review the event more and more the less serious it becomes and the more ridiculous I begin to look. He probably meant no harm. His nature sometimes induces sarcasm, though it is not necessarily to antagonize people.

Tom just walked in.

November 8, 1952 . . . Al went to one of the girl colleges this evening with one of his friends. Dick and I remained in the dorm, as we both have several hour tests Monday. All we did was to study and enjoy the delights of the luxury with which Al has bestowed the room. The $150.00 sofa arrived this morning to complete the final array, which now consists of an expensive leather chair, a built-in bar, gold-plated andirons, black window cushion, oak coffee table, long flowing red drapes with a flower motif, a cotton tufted rug that completely covers the floor, and a high fidelity radio system with a loud speaker.

We turned on the fidelity system and let the music drift through the room with all its splendid luxury. About 10:00 P.M. Dick went to the drugstore to buy some ice cream and French-fried potatoes. He knew that my wallet was bare but bought the food, anyway, and told me to enjoy it. There was nothing to worry about, nothing to harass the mind.

November 10, 1952 . . . Marguerite is going to Iowa for a three weeks' vacation. At least, that is the answer she gave me in reply to the invitation to the college dance. She tutored me some in the phonetics of French this morning, but that was just about all. She never looses that wistful way of looking at a person, though. I hope that this is an indication that she is really going to Iowa and not just saying that to give me the brush-off.

When I arrived at the dormitory after the twenty-minute colloquy with Marguerite, there was a missive from Jane. That last letter that I had written her, the one accepting her invitation to Smith, requested a date for Bill but contained no details as to the type of girl he likes. Jane's response was rather droll:

> Am answering so quickly mainly to ask you about your friend, who is he? What year? What height? And what kind of girl does he like? In short, I can't just get him "any" date—the girl is bound to want to know who she is spending the day with. (I don't mean it from the "un-experiment" point of view . . . .) Just want to please him.

We get pretty frustrated at school with no women to talk to or associate with. When one thinks of going to one of the girl's colleges for a weekend date, his puritanical conscience generally plays against his natural instincts. Generally, after we have been with the girls for a while we once again gain our sense of balance. But before we get up there the question is hard to decide. Shall I give vent to my pent up suppressions or should I let myself be controlled by the religious and social training that my parents have tried to instill in me? Bill did not know what type of girl he wanted. The inner debate had not yet been decided. Here is the first letter I wrote as a reply to Jane's inquiry:

> Ed, the fellow for whom you are getting the date, is about 5'9", medium build, well liked socially, etc., etc. Does not drink, though he says he can get along with a girl whether she drinks or not. Says he would like a girl who would not

consider the date unsuccessful if he didn't want to "make out," or one who would consider the date unsuccessful if the spirit moved him to the contrary. You can use your own judgment. I wouldn't know how to choose myself.

The final draft went as follows:

Got your letter today. Sorry I didn't mention anything about Bill more than his name. Did I even mention that? He is about my height, very well liked on the campus, etc. Is a sophomore from Indiana and can speak pidgin French. Think he would like the opportunity to try his French at your "maison" (her French club house). As for the kind of girl he would like, that is hard to say. I would say that he would like one that is neither too prudish nor one at the opposite extreme. Is that what you mean? He hasn't started drinking yet, but I rather think that is immaterial.

November 11, 1952 . . . It seems rather ridiculous that a simple letter explaining the personality of a friend should work so havoc on my mind in trying to give an answer that says what my heart wants to say and at the same time not bring any social embarrassment either on the friend or myself. After thinking about the last letter I wrote to Jane, a feeling of uneasiness began to creep over me. Before the letter was mailed therefore I tore it up and wrote the following:

> Ed is about my height, very well liked on campus, etc. Comes from Indiana as a sophomore, has played a little intramural football, fairly good student (rather the opposite of what you might term an intellectual, though), and can speak French to some degree. Think he would like the opportunity very much to visit your "maison."
>
> As for the kind of girl he would like, I would say the average—neither particularly dumb and certainly not too smart. Something in between—neither too prudish nor too much the other way. Ed does not drink. Whether you think he would have a better time with a girl who does drink or one who doesn't, let that govern your decision. I don't personally think that it makes much difference.
>
> Hope this is the information that you are after.

My conscience is at rest now. But already my mind is beginning to waver between two courses of action. Will this weekend be the kind that one is inwardly proud of afterwards or will it be one that lasts for the moment only and then is forgotten or perhaps remembered and told to the fellows? Is there a compromise between these two extremes? Can one have both a spiritual and non-spiritual compensation for the weekend? Does one exclude the other? Or is there a medium as there is in most things?

November 15, 1952 . . . A letter came from Dad about three days ago, in which was enclosed the money to defray the cost of the Thanksgiving sojourn in Indiana with them. The check will more than cover the trip, so that I may have $25.00 left to put in the bank for the trip to Cuba this summer. My eagerness to see the folks has been growing day by say since they first extended me the invitation to visit them with all expenses paid. It has been a year and a half since I have seen my nine-year old sister and a year since I have seen the rest of the family. But there is something in me that says such a trip is retrogression into the past. For four years, since the age of sixteen, I have tried to escape the hates and envies and distresses of a broken family. Every time that I think of my mother the heartaches of that life come to mind. And every time that I see Dad I think of mother. I want to get away from this. No one can imagine the tension my mind goes through when these unpleasant memories come to mind. An outsider would think me the apex of cruelty and unsympathetic feelings toward filial devotion. But the outsider does not realize that I am not trying to separate that past from the present merely for selfish reasons. Certainly, some of the reason are selfish, for it is my happiness that I am considering in taking such a drastic step as alienating myself from my mother. But there is more to it than that, for I know that no manner of relations with my mother will lead to happiness for either her or me. Every time I see her husband, my heart begins to pound with revenge. Sometimes that emotional tension becomes so great that I think the only way to stop it, is to kill this man. Many a time I have thought of means to torture him to death. Call it sadistic, if you will. But if you knew how horrifying this tension can become, you would not think I was EXAGGERATING.

Last year just before the final examinations were taken, I was in the library studying. It was a Sunday evening. That was when this attack began to become excruciating. It had been an exciting weekend. Most of the fellows had had dates. The majority of the girls returned to their respective colleges that morning. But one student had brought his girl to study with him in the court that lies adjacent to the right side of the library nave. The sun shown beautifully on the green grass. Through the library window the rays of sunshine ignited the small particles of dust into a confused marathon dance. I glanced out the window and looked at this student and his girl. I tried to study. There was an examination coming up the next day. I had to study but I could not. I delved into the studies with ardent enthusiasm at 2:00 P.M. But by the time that the afternoon was finished my will power was dissipated. There could be no more studying. For some unexplainable reason as I sat in the library chair trying to study these two youths brought Mother to mind. At first the effect was negligible. But it began to grow until it was impossible to think of anything else but Mother and her family. My head turned in a dizzy and heavy consternation. Nothing but the past life at home could enter my head. And nothing I did could banish them. They grew and grew into this horrible incubus. I thought of my stepfather and his brutality in breaking up our family. Thoughts of hatred racked my body and mind with unbearable agony. Reflections on the good relations he had always kept with my brother made the heart palpitate even more. He hated me as I hated him. The hatred was growing from the time that I realized what was the situation. It took several years before I could analyze his clemency toward everyone else but me. The words he said when I left them for good to go to Denver hit like a poison dart and stung and made me bleed with unhappiness. "If you can't get along with your father, do not come back here." The many times that he belittled me before the family and others can never be erased. He always talked of my stepbrother as being so superior both in school and out. He was a genius and I was a nothing. How could I forget the two times he tried to put me in the reform school? Even now while writing to you, my feelings have not changed, though I realize there is nothing that can be done to avenge myself. The only way to heal these hatreds is to never see him again. Then this horrendous confusion pushed to the foreground in bold type these words: "You have a brother who might come to this school." He would come in my senior year. O God, do not let him come here. I do not want to impede his success if the wheel of fortune has a grand future before him. But

I do not want him to have the opportunity to bring this heinous stepfather and all the accompanying memories, into my life again. Maybe I am supposed to be a man but man is only human. He cannot suppress his hatreds forever. It is for their happiness as well as mine that I am trying to keep this separation. But I am powerless to enforce it if they are adamantly determined to find me and visit me. I am running away from them but there is no place to go. Wherever I go they can follow. But do not follow me to closely. Do not try to stalk me like an animal that can be beaten with impunity. I will run but when there is no longer any place to run I will stand and fight back and that fight will be final. Leave me alone.

The day had been dissipated. A constructive work had been accomplished. I failed the test. It had taken a day to rid myself temporarily of these agonizing memories that I had been trying to suppress for so long. But that was not the last attack. They happen often, especially when a trying circumstance presents itself. Then I am free from this curse for maybe a month or two before something else reminds me of the past. That is why I have been so reluctant to visit Dad. He will invariably talk of Mother or my brother or stepbrother. During the trip from Denver to college, I paid Dad a two weeks vacation. One of those mornings was spent talking to Sandra, my stepmother, about the decision to sever all relations with my Mother and her family and relatives. I tried to impress on her the significance of such a move. I thought that she had been convinced and would be able to convince Dad. But when he came to the campus last year he could not refrain from telling me of the latest news from my brother. I said nothing but to impress the firmness of my decision uttered a very gruff "mmm . . ." From then until now nothing has been mentioned in any of our letters about this other half of the family. That is, not until this week. I think the letter merits being quoted in entity.

Dear Son,
    Your much welcome letter came yesterday. And we were certainly glad that you are planning on a trip here for Thanksgiving. We shall be glad to have a letter from you

explaining your plans when they become more definite. Enclosed you'll find a check which we hope will cover expenses.

Indeed, we are happy about the outcome of the election. However, I must admit that I was and still am a great admirer of Governor Stevenson. In my mind there is no doubt but what he is a great man and would have been a fine president. But we felt the Democratic party had become so entrenched in power and position that he would have had trouble making so many necessary changes because of party affiliations. We are hoping and praying that many of the economical problems will be solved and that war and international trouble will become little problems. Most of all, I hope and pray for peace. The hell and horror and misery of Korea is one thing I can't see.

Next Saturday we are planning on going to see the Indiana-Wisconsin football game at Bloomington. We are to meet friends in Bloomington and go with them to the game. If the weather is bad we are not going. So far we have had a beautiful fall. Has not been cold at all to speak of. Of course, such nice weather surely can't continue indefinitely.

I am sure you have been wondering just what my ailment has amounted to since I have not discussed it with you in any of my letters. Even at this point I do not have the complete picture, but slowly the puzzle is being put together by the doctor, the psychiatrist. If you have formed any erroneous opinions about my condition, you are going to be surprised when you see me. Actually for friends who know me they see, so they say, no difference in me now than they did before I went to the hospital. It was a constellation of emotional conflicts that have been busy within me for a longtime; conflicts which were disturbing in a small degree, which I was for years able to suppress and sublimate, but which when I was no longer able to suppress them, they exploded. And when they exploded they became unbearable monsters which I could not handle myself. That is when I had to admit defeat and seek help. If you have ever studied psychology of the emotions or mental hygiene, you will no doubt have some idea of what I am talking about, or if you have ever seen a person overcome by emotional disturbances, you might have an idea of what happened to me. Even at that, it might be a bit difficult for the average person to understand his own emotional peculiarities. In my own life, I have done quite a bit of study on emotional problems from the psychological standpoint yet was not able to understand my own emotional pattern without help.

Here I have given you a very brief idea of my problem. It is by no means complete—and there is much more I could tell you, but it is so difficult to put on paper. It is such a tricky thing to explain. Even when one thinks he is being clear, it can be confusing to the reader. That is one reason I hesitate to say too much about it. A much better understanding can come about in a verbal discussion. So I'll tell you more when you are here.

Sandra and Betty (my half-sister) are in bed and I should be there too. They are also looking forward to your visit with us, even though it will be a short one.

Betty is in the third grad and likes school very much. She is doing fine, too. You'll be surprised when you see how much she has grown. She is quite a gal, if I do say so.

Sandra is not doing regular teaching this year but is substituting now and then. Last week she spent a day teaching English to seniors. She also is teaching Sunday school to a group of high school youngsters.

Had a letter from Mrs. Pollack. Her daughter is in school at Ft. Collins and her son is going to Aurora High School. Arnold (her husband) is out of the Army. They had seen your mother. She had made a visit to Denver to see your grandmother, who had an operation. Said your mother said your brother was really going places with his magic work. I have not written to him in ages and should be ashamed of myself. But I do promise to write in the near future. I am not sure he even knows I am back. I did write and tell him I was going to Europe.

Certainly looking forward to seeing you. We'll have lots of things to talk about since we last saw you at school in March. At this point I am thinking I'll be here for Thanksgiving. But if I am not, I'll let you know just as soon as I find out. But we'll plan it that way and hope our plans are not changed.

Good luck and good night from your Dad.

P.S.

The welcome mat is out and we are so very happy you can come.

Sandra

Why did Dad have to mention Mother? Why did he have to mention my brother? Is there nothing I can do to persuade him that what I said to Sandra last year still stands—that I have not and will not renege on my promise? Before I sailed for the Continent last summer, Mother sent me a letter, saying that my grandmother had to have an operation for a chest cancer. For one solid week I mulled the question over, trying to think of some way to let my grandmother know that I held nothing against her and that I wished her rapid recovery and at the same time maintaining the rigid separation that I was trying to impose. If I wrote her or Mother a letter all the past months during which I had not answered any of their letters, would be but in vain. Yet if I did not send some encouragement to my grandmother, the years to come might find my heart burdened with the thought that it was my fault that she did not recover—that I had sapped her will to survive. To solve the problem, I ordered a bouquet of flowers for my grandmother, specifying at the time that my name was not to appear on the card. The card was to wish her a speedy recovery, but there was to be no mention that I had sent them. Of course, she would know who had sent the flowers. But I thought by that tactic she would realize that I still wished to sever relations. Mother continued to write me. After returning to school after the end of the summer, I found a card from her, thanking me for the flowers and telling me that Grandmother had pulled through. She does not know my address now, though it would be easy enough to find out by asking my father. But since that letter, addressed to my freshman post office box, she has not attempted to contact me. I hope she does not think that this separating is because I do not love her. But we are only human, not divine. Man can forgive but he cannot forget. I have tried both. I have forgiven her for any misery that she might have caused me and I hope that she has forgiven me for any misery that I might have caused her, for I certainly was no angel as a child. But it is impossible to forget the unwarranted hardships that my stepfather inflicted on the family. Never can it be forgotten that he tried to have the Army priest annul the marriage of my father and mother, thus making my brother and me illegitimate children. I can forgive these things, because as time wears on I begin to realize more and more how feeble we all are. But to forget these things is impossible. I am trying, though I know that success will never arrive. Can you not see this, Mother? Can you not see that I am not running away from you because I hate you but because I love you? Help me as I am trying to help you. My stepfather and I can never be reconciled. There will never exist between us anything but intense hatred, no matter how desperately we might try to feign the contrary.

When I return to visit Dad, undoubtedly this undesirable subject will arise. What shall I do? I have already tried being harsh and stern. That has not worked. They think I am only putting on a front and would really like to be reconciled. It is as though one had come to a wall, being chased by snakes and scorpions whose piercing stings were striking at my body, and tries to scale it, only to find that it is too high. I must get over that wall. On the other side of that wall, I feel sure, there lies happiness and joy. Mother can scale it too. So can her husband and my brother. But to do this we must try to forget the past and our blood relation, for we cannot scale this wall together. It is an individual project that calls for the release from the fetters of the past. It seems an impossible task to persuade Dad of this. Right now I do not have any definite plans.

But I think the best thing to do, is to ignore the problem. No, I cannot do that. It is certain to burst one of these days. It is better to settle it now rather than wait until I am married and thus put another marriage and other young lives in jeopardy. Dad himself, I think, is suffering from this same decision. That is beyond a doubt a large facet of those things which he says he has had to suppress and sublimate during the years. That is why he is talking freely of my mother in the letter. The psychologist has told him not to suppress these feelings any longer. Tell them to someone and get them off your chest. I feel sure that this is what he will tell me during this vacation. If he persists, though, in pressing me into reconciliation with my mother, the only thing to do is to sever relations with him also. This would be dreadful, probably harder for me to bear than him, since I have no relative other than him to whom I can confide my secrets and tell my troubles. But it is decided. If he persists, our relations shall cease.

During the voyage to France this summer, I never once told anyone that my parents are divorced. It really felt good to be on a par with the other students, not having to say that my life had been blighted with divorce and its attendant discomforts and pains. Never once did I tell Alice anything about my family. I did not tell her that my father was in the Army. She thought my life had been nothing but happiness, as far as humans can attain happiness. She knew I did not come from a rich family, since the trip to France was financed through my own work on the campus. That she gleaned out of a conversation in which we were talking about the Divinity School. Her friend had gone there. I mentioned in a jesting manner that I too had gone there, as a carpet cleaner with the Service Bureau. I made up my mind that she should not know the truth. I made up my mind to tell Sandra that neither she nor Dad were to reveal anything of my family history to her if she ever visited the home. But now she has not written and all is in vain.

This is the evening I hoped to have a date with Marguerite. It is just as well that I did not, though, for that leaves the evening free to sell miniature footballs to finance the trip to Cuba this coming summer.

November 16, 1952 . . . Six people bought footballs from me last night. I was able to get into the dance free so that there was a better opportunity to sell to the students. It is part of the college aide's job to take pictures of the social events. My job is taking care of guests, but the student who regularly takes pictures wanted to "flick out." So I got some free punch, sold some footballs, met several people, and took some good pictures. It was so dark in the dance hall though, that it was practically impossible to sight. I missed one excellent picture of a rather quaint osculation. But when the couple saw that I was trying to take their picture and having difficulty sighting, they abruptly put a stop to it with a pleasant laugh. The different kinds of people that I saw and met was amazing. It would make a book to tell of all the different personalities—the ones that were agreeable and the ones that were iracund.

I had been at the dance only a few minutes when a low whisper beckoned me to the window. The young lad wanted to know if I could sneak him in past the ticket man. I thought for a moment. I remembered last Christmas when one of the faculty invited me and a friend to live in their home and take care of it while they were away on vacation. This other lad and myself betrayed our trust, though. For we had been there for only a week when one of my friends paid a visit, suggesting that we throw a party. I was game if he would get me a good-looking date. He said he would. One night before the party he and half a dozen of his buddies came to the house. They had come to make final plans and to coax me to increase the number of guests that would be invited. I was reluctant. But not being willing to be considered a prude, I half-heartedly consented, setting at the same time a number which was not to be exceeded. They came the next night and so did six or seven other fellows whom I had never seen before. I said nothing but hoped that the master and his wife would not return. The party continued until after we had welcomed in the New Year. The master returned the next day and was furious when he heard the report of this party. Suddenly all my hopes of success crumbled into a jumble of confused memories of the party and the past. It was to be popular that I had sacrificed this opportunity to form a lasting friendship with a man and woman who had been so kind to me. Nothing mattered to my friend and myself. He was a college aide and was thus in a more immediately embarrassing position. He would have to work with this master, while I did not even have to get in this particular residential college. I did apply there afterwards but was put in another one. My friend stood up under the test, but I became disgusting infantile and broke down in tears as he interviewed me and quizzed me concerning the happenings of that evening. His wife has invited me to visit them several times since then. But I know they will never be able to look at me without thinking of that evening. It was then that I decided never again to betray a man's trust for social recognition.

Thus when this soused boor tried to enter by having me open one of the windows to the dance hall, I politely told him that there were no windows to open. He immediately grew angry and called me that nasty word that starts with "s." He then came in from the patio, walked past the ticket man, and gave me an antagonizing look. Why he did not walk past the ticket agent without trying to test my venality, I have not yet been able to determine.

Perhaps he was trying to be the cynosure of the party. That party that we gave at the master's house found me not inebriated but certainly pretending it, mainly because I was insecure and wanted people to know that I was willing to be friendly. I had had only two bottles of beer, though. Every time anyone would pass by, I would ask him if he was having a good time. If the guy passed me fifty times, he was asked fifty times if he was having a good time. That was the last time that I had anything to drink until just recently. I decided that it was too difficult to fight a conscience that leaves one in mental agony when he does drink. I thought also that through drinking too much, or acting as though I had, some of the people at the party were disgusted with me. One of the students who had not gone home for the vacation and who had not been invited to the party, came into the master's house through the ping-pong room. I did not like him since he was too possessive. I immediately sprung up from the sofa and attempted to prevent his entry. He was not to be persuaded and neither was I until one of my friends took the lad with him to the party upstairs and gave him something to drink. The whole evening was gay and confused and without any satisfaction. I had feigned drunkenness (very successfully, too—of that I still boast to my friends) so that it would be possible to get away from the others. I left my date upstairs and went to the ping-pong room where another couple were saying their valediction to each other before breaking up their engagement. I capitalized on the situation since the girl was rather attractive. She accepted my invitation to come to the freshman prom, which irritated her date, no end. That is why she accepted. Everybody else was having a good time but me. Even this girl seemed to be having a good time in breaking up with her fiancé. Upstairs some of the boys and girls were singing to the tune of an old banjo. I began to feel empty. When that student tried to enter without an invitation I prevented his entry in the most pugnacious manner simply because there was something lacking inside me. My whole heart was seeking friendship and when the friendship was found unavailable I grew pugnacious. How I regretted it later. I made a fool of myself without making any friends. When school started the so-called friend who had been the instigator of the party considered me no more of a friend than before. I was just a simple tool who was at that time too naive to know that it is the extremes in life that make one look silly in the eyes of others.

Last night I was able to over look this pugnacious individual who tried to make me feel chagrin because of an unwillingness to cater to his commands. I did not become soused nor did I refrain from indulging. I imbibed inoffensively, retaining my manners and trying not to offend anyone because of ill-becoming manners. After my head began to feel a little cloggy, the bed felt like a good haven of rest after a happy and lucrative evening as a spectator. I think it was really more fun being a spectator than being a real part of the party with my own girl. Of course, the chances are that with the right girl, one that is compatible, the evening would have been just as much of a success.

November 17, 1952 . . . It seemed like a minor thing that could
easily be forgotten when one of Al's friends from Texas taunted me
for studying too much. It was Sunday morning and the dormitory
was cluttered with debris from the preceding night. The room was
stuffy and no one was in his best mood. I arose before the others,
ate breakfast, and then read the newspaper. I did not go to church.
It has been three weeks now that our chapel has had one less student
worshiper on Sunday morning. The sun was radiant and bright
and the weather was not too hot. The success in selling musical
footballs still kept my spirits up. But this friend of Al's from
Princeton put the damper on any prospects that the day held for
joy and freedom from worry. This irksome lurdan could not have
been any more irritating. He hit at a sore spot and knew it. "You
must make pretty good grades from all the studying you do," he
uttered with sneeringly puckered up lips. This was the height of
irritation that the weekend had offered me. I had not had a date.
Dick looked on me with pity as though such a weekend without a
date indicated that I would be extremely unhappy. Al was not too
different from usual, but he had a very sultry and unfriendly date
who more or less sneered at my efforts to sell her a musical football.
It was as though I was a miserable creature either to be pitied or
despised. And when that son of a bitch started to revile me because
of studying, there was little strength left to suppress my feelings.
Probably, it would have been possible to have said something in a
jesting manner that would have both squelched this fellow and at
the same time prevented him from feeling antagonistic toward
me. But I did not. Instead, the reply was a typical denial of excessive
study said in the epitome of causticity. "Study! Oh, yes, I believe
in some study. But there should be very little. Just skim the book."
The satisfaction would have been unlimited that would have been
derived from punching this tactless boor in the belly.

All yesterday this event bothered and troubled me. In the library
Tim, the friend who has interested me in joining one of the
fraternities when rushing begin after Christmas vacation, was
looking over some work for accounting. We began to talk. He
recounted his efforts to bird-dog one of the freshmen that works

for him at the concession stand at the football bowl. Then we talked about accounting and then the girl he was pinned to last year. It was almost in nostalgic tones that he spoke of this girl, how he had spent so much money on her through buying simple curios like a mechanical monkey at Central Park. At least all the world was not against me. Then there were other friends who jokingly asked me if there were any more footballs for sale. The remarks were not profound. But they were welcomed as friendly gestures and warmed the heart against the insult that less noble individuals doled out freely throughout the whole weekend.

Today the examination results were given out in English. I got a 73. Last week the results of the other tests were made known. In Air Science the mark was 70 and in French the mark was 79. My grades are going down. From an 82 average the first semester of last year, the grades have steadily decreased, first to an 81 average and now to this horrify average of probably 75. What will the scholarship board do? I am loosing interest. Hardly any time was spent in preparing for these final examinations, though much time was given to the history preparation. I thought that all there was to know was firmly in my mind. But it was not. The conversation between Dad and Sandra when they last visited the campus comes to mind vividly. They were proud of that high 82 average which put me on the Dean's list. I told them the truth, though, that my enthusiasm was always great at first but gradually dwindles to nothing in the end. It looks like that is what is happening now. Maybe I am spending too much time heeling this selling agency. If I succeed in heeling the organization, there will be an opportunity to join one of the fraternities without having to borrow money and there will be sufficient money to defray the expenses of any number of dates. I do not know what it is, except that everything looks so bleak now and I fell so mentally and bodily worn out and sick. It is impossible to battle against the opposing forces all the time. A man has only so much strength to expend in warding off debilitating worries and then he succumbs. If only I had some one in whom to confide. But even that is not practical, for people do not understand. Alice has not written since I confided in her the worries and anxieties of the summer in France with a group of boys and girls. Every time that I confide in someone who appears understanding and sympathetic, that person lowers his estimation of me. Man has to have a strong equilibrium to be highly considered by his friends. But what if a person does not have that equilibrium, but is desperately searching for it so that he can be happy like other people? There is no one in whom I can confide. I have tried it before but never again. Call it the cry of the cynic. What else can you expect? The way things are going now I will probably not get my scholarship renewed. The trip to Cuba is my goal now. But after that there are no plans.

November 18, 1952 . . . Since Sunday there has developed an intangible estrangement between me and my other two roommates. When I talk with either Al or Dick alone there is no feeling of distance between us. But when we are all together I have to try hard to get them to listen to me or laugh at my jokes. The situation is similar to the one that developed after the group had visited Mont St. Michel last summer. The French girl with whom I had been spending much time, suddenly became oppressively antipathetic toward me and even tried to avoid my presence. It was during the evening that we arrived at this Mecca. This girl, a couple other Frenchmen and myself had preceded the others to this spot by about two hours. Mont St. Michel is a former abbey located half way down the northern coast of Brittany. There is a modern asphalt highway that covers the causeway, which leads as the crow flies from the small hamlet of Beauvoir to the center of this chateau-like abbey. We all reached the abbey ensemble; that is, the ones who had gone ahead of the others. The French girl and myself looked around the grounds and then proceeded to return to a place about two kilometers up the road to Beauvoir, where we were to meet the rest of the group. On the way back I preceded her by about twenty-five feet. But when I arrived at the designated place she was no where in sight. Had she gone back to the abbey, perhaps to return with the French lad who seemed to intrigue her or had something else happened?

She did not return for about a half hour. In the meantime the rest of the group had arrived. The first to arrive was the brother of this girl. And the first words he said were, "Look at Alex, by himself 'comme toujours.'" The sting was bitter. If it had appeared to the group that I liked to be isolated, they were wrong. Perhaps I had been reading too much. Perhaps some of the disgruntled members of the group were becoming jealous. Our leader soon arrived and invited me to have an alcoholic beverage. In Normandy the people drink strong cider instead of red wine at the table and for between-meal refreshment. I was becoming keenly aware of a certain antagonism developing among the others because of my teetotalism, though there was one other fellow who did not drink. But he did not seem to have the same difficulty that I did in preventing the group from considering such an attitude the reflection of extreme egotism. Thus I persuaded myself to take some of the cider that the leader purchased for the few who were there at that time. Several of the others had already departed to see Mont St. Michel. At the table I felt uneasy. Why, I do no know. There was just a sensing that the others were feeling some animosity for me. I could not really analyze it, though another probably could. The ones in our group could not analyze it. Only an outsider could. One thing is certain. The Americans were becoming jealous of my demonstrated large vocabulary. They were starting to retaliate at every moment conceivable to demonstrate their ability also. Alison mentioned that we should not "gaspiller" (waste) something and Mae immediately riposted that she should not try to show off her intelligence. I told Mae that this word is not sesquipedalian, that the French use it all the time, though it may be a very extraordinary feat for an American to be able to muster it to use in conversation. Immediately, there was an inner warring of feelings set up between us in an apparently non-bellicose conversation. My use of a large vocabulary was being attacked by both of the girls. One was fighting it by using supposedly ten dollars words herself and the other was belittling such a thing.

That evening I intentionally separated myself from the French girl friend. And it seemed that people were beginning to avoid me. The next morning I spent reading a biography while a couple of the girls shortened my shorts to correspond to the French style. It was an effort to become less individualistic. But people seemed to avoid me, either speaking in unfriendly tones or in tones of disgusting pity. At the abbey the day before the French girl friend had said that she was not going to return to see it the next day with the others, since one visit would suffice. But the very next morning she changed her mind and haughtily informed me of this abrupt change of plans, expressing herself in such a manner as would lead one to think that I was to be always at her beck and call and do just what she did. I rebelled and expressed the desire to remain at the camp. From that day forward the atmosphere of the group changed. Something subtle developed so that the girls and boys tried to avoid eating with one of the opposite sex. Skip managed to maintain his good relations with his French girl friend for a much longer time than I had been able to do with this other French girl. It was not that I did not want to keep on friendly terms with her. It was that I could not. The antagonism between the two factions grew and grew. The last night was spent at Vannes, where the French and the Americans gave each other a surprise party in which each person of the camping trip was caricatured. I did a trite burlesque on my former French girl friend, imitating a coquette. Everyone laughed. She expressed a certain appreciation in saying with a warming smile that she thought I was imitating Skip's girl. And her brother thanked me. The way he said thank you indicated that he thought this little burlesque had heightened his sister's popularity. I did not understand. There was something in that statement that warmed my heart and yet left me nonplused.

As the panorama of the summer passes before me, this statement begin to loose some of its cryptic meaning, though not all. As far as anyone could observe, this French girl was as normal as anyone else in the group; that is, up to the night of the big festival in the small Briton town of Le Faou. At last after a week and half of bicycling and rough living, we had come to a town that was going to have a fete that evening. The emotional warrings of the group were temporarily forgotten. The girls immediately began to radiate with pleasantness. Mae began to pursue me once more but I tried to ignore her. This was a chance to forget the worries of the emotional strain among these people who had lived together under the hardest of conditions for a week and half. The evening began when Skip, a fellow from the southern United States, my French girlfriend and one of her friends began to converse with a tall brawny sailor who immediately invited us to attend the town dance in one of the buildings on the other side of the concession stands. For two hours we gave way to our inhibitions and danced with everybody that wanted too and even some incredulous French filles who were not too eager to. Then we left and went to a bar. The sailor bought us all drinks. By this time the others had gone except for Skip, the two French girls and myself. Skip and I did not drink. But the girls did. They drank and drank without any apparent affect until we returned to the barn in which we were to sleep that evening. Then my girl friend became delirious, laughing and crying as she stumbled and fell along the ground before the hay loft. Her body was limp like a helpless baby and her cries pierced the sleep of those who slept above. Her girl friend dashed cold water on her face and put her to bed. Nothing more was said of the incident, for we all agreed that it would be best to refrain from telling the others of what had happened before during the evening. Nothing was said further but this girl undoubtedly suffered inwardly from what the others might think of her for such unbecoming deportment. Maybe this is what her brother was speaking of when he said, "Merci, Alex."

Thus a certain subtle tension has been developing in our dormitory since Sunday. I cannot analyze it. But it is certain that I am the cause. Is it because I unconsciously give people that idea that my whole personality is seeped with egotism and conceit? Is it that something of my past accomplishments, which are few if any, causes jealousy. I remember that Dick mentioned when Tom quit school that Al would suffer, since he and Tom were buddies just like he and I. Is it possible that Dick is trying to prevent Al from feeling out of place? But if that is so why is it that the same situation seems to develop no matter where or with whom I live? Is it that I develop contempt for people after living with them for a time and show it in my attitude, or vice versa? Maybe I try to be too subservient to those around me and thus create an atmosphere of tension. That is the theory that I worked on this evening. To date I have looked the roommate in the eyes to whom the conversation was directed, or have looked from one to another. This might be what the Army calls "bootlicking," though it is not intentional. This caused my roommates to think that I am trying to play one against the other. Or it is possible that they take me to much for granted by my sycophant attitude. Thus this evening, for the first time, I tried not looking anyone in the eyes when talking to them. Instead I gazed off in the distance as though I did not give a damn if they listened or not. And it worked—they listened. When they talked without including me in the conversation, I sat still and comforted myself by noticing that in the other groups in the refectory that there were private conversations among two roommates to the exclusion of the others. I really think that it is my immaturity that causes this social distress. But I am determined to live with these roommates and get along well with them. Yes, I think that this perhaps seemly idea about not looking at either of the roommates when talking to them together may solve the problem of giving our room unity without contention for the highest recognition.

November 19, 1952 . . . This afternoon in the seminar Dick fell
into a somnolent torpor two or three times. He got to bed at 2:00
last night to rise sharply at 6:30 this morning to resume his
studying. The weekend really was hard on him in eliminating some
necessary sleep, but it gave him a chance to get away from the
grind for a while to come back with new vigor in tackling the
studies. Dick might be inclined to challenge that "new vigor" idea,
though. The lucubration had stopped completely for two and
one half days, so that when he did resume studies they must
have looked like a formidable, if not impossible, barrier to cross.
To aid in putting him in the nadir of good fortune, the mid-
term history examination came back with a menacing fifty. All
this combined to change Dick's mind to go to Harvard this
next weekend. It was yesterday in the library that he told me
that. This evening in the library, at the same time, he asserted
his intention to go to Boston, anyway. About five minutes ago
the singing group that he is in just serenaded the college for
about fifteen minutes. What is that saying—if you want
something done, get a busy man to do it?

After the seminar was terminated for this week, I told Dick we
could meet in the lounge about 6:15 for supper. Al was there.
Where Dick was I have no idea. Al and I ate dinner with an
intangible freedom from a tense atmosphere of small irritation or
competition to excel in conversation. One of Bill's roommates was
seated across from me; and there was conversation with an equal
bit of silence, which was not filled with tenseness. Rather those
moments of silence meant that we were beginning to understand
one another—that it is not necessary to talk to a person all the
time to keep his friendship.

On returning to the library I found my Classical Civilization
paper with the following caption scribbled on it, "Evelyn eats it!"
There across the table was Dick seated with a smug grin across his
face. "Why, you son of a gun," I said, "what in the heck do you
mean marking up my paper." After a little conversation he then
breached the new plans to divagate to Boston this Saturday for the
football game.

There is something in a social mixing that binds people together. They see each other's faults and realize that the other fellow is not a god free from all blemish. Even in drinking there is some good. When one does not drink, others might think he is just too proud to break the teaching of his egotistical self-concern. There is something in total abstinence that sets up an uneasy atmosphere in the social circle. Not only does it cause discomfort for others but it makes the teetotaler uneasy. However, there are those who can refrain from drink and still maintain an exceptionally warm relationship in the group. I am not one of those. Skip was, for though he never drank, his popularity very seldom waned during the whole trip abroad. Man is a feeble creature and knows it. And he feels great comfort when he knows that he is not alone, but that there are others among the human race who also have weaknesses. Drink is a weakness. But why is it a weakness? It is a weakness only in excess. Otherwise it is a good and a boon to humanity. The reticent become pleasingly voluble and the disagreeable become agreeable. Drink is to loosen the tongue and to develop a feeling of camaraderie by letting others know that we really do want to be friendly and are not aloof to indulge in their social habits as long as these habits do not essentially run counter to the Christian religion. But an excess is evil and destructive. Indeed the social gathering might be difficult for the parvenu, as it has been for me, but as its nuances are developed, there is something intangible that one gains. It is like going through a difficult experience with others and afterwards being bound to these people through these experiences. Surely, this last weekend has drawn us closer.

November 19, 1952 . . . For dinner this evening I invited the
president of the French Club. But since it was "college night" he
could not eat here. After a little debate we decided to postpone the
date until some further time, in view of the fact that his college
had had steak the night before and we were having it this evening.
Dick went to one of the other colleges to eat with one of his friends,
probably his last year's roommate. Al probably ate here this evening;
but I do not really know, since my French friend came to get me in
the library a half hour before the scheduled rendezvous. He had
been to the room where Dick and Al had told him that I was—in
the athenaeum—in close scrutiny of Thucydides' historical chef-
d'oeuvre, trying to discover some profound thought for a seminar
paper.

This morning after classes when I entered the room Al was
seated in the arm chair, reading a letter. I greeted him but there
was no response. After about five minutes he came in the bedroom
and informed me that he was going to the gymnasium to donate
some blood. I asked him what time his appointment was scheduled
for and he replied that there was none. "But I am sure that you got
a post card in the mail, setting a specific time for the donation."
We looked around under the stacks of books and dossiers but found
nothing. "A hell of a lot of good that does me!" he muttered.

Bill was in the library this evening, setting across the table
from me. After about an hour or so he left and did not return for at
least a half hour. By that time Dick had come to the library to
crack the books for a little while before hitting the sack at the early
hour of 9:30 P.M. and I had moved into the adjacent room to read
some more of Professor Leyburn's book on Haiti. After being
leisurely lounged in the chair for about fifteen minutes, I saw Bill
return and enter the room where Dick was studying. I heard them
pass some pleasant remarks and jests. As Bill made his exit from
the adjacent room, he glanced rather unnoticeably in my direction.
He was hesitating whether to greet me or not, though we had
greeted each other earlier in the evening. I did not raise my head,
for there was an inner reaction, which said that the time did not
call for a greeting. He would have greeted me if I had raised my

head. Perhaps he thought it was I who wanted to greet him, though he himself knew that this was not the proper moment to extend salutations and was thus reluctant to look in my direction. Too much greeting become effusive and makes the individuals appear subservient to each other. An excess in greeting is as bad as being a misanthrope who never greets anyone. These things may be considered insignificant by the man or woman who does not have to live daily with many different people—and live with them harmoniously so that no one tires of the other. These little facts when put together form the basis of a well-rounded mature individual. To me the college education consists more in learning how to live with people than in learning in what era a certain king deposed a certain other king to marry his daughter. The people of the past lived and so must we. I made that mistake the first year here. There was all study and no play, though that situation would really have been hard to rectify since I had neither the time nor the money to do otherwise. The first year was hard. Working in the commons, going out for swimming, and my studies took too much time. But this year I am determined to live, not just to be the intellectual who cannot live with others. If I am to be an intellectual it will not consist solely in learning. Richard Baxter expresses himself well in his *Christian Directory*: "And he that will do nothing but pray and meditate, it's like will (by sickness or melancholy) be disabled e're long either to pray or meditate." Man needs diversion and the student is just as much of a man as anyone else.

The morning paper had a small biography of our college master. During the war he was in the Navy, doing special work at Washington. After the war he returned to the campus to do graduate work and some teaching, while his wife remained in a town several miles away. That last sentence struck me to the core. This man did not have his wife in town but was carrying on his life normally without her except for weekend trips home. Could this man still love his wife and keep her in another town? Obviously, he did. Circumstances did not permit her presence here. I then began to put myself in her place. Would my reaction have been a mature one or would I have thought myself unloved if my conjugal partner had to be in another area than my personal stomping grounds. I began to think. What is this business of human relations? At parties the adults whom I have noticed, are not always with their spouse. As a matter of fact, in the majority of parties one will find the couple spending the evening more with others than with each other. The problem is hard to analyze, but it must be solved. Oh, how I want to be mature and free from the troubles that do not seem to bother the well-balanced person.

When the group was in Paris this summer I noticed that the girls were more eager to go out with new American boys than with the ones who had been accompanying them all summer. In pondering over the number of steady girl friends I have had, the reality is only too clear that we all became mutually tired of each other as the glitter of the romance wore off. Is this then what marriage life is? Is it just like the last weary month of going steady with a girl that you know perfectly? Is Montesquieu right when he says: "Un mari qui aime sa femme est un homme qui n'a pas assez de mérite pour se faire aimer d'une autre?" Is it impossible for people to live together for a very long time, since familiarity breeds contempt and the monotony of one person become too onerous a burden to carry? I hope this is not true. I hope that the history of divorces that have preceded in my lineage will not be repeated in my marriage. Mother once said that when she was a young teenager she promised that no divorce would ever taint her soul. But look what happened. If she had been more mature, perhaps this marriage would not have been destroyed for a man who caused more unhappiness than can be forgotten in a generation. I am no more mature than she was. But it is for this maturity that I strive. There must be, there has too be, a stage where a person can mount where he is free from jealousy for a wife who talks to another man, abounds in trust, and does emotionally not require that one's friends continually give personal recognition to still be considered friends. If you do not understand that which my heart wishes to say, it is that I myself do not know exactly that which it wishes to say. If I could analyze it more profoundly perhaps the realization of my maturity would not be far away. But someday this maturity will come.

November 21, 1952 . . . Jane sent me a letter a few days ago, telling of her proposed plans for the weekend and of the date she had gotten for Bill. It read as follows:

> All arranged—my roommate Patsy will double with us Saturday. Lunch at house is at 1:00 P.M. So if you could arrange it to come by 12, that'd be best. Should you not be sure of being here by 1:0 0 o'clock, let me know immediately so I can plan accordingly.
>
> Have you seen the film "Cry the Beloved Country?" Twas a book by Alan Paton made into a play (musical-drama) several years back, with Todd Duncan. (Saw it & read it & love it!) The story is of a Negro minister and his family in and near Johannesburg. Anyhow, the film, starring Canada Lee, will be here Saturday nite—if we want to go.
>
> Am having the members of the St. Etienne and Rouen groups, who are in New York on Thanksgiving—up to my house from 4 P.M. to 7 P.M. Hope you'll be able to come! Should you see any other of the boys . . . Tim and Frank, etc., would appreciate it if you'd pass the word on.
>
> Well Alex, j'attend notre petite réunion avec plaisir— rappellez-vous d'apporter vos photos de l'été si vous y pensez
>
> à bientot.
>
> Mes amitiés sincères,
>
> Jane

To say the least that second paragraph enraged me. What the heck does she think I am going up to see her for—to see movies? My response was as follows:

> Glad you could get a date for Bill. Will try to make it to Smith by 12:00 noon Saturday. Will start probably very early Saturday morning and if the rides are good should get there by 12:00 or before.
>
> Weather was one hell of a disgusting mess for the Princeton weekend. After about five minutes from the first

touchdown, it started to rain. As for the results of the game—
well . . .

Mid-term exams are finally over. Were not too hard but
always are annoying when there are other things to do.

Sincerely,

Alex

I thought this might give her some insight why we are going
to visit her. But I guess she had not yet received it before writing
the card that came in the mail this morning:

We are being swamped with work from all sides. My
roommate finds she has too much exam pressure to make
it—but I am standing up under the strain—(though
wavering). Have gotten another gal who is very nice—so
have no fears for Ed. Only if you have any portable work,
and wouldn't mind spending at least some of Saturday
afternoon "at the books" we would be "d'accord"—am a
little desperate for time. See you soon, in any case.

And she had "very nice" underscored.

As I anticipate the weekend the vacillation between two
decisions becomes greater and greater. I want to get rid of this
frustrated feeling and do it without harming my conscience. If the
conscience has to suffer to relieve this frustration, it is like deciding
to kill oneself with a canon than with a gun. All the years I have
tried to develop some set of ideals through reading religious works,
psychological tracts, and by trying to emulate noble men who
have had the courage to assert themselves as embracing a certain
high moral standard. Those men who have succeeded in life and
yet had enough fortitude and strength to succeed without
compromising their conscience, have always offered me courage
and inspiration in trying circumstances. General Marshall comes
to mind and the incident that the newspapers spread one day after

a big social gathering in Washington. One young socialite at the party tactlessly remarked to General Marshall that she had never before seen a general who did not indulge. He so magnificently replied, "Well, young lady, you've met one now." You remember the night that I visited that faculty member and as a result of the evening decided to join a fraternity. As a freshman I was told by him, "If you don't want to drink, then don't." Skip did not drink on the trip to France and he was popular. The master with whom I had the Christmas difficulty said he did not drink beer and he has risen to be a man of great consequence on the campus. Yet on the other hand, there have been great religious leaders, like Martin Luther and others, who have moderately indulged. Each time that I read of some one, who is great and does not drink, my mind reverses its decision to indulge moderately. But recently there has been little vacillation. After the party and dance of last week, I felt no compunctions of conscience for drinking; because it had been done temperately. The people of the social circle had seen that I was not aloof to them and God had seen that I was not indifferent to him. But this weekend presents another problem just as hard to resolve as has been the one of drinking. Is this weekend at Smith to be a strictly puritanical one? Will there be no way to relieve this inner tension that is tearing me between two decisions.

As the pantasmagoria of the coming weekend passes before me, there are two voices that cry out differently but with equal intensity. One says that I must and would like to go beyond the stage of just seeing Jane. Through my mind the beast of man sends these prurient thoughts and salacious scenes. I can picture the evening as we sit on the couch, listening to a dulcet music that lulls our senses into a sweet reverie of love. The room is lit by one lamp that strives to remove the tenebrously pleasant overcast of blackness. No one else is in the room. Infatuation of one another is all that runs through the mind as worries are dissipated into the darkness. The one voice says how pleasant this evening will be, and the other voices answers with all ruthlessness, "Come away. Do not do something that you would be sorry for." But the other voice so impels me that great doubt arises as to the complete right of the one over the other. In years past the restraining voice has wielded much more power than the constraining voice. But things are changing and I am growing up. Is there not a medium in the solution of this problem? And yet the constraining voice says I do not want to find a medium this weekend. Never before have I really gone on a true saturnalia. I do not know what it is like. I do not know what happiness some people seem to derive from completely relaxing mundane tensions that are created through the week. Of this Pascal might say:

> Man is never unhappy in not having three eyes. But he is disconsolate in not having had any.

November 23, 1952 . . . Bill and I started for Smith about 9:35 Saturday morning and got in Northampton at 4:00 P.M. It took nine rides to get us there, about three more than usual; since the second driver that gave us a lift took us unwittingly half way to Boston before he realized what road he was taking. From the lowering skies there fell a cascadal inundation that that fell on our clothes and bodies until we arrived as poor waifs from the grisly streets of some large city. All day it rained and for seven hours we tried to reach a destination that for a good many hours was becoming farther and farther from us. One car would let us out and we would stand without any shelter, as the rain rolled over our heads into our garments.

When we arrived one of the girls went to fetch Jane as we followed closely behind her. Bursts of laughter filled the damp air as she gazed on these two ridiculously soaked bumpkins. But I lost no time, knowing that this trip was for one reason and that everything would be done to realize it. "Jane!" I exclaimed while putting on her rosy cheek, an affectionate osculation that was made all the more pleasant as her opulent breasts concealed in a tight-fitting sweater brushed against my side.

We followed her into the guest's chamber, where we changed into some of the girls' raiment. To cover my dampened torso, Jane gave me one of her short-sleeved blouses that pulled my shoulders together like a vice. One of her girl friends donated a pair of blue jeans, which closely bound my lower extremities so that it was difficult and unwise to move too much lest they rip or undue discomfort be inflicted on me. Finally, to put the climax to my comfort they let me have a jersey that had its tensile capability tested to the utmost. After the garments were reasonably dry the girls pressed them and sent us on our way to Rahar's Restaurant.

It was decided from the beginning of the trip that this weekend would be a success, if only from a selfish standpoint. Too long had people been regarding me as the man of great fortitude who never bowed to temptation or who was too sad or melancholic to be able to have a good time with a girl. But the universal cure-all for reticence was to open up my heart and mind so that the evening would be a glittering success. Jane meant nothing to me and still does not. She was to be solely an ego-boaster. Too long have I been denied those natural satisfactions that the human body and mind cry for. She did not know that I had once again decided to imbibe. When I ordered a Daiquiri she was rather surprised and ordered one herself in remarking, "Oh, is this going to be a drinking evening?" She then knew why I was there and knew more thoroughly when I made a boorish reply to a remark concerning the menu. "This menu really tempts me." To that I unthinkingly replied, "That's what you are here for." I tried to covered up this true but tactless faux pas by telling her that we were there to eat well. After the Tourmaise appetizer, the waitress brought two orders of delectably crisp and brown chicken. I wanted no desert, but Jane enjoyed some strawberry shortcake.

The band began to play and my head began to whirl pleasantly, though I kept my social balance throughout the evening. If I was drunk, which was far from the truth, no one could have told it. I tried and tried desperately to be amiable and friendly toward Bill and his date, trying not to belittle any one of them or make myself offensive, disagreeable, or too aloof. I did succeed. For in spite of the fact that neither Bill nor his date drank, they never became distant from me or said disagreeable things to reward me for any egotism or selfishness that might have been shown. Now that I look back on this, sentimental tears fall from my eyes to think that I truly passed an evening without showing offensive egotism and yet retaining the respect of these friends. But Jane was afraid. She was with one of her friends that refrained from drinking and did not want this girl to feel uncomfortable nor did she want to give herself the reputation of being too lax and easy to conquer. But she was not drinking just because I was. She has learned how to temporize. She was ready not to drink, because she thought that I did not drink. But when we started to order drinks it would have taken no expert to realize that this was not the first time she had engaged in drinking. She did not even have to look at the menu to order. I did have to use one, hoping all the time that the drink being ordered was not out of place with the meal, time and atmosphere. The only thing I did hold against her was the fact that she was temporizing. With me she could have gone without drinking, but what would she have done with someone who was a real drunkard? Was this temporizing merely an indication of insincerity on her part? But I did not care. I was there for one thing—to satisfy these frustrations, which say I am incapable of holding the affection of a person very long. I have tried being like a true man is supposed to be. I have tried to be fair with the opposite sex, but they consider me the less for it. They would rather go out with a man who is considered no sissy. I had given up any desire to leave a good impression on her. My sole object was to quench this desire to be recognized for my masculinity. And to implement this plan, I began to think of drinking just enough to add gaiety to the party and at the same time go as far as possible with Jane. It is supposed to be the girl's prerogative to say when to stop and the male's prerogative to try to go as far as possible. I tried and it was fun.

We arose from the table, being far from intoxication, but free from reticence. As the first dance beat a lulling rhythm, which our feet followed with a languid release from worry and sorrow, Jane moved her soft black hair against my cheek as I tightened my embrace. The evening passed with dance and drink. We walked into the softly lighted bar and I drank a beer as her beautiful eyes gazed into mine and we reminisced about the summer. As the bottle of beer dwindle, I handed it to her and she smoothed her throat with a small quantity. We sauntered back to the dancing room, hand-in-hand, and once more joined Bill and his girl friend. Bill and Jane were talking about nineteenth century music and philosophy. Suddenly, the dance floor thundered with a ravenous piece of boisterous tones, which someone had requested by the name of Charleston. The urge hit me and we were soon in the midst of vociferous pounding of feet and exotic waving of hands.

As we returned to the table, the sweat poured from our amorous faces and my mind thought of nothing but one thing. The cares and worries of the world about me disappeared and my heart grew light and set on one thing. We sat down with the others for a few minutes and contributed a few words about Descartes' theory of being. As a new fox trot rolled from the band, Bill and his girl joined the happy dancers who were now surrounded by the fuliginous smoke that rose from nearby tables and concealed them in nepenthean bliss.

I then suggested that we take a walk on the veranda to cool off. Through the crowds we made our way until the porch was reached where she refused to go any further without a wrap. Since it would be too difficulty to weave our way once more through the crowd to find her coat, we decided to remain inside. I offered to give her my coat but she politely refused. Thus we sedately and disgustingly sat ourselves down on a window ledge, saying very little as I sulked because she would not go outside. We returned to the table and I told the others we had been outside to get some fresh air. Jane's immediate and almost apologetic riposte was that we had gotten this fresh air outside in the lounge on a window ledge.

The evening was drawing to a close and it became apparent that she was fulfilling her part of the feminine role, but perhaps my masculine role was not being aggressive enough. Once more we began to dance to a low and mellifluous tune that caused oblivion. The floor was crowded and we could not move far. I began to move a little bit forward and then to the side. As we remained in one spot lulling back and forth to the rhythm of the music, I occasionally made an aggressive and unexpected step forward. Our thighs touched and rocked back and forth together as I felt my phallic weakness rubbing against her stomach. I pulled her tighter in the embrace as her comforting head rested on my shoulder and our hands clasped in ecstasy rested between our hearts. Suddenly, with an unpleasant jerk, she raised her head, looked around and remarked that the floor was crowded, and then rested her tempting head once more on my clavicular joint.

The evening enchantress had flown away and once more we were in the world of bitter worries and poisonous stings. The seducing music had slipped away into the night. But its happiness still lingered as we marched up the sidewalk in military fashion until I stepped on her toe in a "to-the-rear-march." "Carry me,

Alex," she cried as a happy little baby. And so through the town we went, she in my arms and laughter in the air and one thought in my mind. I let her down in front of her house as suddenly the wild and unthinking gaiety of the evening came to a distressful end. Bill's girl went inside to fetch our gear, as Jane and I walked around the parking lot. We walked to the rear of the minuscule parking lot but turned to the left when the faces of many students were seen through the window studying their books. We made a circle around the parking lot until we finally came to a shadowy, excluded spot. I turned her quickly, taking her in my arms, squeezing her like a beast, trying to get some satisfaction—some response. But her body was limp like a hanging cadaver. I wanted to continue the kiss, but she unenergetically turned her head. We walked to the porch. She explained how to reach the house where Bill and I were to catch a ride. I grabbed her once more in my arms, but she turned her head. We walked over the pavement to her room. On the veranda one of her friends was standing with her fiancé. The only thing Jane said was, "It's all right in public for them. They're engaged." Nuts! The purpose of the evening had been thwarted.

As we drove home the evening passed before me in a beautiful and uncynical panorama. The phantasmagoria of anxieties that so many dates have drawn for me was not present. I sat back in the seat of the car, reflecting on Jane with great respect and on the evening with great joy. I realized that she was not the kind of girl that had been painted in my mind of her. She has real values in life. She can temporize, true, but so can I. The few moments that I have had to reflect on this date were replete with guiltiness and trying to convince myself that Alice would not have to know anything about it. When Alice comes to visit me, if she ever does, I decided that I would not drink with her. But since Jane does drink, I decided to drink also. I had played the masculine role well and she had played the feminine role well. How much more respect I have for her now, knowing that she does have morals and very high morals! I know now that her laxity in morals does not go beyond a kiss and that kiss can be pretty cold if she wants to make it thus. I respect you, Jane, and though I do not love you, I thank you for having enough courage to protect your girl friend from social uneasiness, for talking of things of spiritual value with sincerity, and for playing your feminine position well. You have helped me to find that medium in life that I am seeking.

November 25, 1952 . . . The Air Science examination was finished early this afternoon so that I could spend two and a half hours at the gymnasium in swimming and exercising. The release of the pre-test tension and the free time given to exercise after the test created in me a sense of tranquility and a certain oblivion of harassing worries. The tired and fatigued but mentally rested body that I carried with relaxation from the gymnasium caused a few moments of fleeting bliss. Today was the first time that I had been in the swimming pool since the very beginning of the semester in September. At that time my form was not in perfect shape, since the summer offered little chance to practice for competitive swimming. My thighs were in fairly good condition, though, since we had done considerable bicycling through the Armorican Massif during the two and one half weeks preceding the fifteen-day trek to Paris. But the rest of my body was not in too good condition.

Last year I swam on the freshman team—one time in a meet with a high school group. I had never swum competitively before and could do little more than stay afloat, whereas the majority of the other students on the team had done a great deal of competitive swimming in their prep schools and high schools. But I wanted to become a good swimmer and I tried. Many were the nights, though, when I walked from the gymnasium sick and manly holding back tears, for the coach had no use for me. I had started too late and did not have the potential to develop into a good swimmer. Certainly, others had developed from little or nothing into great swimmers, but most of them knew how to breathe and stroke. I did not know how to breathe while swimming. And there as the others magnificently performed, I sat by myself—the cynosure of mocking ridicule. Nobody said anything. But it was not hard to see that they considered me inferior. But I was able to develop my ability and form as the year passed by. The coach never put me in any of the big meets. And one time he looked at me and said in biting words, "I don't want you."

On the boat to France this summer one of my fellow journalists asked me why I was not on the college paper. To this piquing remark I enumerated my college chores of the freshman year—

dining hall work, French club, and swimming. This ferocious young journalist immediately seized on this piece of information. In a few days the boat was rolling with the reputation of the great Alexis Evelyn—the incomparable champion of varsity potential. "Don't be too surprised if you see Alexis Evelyn jumping off the side of the boat," read a portion of the next day's newspaper. In the lounge on the bulletin board someone had put up a picture from some magazine. The picture showed a young man clad in a bathing suit, jumping into the ocean. Underneath was my name. Undoubtedly this copemate was merely trying to increase the camaraderie of the ship by using this good-natured joke on one of the members of the newspaper staff. There was nothing I could do. It would have been pure tomfoolery to have printed a contradiction to my vaunted talents. Yet I was capitalizing on something that was not mine. Throughout the whole trip I tried to play the role of a big swimmer. Indeed, I was the best swimmer in our group so that the task was not too difficult. But there was never a moment that I did not fear that some one in the group would find out my real capabilities compared to the other members of my college team. On the other hand, the old saw says that anyone who does anything has those who talk about him or her and I let it go at that.

Today this chagrin passed away. I did it. The time spent in bodybuilding has not been in vain. I swam one lap and stopped and then two. I worked out with the flutter board for two or three laps. Then I decided to try the ordinary ten laps that the coach gave us to do last year. Only during the very last part of the year had I been able to complete ten laps in medium heat. So I was dubious whether or not it would be feasible to even try to do these ten laps after a summer of little exercise. I tried it and failed. I did four and could do not more. The water got in my nose, my stoke became a confused pattern of blows which struck the water like a windmill, and my arms became fatigued. But this was not to discourage me. After one year of failing, I did not care what the coach thought of me. I was not trying to do these laps to help me make varsity. They were tried because I wanted to be as good as the fellows from last year—the fellows who ignored me and thought me unworthy to be considered as a swimmer. For one hour I did not again try to accomplish what seemed like an impossible feat. Instead, I did one or two laps and then rested. Finally, the courage ebbed up until I could no longer wait. I started to swim, trying to perfect a method of blowing the air out through my nose while it was turned under water without getting a mouthful of water in my mouth. I swam one lap and turned to complete the second when I succumbed and could no longer suffer the discomfort and frustration of swimming and getting small quantities of water in my mouth. After returning to the end of the pool, I once again recommenced this unrewarding project. And then with the shocking surprise of a speeding hurricane and the peaceful happiness of a dove in flight, I felt myself suddenly released from this tension and fear of the water and of reaching my destination at the other end of the pool. My body relaxed as I blew the initial exhalation out of my nose and the rest out of my mouth, following the last movement by immediately turning my head to inhale in my right armpit. Before I had had no system of exhalation. I would try it one way and then the other way until finally it chanced that this particular combination of mouth-nose exhalation with its peculiar timing gave me the breathing comfort to swim indefinitely if my body could stand up under the stress. And it did. It was as though someone had given me an ampoule of some energizing liquid. My body relaxed, my mind relaxed, and I swam peacefully though slowly up and down the pool. I felt and knew that I could go on for many minutes but stopped after breaking my personal record. I can do it. I can go out for varsity now and wont have to go out for intramural swimming. All my efforts have not been in vain. Certainly, I will never be a great swimming star—probably will not even get a letter—but the thing is that I will be on the varsity. I know I can make it now. My mother's first cousin had graduated from Littleton High School, just south of Denver, a year after I was born and he went to Harvard College, where he became the captain of the football team, an English major and a Phi Beta Kappa. His father was a medical doctor and Commander of San Luis Obispo

Army Hospital in California during World War II. When we were living in New Orleans, he was there, living with his wife (a Radcliffe College graduate) and working as an accountant—he had also graduated from Harvard School of Business with a major in accounting. Once at his apartment, he showed me the photograph of him and his football teammates that was hanging on the wall. I do not want to follow in his shadow, though I know my mother wishes it. I want to be my own man. Swimming is now my thing— for better or for worse.

November 25, 1952 . . . Last night after working out at the gymnasium, I returned to the college dining hall where Al had promised to meet me at 6:00 P.M. I was a few minutes late, though, and therefore found him already seated at one of the tables with Henry as his commensal. After a few seconds in line, I was accosted with a friendly tap on the shoulder by Pete, who I noticed was not with his roommates. We went through the line and then joined Al and Henry, who were not unexpectedly talking about some political subject.

There was no tension, though Henry expatiated as usual with the utmost boisterousness and gesticulation. We began to discuss the treatment of communist activities in the country, with particular reference to the Rosenthal case that was just refused a retrial this last week. Henry began his tirade against the government, giving the impression that the government has never been stern enough with the Communists. During the presidential campaign he reflected the same discontent concerning the administration of the government under the Democrats. He is never satisfied and always can talk. He is one of the few persons who really has the gift for gab. His mouth is like a well-fired chimney—it never stops smoking. And thus it was not out of character that he should be condemning the government for clemency in dealing with the Rosenthal's. Al half-heartedly agreed. And then I added my pertinent piece of information, which threw new light on the subject, though it did not stop his infernal griping. During most of the conversation I sat back, hoping that they would stop talking, yet interspersing a few germane remarks when the occasion arose. After about fifteen minutes Dick walked into the dining hall, giving some jesting greeting to Al while saying nothing to me or the others that were seated at the table. I felt uneasy and the more consideration I gave the problem the heavier it began to weigh on my mind.

That evening after selling some musical footballs and beer mugs, I retired at 10:00 P.M., read the Figaro and the New York Herald, and then tried to go to sleep. But this haunting idea that I was being ignored, that Al was getting more respect that I—these and other tearing thoughts began to levitate in my mind from the black and abysmal depths where I tried to suppress them. They broke through and I could not avoid facing the reality. I tried to analyze the situation but could not. I thought again of the events that had brought us together—that Dick and I had chosen to be roommates solely because that seemed to be a last resort. One day after we had chosen to be roommates, he was walking with another friend into the employment bureau as I opened the door to enter myself. In a very cutting and caustic tone that lacked all semblance of friendship, he remarked, "Hi, handsome." This black cesspool of horrendous memories began to ebb up. I thought of my unsuccessful efforts to live with others—my family, my grandmother, and my freshmen roommates. Would Dick be another victim of this person who so wanted to live with other people yet found and still does find his attempts rather abortive? Thank God my fears have been assuaged, for Dick is extremely compatible, though there are moments when his cutting sarcasm does inflict telling blows on a too sensitive mind. But still the fact cannot escape me that we were not brought together out of any real attachment. The two reasons that I asked Dick to room with me were that I did not want to go through the disgrace of having people say I could not live with others and also I knew that he did not drink. He was at that time planning to enter the ministry, though I did not find that out either until several weeks after our decision to room together. This I learned one evening when he expressed a desire to change from the ministry to medicine, since he wanted to be considered like the other fellows. He did not want them to think that he was too puritanical. He wanted to be a part of the undergraduate society. I knew how he felt, since the same decision had occurred with me a year previous. But the main thing I was seeking in a roommate was someone who was not given to continued bacchanalias and was religious to some extent. I am glad we are rooming together, though it is perhaps a shame that we did not know each other better before making the final decision to turn our applications in together, since that might have given us both confidence that we both liked each other.

Last night Al and Dick did not retire until 2:00 A.M. For two or three hours they talked about what I do not know. Last year Steve and Sam had done the same thing. Why is it that I am never included in these conversations? This morning as I returned from classes, I saw one of my friends sauntering along to class and talking to a classmate. Coming through the gates about a third of a block away, I saw one of his roommates. They were both going the same direction, but they were not together. This same fellow who was coming through the gate had asked me to double date with him this last Saturday. But since I was going to Smith it was impossible. Why did he not ask his roommate before asking me. His roommate, a very good-looking individual, asked me a few weeks ago if I knew girls in town with whom he might be able to get a date. Is it true what Jesus said in his sermon of the mount?

> No man can serve two masters: for either he will hate
> the one, and love the other; or else he will hold to the one,
> and despise the other. Ye cannot serve God and mammon.

Jesus knew human psychology better than any other person who has ever trodden upon the earth. He knew that man could not serve God and money at the same time. But he also knew that for two individuals to give the utmost devotion to each other, they must solely be committed to each other. There cannot be a third person, for then tension develops, feelings are mixed up and confused. All three persons want to be liked by the other. And the two who were the closest in the beginning might well be the most hateful of enemies in the end. Is this then why we have the institution of monogamous marriage? When three people live together there is a constant struggle for the other person's favor to the detriment of the next fellow. The person who has the most to offer will be the one to whom all this fulsome sycophancy and petty rivalry will be directed. And money means more than anything else in a situation like this. The richest man is the most influential. When he no longer has any money, then he no longer has any influence unless he has an exceedingly forceful personality.

Dick is sitting on the lounge now and Al is unwrapping a turkey that his parents sent him from Texas. The room is calm—blessedly calm with no inner tensions. Vacation will start for us all in a few hours. I will be going home to see the folks. Already supposedly forgotten things of the past are beginning to appear. I cannot get the thought and image of Mother out of my mind. I think of her words spoken once in regard to my father, "He did not even like me to kiss my uncle." These thoughts they come like piercing darts and woeful reminders of the past. They come in spite of what I may do and come like the image of a kaleidoscope with only black glass. I think of Sandra and what she said one time when I was visiting them on the Army post in Denver. She was going to the movies. She had invited me but I declined. "We have decided to not make each other do something that he does not want to do because the other one thinks it nice." Many years had passed between this remark and the one about which Mother so morbidly reminisced.

Al is going to New York today. He will probably spend the vacation at the Biltmore Hotel, where a good majority of the college students pass their vacation. Had I made plans to remain here, I wish he would have invited me to go with him. But I know that he would not. Our interests are different. That is what results from being haphazardly thrown in with someone else. It is possible to be happy and live in harmony, but it is much more easier if each individual involved has similar likes and dislikes. To be compatible two people must have the same interests, or else the different interests will diverge in such different directions that a truly close feeling cannot be developed. I have decided today that to have a married life, I must have a girl with similar likes and dislikes. Such a person does not come without effort. I am going to visit Smith, Vassar, Holyoke and every other girls' college that there is in the East whenever the chance comes and the financial status thus permits. I have decided that the girl I marry will have to live with me before the person ties the nuptial knot. Whether such a relationship will be platonic or sexual is hard to tell know. Moral fiber weakens under such conditions, but it will be that test that my prospective wife will have to pass. I do not care where we live. But we must live alone and without pre-marital copulation. I will not commit myself to an intolerable situation with a woman who does not have my interests and a personality that will be compatible with mine in such a way that we will be able to rear a large family in all happiness that humans can attain, however small or great that may be. Neither do I want a woman who has no outside interests. But I want one who can deport herself well among others without causing either of us social chagrin by undermining the ego. And yet I want her to be friendly with others and sympathetic. I do not want her to be a snob. But I want her to understand this morbid sensitiveness that is an intrinsic part of my nature. Indeed it will take an understanding and mature individual to give me a sure footing and make up for the love and security that never existed in my childhood.

The excitement of going home is increasing minute by minute, as the final hour of departure grows nearer. There will be unpleasant items with which to contend but there will also be awaiting me a grand reception from the family. But there is one thing I have decided. I will tell them nothing of my accomplishment during the time since we last saw each other. I will tell them nothing of the mental trials and tribulations that are so common in the college life. In other words, I will appear to them as the mature and healthy son that they are proud of. I have decided that people do not have confidence in or respect people as much when they detect a sense of continual unhappiness. Everybody has their troubles and tries hard to dissipate them. They are solaced to realize that others have the same tribulations, but they do not like to hear one talk about them.

Why I do not know—but I have not been able to get my mind off of Jane. Every sentence that I have written today was done in recalling the pleasant time at Smith last Saturday. I wonder if Jane would lower her opinion of me like Alice did if she could read what I am writing.

November 26,1952 . . . There is nothing to do now but wait—
wait until I get home. We should probably arrive in Fort Wayne
tomorrow about 9:00P.M. I wish there were something else to do
but just sit in the car and watch the landscape being swiftly passed
by. The fellow who is driving the car is not too voluble. He cannot
be in this heavy and speeding traffic. The silence is unbearable and
only now and then does a light manage to flicker from some distant
town as the harassing negritude presses upon us. He offers me a
cigarette. I refuse. "I am out for swimming," I tell him, knowing
only too well the falseness of the statement. All the time my face
remains sullen, as I gaze into the distance, hoping that he will not
say anything. My heart is palpitating but I do not know why. I
feel like crying but how silly that is. "I am a man," I keep telling
myself. I do not care what this fellow thinks of me. Let him think
that I am sullen. Whenever I am initially friendly to people, they
afterwards think I am subservient. Yet all the time I was hoping he
would like me.

About 3:00 the next morning we were speeding across the
Pennsylvania Turnpike. Neither of us had slept much and then he
said, "I wonder if it is worth it." I asked him why he was making
this Thanksgiving trip home. He was going to let his folks sell the
car—a Cadillac—and he had not seen them since a year. He had
attended a summer school course in Russian and had not been
able to visit them. I wanted to talk. Suddenly the urge to talk
became irresistible. Here was a student who had not seen his parents
for a long time and was not particularly anxious to see them at this
time. We began to converse first about school in general and then,
when he found out that I had been to Europe, the topic changed
to a philosophical perusal of the problems of different cultures. I
talked about "culture shock" and the gradual effect it had on the
group. I told him how the culture with which one had been
inculcated with since childhood battles against this new culture
and despises it in spite of the conscious efforts one makes to
assimilate it. I told him that the French morals outside of Paris are
much more stricter than in the States and that the nuptial union
is considered more as a business contract than as the culmination

of a courtship of profound love. But I did not tell him the battle I fought to keep from drinking when everyone else in our group except Skip imbibed as Frenchmen. I did not tell him that I had previously attributed the downfall of French power and prestige to the fact that they have one of the best wine-producing countries in the world. I did not tell him that I had once thought that, because now I know why they drink. I was too naive before. The world had to be perfect. And I despised the world because it was not so. And then he said something that stuck like an arrow in a target: "We are not living if we do not resist." The words rang with a reverberating echo and I looked back on this European experience not with shame but with thanksgiving. I looked back on these people and the boys and girls in our group with pride and said a silent prayer, thanking God that he had given me the opportunity to be with these people and to love them for their faults rather than hate them.

We stopped at one of the Howard Johnson's Restaurants about 4:00 A.M. My friend parked the car while I went in to get some coffee for him and some milk or ice cream for me. As I stood at the counter waiting as the crowd was being served, a young girl of about nineteen entered the restaurant with a young fellow who wore an orange and white sweater. Nothing could have stupefied me more—she resembled in every respect the girl whom I had taken on the date to Central City before going East to school. It was with Jabe that we had double dated. The picnic was given by some students from Colorado who were upperclassmen at our prospective college. After the party this girl and I went to Central City. The night was a painful one. She was not going to college or even entertaining any thoughts of college and consequently felt ill at ease among the college crowd. It was my first contact with the college crowd and my conscience tore and beat me viciously. I hated Jade's haughty antics and disdaining attitude and feared the others. I had been taking dancing lessons at Arthur Murray's for a month. The final lesson was the following week. I did not know how to square dance or fox-trot or waltz. I stepped on my girl's feet and was made the cynosure of ridicule in never being able to follow the caller and always bumping into others in doing the fox trot. This was the first dance to which I had been since the age of twelve, when I took Mrs. Pollack's daughter to a formal dance in Aurora (a suburb of Denver) with Dad and Sandra. As we drove home in the car, I put my arm around this girl and closed my eyes, hoping that they would think I was asleep and not merely afraid to talk or sing. I could not and cannot sing well and never will be able to. As the others sung, I wished with all my might that my voice were also capable of the same. As we neared home the jarring of the car from the rough roads caused my arm to slip down into her lap. She moved it aside but it fell in place again with salacious thoughts. They let us off before her house. I walked her to the door, said goodnight, and quickly left as a frightened child who has tried to do something wrong and has been thwarted. She stood there rather puzzled. Two days later I called her up for another date and she said she was busy.

This then was the girl whom I thought had entered the restaurant. I did not think of the unpleasantness of that evening. I did not think of the chagrin and embarrassment that followed from reflection on my immatureness. I thought only passingly of the remark which unthinkingly emanated from my inexperienced month when one of the boys said something in French and I replied that my French vocabulary was limited to "L'amour." This was all passed. The fact that this person might be a friend whom I had known previously was more important. I was a little cautious at first, not wishing to approach her and have it turn out that this was not the girl. My friend had parked the car by this time and came walking in the door. He advised me to go speak to her and quit being so diffident. We walked over to the counter at which they were seated but there was only one seat. So we went to the other end of the room. After peering incessantly through the crowd at her and her man friend, I was able to discern a capital "C" on the male's sweater. There was no doubt then. This was she. I got up, walked over to them and said in polite tones, "I hope you wont consider me impudent but your face looks familiar to me." It was she. But before the conversation had even started she pointed to the fellow to her right and said, "I want you to meet my husband." Little gusts of laughter burst up in my throat but I was able to contain them.

My friend and I left the restaurant. The past seemed pleasantly blissful. That evening did not seem so spiritually morbific after all. The whole evening, which had happened so long ago, now passed in retrospect and what then seemed unbearable was now looked on with sweet reverie. I remembered when we were leaving the bar to return to Denver. My girl and I were walking ahead of another couple when I turned my head and replied rather subserviently, "Are you drunk, ha, ha!" The fellow turned to his girl and very curtly asked her what I had said without answering me. The causticity of his disdaining attitude stuck with me for a long time. We say little to each other at school now and have often passed each other on the street without speaking. One day during the beginning of the year, I was coming from the gymnasium and spied him standing in front of a grocery store, waiting for one of his friends. I looked at him and he looked at me but showed no signs of recognition. So I passed him by and have not greeted him since then. But this all passed by now as something that really did not concern me. It seemed like a movie that might have been seen long ago and only a few of the images remained. The plot was forgotten, as were the names and the emotions of the picture. It had been so boorish that it did not even reach the level of one-upmanship, which might have at least made it interesting.

We were nearing home but my attitude remained the same. I still looked forward with dread. I knew that the past has put an inseparable hold on Dad. He had suffered from the past and every time that I visited him a morose feeling came over me. All we ever talked about were morose subjects. But I was determined to prevent that this time. My friend left me at Fort Wayne at 9:00 A.M. and after three rides I arrived home in Edinburgh, Indiana. My father was now on an outpatient's status from nearby Camp Atterbury. After riding all night without sleeping I naturally felt tired but tried to conceal the fact in a very warm greeting to the whole family. I kissed Sandra and Betty on the cheeks and shook Dad's hand. They greeted me with smiles and quick flowing conversation. In the first fire minutes at least ten topics were covered. We talked about the summer in France, my hitchhiking from Fort Wayne (Sandra said I might have been robbed. This I resented and told her I did not have enough money to be robbed.), school, my new girl friends, the weather and how Betty had grown. Before I could complete the answer to one question they had interrogated me on another. But as yet they had not touched the taboo subject. That would come later and I knew it and began to unconsciously and unwillingly tighten up. Little by little I started to laugh less vigorously and began more and more to feel empty as though my folks were distant from me. The feeling was not new, for every time that I have been with Dad since the divorce there was a feeling of distance between us. And in trying to lessen that distance I would only succeed in enlarging it, for the only way we had during these short visits before and now to unite our feelings was by conversation. And that has always proved unsuccessful. Why I do not know, but it has and did this time also.

That evening we all went to see *Francis Goes to West Point*. Since the film is about the life of this college and a mule, it was quite appropriate for the evening. Maybe the mule was less appropriate. But nevertheless we went and laughed. I was inwardly proud that we were seeing this picture, since my college is of the same caliber in a civilian capacity as is West Point and I knew they would think of me as one of the boys going to school with the mule. For me it was a piece of vicariously living on an elevated plane. I rather resented the melodramatic element of the film, since college is by no means melodramatic. But I was happy in the end when the film turned out in the American fashion and everybody was happy and on the road to success. The crisis came after the film as Sandra and I walked through the foyer. I then told her of resentments for the melodramatic tone the producers had given to the play and thus the indirect romanticism that would be eventually created in the minds of the youngsters for the Point. "They do not really have that much discipline there," I said in a declaiming tone. "They certainly do!" she snapped back like a wounded wildcat. The incident was passed over until we all reached home where it eventually flared up again.

There was an elderly lady and her grandchildren who had accompanied us to the movies and who afterwards came home with us to have something to eat. She was a friendly and affable individual. But she was older than I and spoke to me in too gentle and condescending tones. To counter this I immediately assumed a superior attitude to all that was going on around me. I gazed reservedly into the distance and said little except when spoken to. All the time, though, I was afraid that she might do the same thing to me and she did, it seemed. Just before we arose to go to the table, I interspersed some remark, hoping and praying that it would receive some intelligent attention. I looked at her in the eyes and felt a deep antagonism but tried half successfully to reconcile our estrangement. I did not laugh at anything that was funny, though an effort was made. If my folks had not been there, I know that it would have been much more easier to laugh. I wonder if they had told her my biography and hated them the more if such were true. A flicker of hate and bile began to control me and a sense of uneasiness pricked at my body as I tried to combat them. We repaired to the table. I was decided to talk as loathsome and debasing as the action now seemed to warrant. What could I say. If I said something too erudite they would think me a snob. If I said something too light they would think me childish. And I detested them and loathed them for it. And then I was afraid I could neither think of something too erudite or too light. I stumbled into the conversation when the topic eventually turned to the never failing panacea of stymied conversation, especially among women, however loathsome and disgusting the topic may be to the majority of man. In the most unassuming manner that was possible under the circumstances, I tried to explain that when one breathes in, the diaphragm expands, which means that the stomach also expands. It was to my great surprise when Sandra did not immediately start a dispute over this information, claiming that I was irrecusably wrong and that my benighted callowness in everything prevented me from interpreting the facts as they should be. The evening was apparently saved and the bitterness that was to come deferred until the next night, when the sore was ruthlessly broken open and the pus and filth of the past once more oozed out to sully our minds and attitude and bodies and faces. And the sore may never heal again.

The next day was half dissipated when I arose at 11:00 A.M. Dad paid his diurnal visit to the psychiatrist. But besides that nothing unusual happened until Sandra went shopping and left Dad and me by ourselves in the house. I dreaded this moment but knew that as sure as day is day and night is night that it would be ineluctable. There was no way to avoid it, if I were to spend a vacation with them. There never has been. Someone is always having troubles and nobody is ever happy and everyone pities me and thinks that I have had such a terrible life. The fools—I do not want their pity or their condescension or their moroseness. Can they not see that when things are put safely in the past, it is sheer tomfoolery to bring them out again to cause more hardship and suffering? Can they not conquer this sentimentality?

Dad was sitting on the settee on the other side of the room from my fauteuil. Without too much of a preface he asked if I was surprised to see him in this condition without any physical ailments in spite of his nervous breakdown (depressive). I told him that what had been expected was no other than it appeared. I looked at him and despised him and thought what a little man he was. I decided though that what he had to say would be listened to, for I realized that he had been suffering mentally and that what I could do to help him would be to the good. And so I resigned myself to listen to what he had to say, determined only to listen. And that I did. I only listened. Never once did I mention Mother or my brother or stepfather, though the following conversation brought these memories like a hand that reaches into a filthy and mephitic sewer.

"Alex," he started, "you and I both have had difficult childhoods. What I am going to tell you, I hope will save you from the suffering that I have been through. Not many people have the money to have the treatment of a psychiatrist. And so I consider myself a very lucky man. The doctor has at sometimes been intolerable. But he has started with the beginning and has worked forward. He should be through in maybe two or three months or maybe longer.

"I have not discussed much of my childhood with you, since I thought it best to put these unpleasant memories in the past. The psychiatrist showed me where I was wrong. I told him that I did not think it was necessary for a man to talk about himself. If he were any good others would know about him anyway. The doctor did not say much. He merely replied in stern tones, 'Why?'

"My mother was eighteen when she married my father, a man of thirty-three. He came from Kentucky. His father was a physician born in Tennessee, whose ancestors had emigrated from England via Virginia, North Carolina and South Carolina. As a small child his immediate family moved to Livingston County, Kentucky. My mother came from a large farm family. They met each other at a dance. And so well could my father dance that they soon became infatuated with each other. A few years ago Mother admitted to Sandra that she married him merely because of his ability to dance. I was the oldest of the family and consequently the one who had all the hard chores as the other youngsters came along. Dad drank a lot and Mother became very religious. Mother beat religion into us and what Mother didn't beat into us Dad did. I was unhappy and tried to run away at one time, but not having any money I had to return. One summer Dad promised to give us half of the returns from the crop if we would take care of the fields. Do you know how much we got?" I here interspersed a dry "No, I don't." "My brother and myself each got one dollar. I hated my father and I hated my mother but have always been afraid to say so, since convention says we should love our mother and father. I developed a guilt complex, because I knew I should not hate them yet I could not do otherwise. I developed an inferiority complex. On time I remember when I was writing to a girl and I asked Mother if the letter sounded all right to her. She told me that if I couldn't tell myself whether it was good or not, I should not be writing it. If I could not confide in her whom could I confide in? And to cover up for this inferiority complex, I developed a superior complex. I became a perfectionist. I set high standards for myself and for you and your brother. Here is a list of what a perfectionist does. Let me read them to you. 'He thinks himself better than anyone else. He boasts of good health. He cannot stand to be sick. If he is sick he blames himself and develops a guilt attitude. He works all the time and exhausts himself so that he is eventually unable to do anything. He sets high standards for himself and others and cannot stand shortcomings in others. He is basically frustrated and is trying to cover up an inferiority complex.' That is what I was, Alex, a perfectionist. I was afraid of the past and tried to cover it up by being a perfectionist until the past developed into a monster that tore open the cage and I could not longer ward it off.

"You remember yourself how your grandmother used to fight with me all the time. And you remember the divorce and that I was so heart-broken that I did not even go to the trial. Your grandmother testified against me—accused me of atheism and cruelty. When I was in the Pacific your stepfather wanted to change your surname but I refused.

"Sandra has done a lot to bring me out of this insecurity. When I was in Europe without her, I could not stand it having no one with me in whom I could confide. It was then that this monster became too large for me to contain. When I reached the States I was a broken man. I came back crying like a baby and blaming everything on the Army. The personnel at the base have been swell, though. They have done everything in the world to help me."

Sandra opened the door and walked in with several large bundles of groceries. After a few minutes Dad got up and went downstairs to regulate the furnace. Sandra took this opportunity to heap more coals on the fire, for she could see by the sullen and morose atmosphere that we had been perusing the subject of Dad's mental illness. There was not much she could say in those few moments. She could not elaborate too much. She did tell me though that the I.Q. test they had given Dad showed that he has a superior intelligence to the majority of the cases that they had previously dealt with and that he had the natural endowment to have become a general. They gave him credit for the sophomore year in college as the result of the test. That is the trouble she said. Then I remembered the words of my mother at the time when my stepbrother continued his kleptomaniac escapades. The people of the juvenile delinquency bureau said his tests showed an I.Q. exceedingly above normal. I remembered how they used to think I was so stupid and my stepbrother so smart.

As the groceries were put away we continued the talk. It did not cover new ground. They just kept mulling over the past. They were throwing it at me. Whenever they mentioned anyone's name whom I did not want to remember, I turned my head and made a noticeable scowl. From then to the end of the vacation I did not laugh once. I could not. I wished that I could but already my head was becoming heavy and I was becoming weary. They had broken their trust. They had opened the sore and began to talk about things that were well in the past. Why did they not stop this incessant torture? I hated them more and more as those dreadful last hours with them lingered on. I hoped that the time of departure for the campus would soon arrive.

After the evening repast, we all vacated to the living room, where we continued the evening in hot debate over every and any subject that happened to come to mind. Sandra would never agree with me. She never has agreed with me—whether the question be merely a hypothetical one for discussion or whether it be a pressing problem that must be resolved. We first began to discuss the various cultures of the world. Immediately, her idealistic mind began to work and she adamantly declared that cultures meant little, that the world could be united under one ruler and that all cultures could be assimilated into one. I tried to point out the infeasibility of such an idea, telling her that a person requires a lifetime to change from one culture to another. With the better communications system that we have today, I admitted that such an idea is more feasible today than it was fifty years heretofore. But I could not convince her that the French will not and cannot give up their culture for a united world. But she argued like a simpleton to the contrary, never willing to concede that her theory had certain desirable points but that it also had certain defects. She had to be right and I, the little boy never grown up, had to be wrong. I did not have enough experience, in spite of the fact I had been in Europe, to make a judgment on such a profound subject.

From there we digressed to college styles in clothes. The evening before, when they asked me what I would want for Christmas, I told them I needed a new suit and would like to buy a dark flannel one, since that is the style on the campus. Immediately, she disagreed and carried the topic over into this evening's discussion. Such suits are too dark and lugubrious was her contention. I tried to explain to her that the East is more conservative that the West. "Oh, yes, 'In Rome do as the Romans do.'" she retorted. But still she remained adamant and finally declared that even that was wrong. She had lived in the East and had never found that to be true. I was wrong and never could be right. Then I realized that it would do no good to argue sensibly with this woman. She would not listen. The only thing to do, would be to argue as irrationally as she. I then began to get bitter and have utter disregard for feelings and for any kind of tact. She had done the same thing to me. Why should I not do it to her? I then began an unsystematic and irrational humiliation of her. The schools of the East are much better than the school you went to. Once you have gone to them, whether you have money or not, you are in the aristocracy. The only way a girl can amount to anything is to go to one of the better-known Eastern colleges. There is no other way to happiness. That is the way to marry a rich husband. Immediately, she replied that she would not want to marry anyone who has gone to my school. She would rather be happy instead of being so financially and socially ambitious. "You cannot tell me that people with riches are happy," she said. "And going to your college does not insure social prestige. I wouldn't want to marry anyone who went to your college. I would rather be happy. And I know that the East is not any more conservative that the West because my fiancé went to Columbia." "That was the one with whom you broke up when he went to Texas during the war?" "Yes, that is he." She continued the argument and culminated my ire in saying that no daughter of hers would go to Smith College or Mount Holyoke College, where all the girls are debauched. I could not persuade her with any information that these girls are not debauched. She then began to claim that anyone who goes to an all boys' college is unstable socially and does not understand women. The same thing is true of girls who go to all women's colleges she claimed. Everyone who goes to a non-coeducational school is doomed to an unhappy marriage. That, of course, gave me great inspiration and hope for the future, considering my family history of divorces. I went to bed in a huff as did she. I know Dad was suffering through the whole thing but I was just as estranged from him as from Sandra.

When we were in Denver during the early years of their marriage, she never agreed with me. She never agreed with me and she never agreed with my brother. The first incident that comes to my mind concerned my brother. We were spending the summer with them, having left the family in the South. One evening a rather disputed film was playing. It was entitled *The Hucksters*. She expected it to be rather risqué and forbad my brother from seeing it. In spite of her orders, however, he went to see it and strode down the aisle with impish deviltry and called to Sandra, "How is your boy friend?" Nobody was more enraged. That was the first time I saw her in real anger and can see she her justification, though the film was not really out of line. The next summer I visited them alone. This was the last summer I spent before going out on my own. They did not know what the situation was at home and I would not tell them. During this particular phase of my life I was deeply religious; having no parents in whom I could confide, I thought, and justly so, that perhaps the church would give me some comfort. It was not unusual, therefore, to find us going to a revival meeting one Sunday in the City Auditorium in downtown Denver. As we were going there, we began to discuss the meaning of the word "pulpit." She claimed that it was the desk from which the speaker delivered his address. I tried to tell her that she was wrong and was confusing it with a lectern. But she would not listen. She was right and I was wrong. The pulpit was not, never has been and never will be the platform from which the speaker delivers the sermon. She wrangled about it and we both became angry. Another time she argued that in the word "habitat" the "a" of the last syllable is like the "a" in father. Her professor at college had pronounced it like that and therefore that was the accepted pronunciation. I tried to tell her that the correct pronunciation was like "a" in dad, but she would not listen and became angered, as did I. When I told her that I was leaving to go on my own, she berated me as though I were the worst scoundrel that ever lived.

Just before we went to bed the conversation turned to Lincoln. This resulted when I told her that colleges are trying to turn out leaders. She said she preferred Lincoln and his simple vocabulary. And she stressed vocabulary and made it sink in deep so that it stung. She said she preferred General Eisenhower to General MacArthur. I guess she was comparing me to General MacArthur because by that time I was so disgusted that I simply assumed an insufferable haughty attitude. In any event, the comparison to General MacArthur made me feel rather elated, though some people might have difficulty in finding the mental resemblance.

As we drove to Indianapolis the next day, I was reticent. Sandra breached the silence by asking me to explain existentialism. I was perhaps now more ready to explain existentialism than I ever have been. I told her how the French existentialists of Saint-Germain-des-Prés in Paris wear all black apparel, very seldom take baths, and try to get back as close to nature as they can. This is on the left bank south across the street by the same name from the University of Paris (branch V), which is also in this district, and about one mile northwest of the Sorbonne lecture hall of the University of Paris (branch VI) in the Latin Quarter, all south of the Seine River. It is the left bank because one faces its source the Atlantic Ocean to determine south or north bank. Students saturate the area. I stressed the black, though I am afraid that would rather astound the student body that they were compared to existentialists. I told her that they did not believe in God and that it seemed to me that this sort of cynicism developed from the misery that the French people have been subjected to during the war years. I could really see why these people might embrace this kind of religion or lack of it. Then I told her of some of the great French authors and their pessimistic attitude toward life. I told her that LaFontaine lived in Paris on the other side of the city from his wife. One day he went to visit her and saw a beautiful butterfly in the field. He spent the afternoon chasing it and returned to his coach too late to visit his wife and children. I told her of Voltaire's *Zadig* and how the old man from heaven threw the young boy into the river, because he would have brought only evil in the future. This and this alone was the extent of our conversation throughout the trip to Indianapolis.

All this time the conversation with Dad the previous day weighed on my mind. Perfectionist, perfectionist, perfectionist . . . ran through my mind. "Prefer General Eisenhower to General MacArthur." "I prefer Lincoln's simple vocabulary." "He thinks he is better than everyone else." "He is unstable and insecure." My head buzzed in vertigo of confused thoughts and I hoped the train would soon depart. I wished that I were away from my folks.

Dad parked the car while Sandra and Betty accompanied me into the train depot. I asked Sandra to get the ticket. I walked hesitatingly to the cigarette counter and asked for a pack of Chesterfields. I then gave a surreptitious glance in Sandra's direction, hoping that she would not see me. I put them in my pocket and waited for the train.

On the train I had all night to think about what had happened. There could have been no greater cynicism than that which wracked me. But there was a distant hand that kept calling to me that there might be some hope for happiness in this world, that there had to be some hope. I decided never to visit them again. And then Sandra's words came to me, words which she had said jestingly in considering my future: "You'll probably disown us when you get to be a millionaire." And I thought that perhaps she was so disputatious merely because she felt that I would some day think that I was too good for them. But I could not explain why she had been so disputatious before anyone knew that I might amount to something. Why was it that she always had to be right when she really was so wrong? The year I graduated from high school and spent two weeks with them before continuing to college, we spent one whole night in which she earnestly and righteously accused the professors of my prospective college as being Communists. Oh, how I wished that Mother and Dad had never been divorced, that I had a family like other boys and girls do! How much more fun would it be to go home, knowing that no one would be jealous of my progress! Did I remind her of her fiancé that went to Columbia? Is that why she never would agree with me? Then I remembered that she had said something about going to a psychiatrist when she was in New Orleans. I reached into the side of my coat pocket for the pack of cigarettes and then stepped out to the compartment joining the two cars. I lit a cigarette and began to smoke my first cigarette. My conscience oddly offered no qualms. I was determined to leave my perfectionism back at the train station. I was determined to be what Pericles meant when he said, "We cultivate the mind without loss of manliness." Life is a hard voyage and anything that will make the trip easier for the individual should not be condemned. I had never before been able to understand why people smoke but as a certain manly serenity and satisfaction came over me my conscience echoed: "What are you, Alex, that you want to be so perfect? God himself had more compassion on the poor outcast woman than on the righteous Scribes and Pharisees. You are no longer a child, who can live in his innocence and be happy. You are a man just as weak and helpless as the next fellow."

I still had not resolved this ambivalent feeling of hatred and love toward my folks, when I walked into our dormitory Sunday afternoon to find that Al and Dick had already returned. "Here is Evelyn and, God, with a weed in his mouth," greeted Dick. I walked in a rather unjovial but friendly disposition, still not recovered from the vacation. Dick and Al had already eaten, so I soon left them to replenish my empty stomach. As I sat over a hot plate of spaghetti there was a certain calmness after the storm, but my mind kept returning on something Sandra had said just before asking about existentialism: "How do you like your roommates

this year? Last year you . . . ." And then the sentence died down so
that I did not hear the finish and she did not get a reply. I knew
how I liked them. Al and Dick have had their faults and there has
been some tension but I have liked them. But these caustic words
spurred me on. From now on my roommates would see and live
with a new man—not a man who goes to bed while they talk, not
a man who holds himself aloof because of insecurity and jealousy,
but a man who esteems them for what they are and a man who
would endeavor to endear the relationship. I thought of double
dating with Dick. Maybe he is not the handsomest fellow on the
campus but he certainly has more than that—he is friendly. Maybe
Al does have a rather nonchalant attitude toward his studies. Maybe
he has realized that living with people is more important than
storing knowledge.

About 5:00 that evening I asked them if they were ready to go
eat. "We are going to eat here," they replied. I had almost forgotten
that Al's folks had sent him a large turkey. "Let's invite some more
people," Dick spurted out from under his books." Heck, yes,"
replied Al. "We can't eat all this." Al and I dispatched ourselves to
the nearest restaurant. Before we entered the restaurant we both
threw our cigarette butts to the ground. We first bought three
milkshakes and as I went to pay for them, Al waited for the ice
cream. He not only got ice cream but French fried potatoes and
rolls, which he paid for. As we were leaving one of the students
from across the hall opened one of the front doors. We invited him
to our feast and he said he would be there shortly. Our little
banquet consisted of five people. Dick had a blazing fire going in
the fireplace when we returned and had moved the coffee table
and the divan closer to the fire. While riding to Indiana, I had
heard an announcer tell how to slice a turkey. So that gave me the
privilege of being the official turkey cutter. Al passed around the
port and we all ate heartily. We even took a couple of pictures.
After finishing this sumptuous meal, I reclined in the armchair
with my cigarette and for the first time in ages really felt at home
as the warmth of the fireplace seeped through the room and the
conversation waned and dwindled with the glowing flames.

December 6, 1952 . . . Last Tuesday I went to the gymnasium. I had smoked at least a pack of cigarettes since I first got up about 7:00 that morning. I was just finishing one upon entering the gymnasium. My mind passed lightly over the taboo most coaches put on smoking, for I knew that I would never be a good athlete. I knew that I would not make varsity and I knew that I would not try. The humiliation would be too great to bear as the stars watched me sitting on the bench doing nothing and unable to keep up with them in the exercises. It was the second day of official varsity practice, but I went to the pool on the second floor instead of the basement one where the varsity was practicing. I stripped and took a shower and then walked to the pool, not with a feeling of frustration or despair, but thinking that nothing mattered if I could be happy and make those happy around me. This hour of exercise was only going to be for relaxation. There were no hopes of eventual recognition as a swimming ace.

The water was cool and green rays of chlorine shot from side to side as the freshmen swimmers dove in at the signal "go." The partition across the center of the pool separated the freshman team from the right side of the pool, where anybody could swim. I sat down on the bench and looked at the swimmers for a few moments before plunging. One lap and my heart started beating—two laps and it still was beating. I was not tired. I was afraid. But of what I do not know. I was just afraid. "Take it easy," I said to myself. After a few more laps of the crawl, I got the flutter board. I began to limber up. I began to think that this was fun and finally realized what I had been saying to myself: "It does not matter whether you are a great swimming star or not. Think of all the other people who can't even swim. This is just for relaxation." I dove in and began to swim slowly. I forgot the varsity and thought only of the personal relaxation received from spending a few minutes in the water. One, two, three . . . . then twenty, twenty-five, thirty, forty. I had done it. I had broken my record. I had never swam more than fifteen consecutive laps before. That is all the varsity had done the first day. And I could have done more. I got out of the water and was not fatigued in the least.

Outside our first snow of the winter, spread its twinkling little stars over the streets and buildings as the dusk swept in over its virgin whiteness and speeding cars sullied its beauty. I put a cigarette to my mouth and felt its warmth penetrate to my lungs. For a few moments nothing came. I looked around and began to wonder just what is nothing. The swimming season starts after Christmas vacation and our college has an intramural team.

Dick had a rehearsal with the singing group, so Al was the only one to meet me in the refectory. I began to think of what Dick had said Sunday, "When I left the folks, I told them I'd have to get back home now because there was a lot of homework to do. I guess they were rather surprised." Henry sat down at the table with us and began his usual barnstorming and I got right in there with him. I did not laugh boisterously with him at all his jests but I tried hard to be one of the conversation. I tried not to be aloof. I remembered something read in putting one of the books away in the library the day before. "The results are not always immediate." I did not feel uneasy. I did not feel superior, nor did I feel inferior. I felt like one of them. Al and I finished our cigarettes, pushed the table forward and left the dining hall.

We all retired rather late that evening. It seems that lately we have all been staying up fairly late. Al and Dick usually do retire somewhat later than I. But this last week we have all been going to bed about the same time. We had some of the turkey that was left from the Sunday debauchery and then repaired to our bedrooms. As fresh air blew in through the casement window, I grew pensive and philosophical. "Tell me, Dick, do your parents treat you like a little baby?" "I don't let them," was the reply. "Yeah, you know I would go home more often if they would only treat me like a man." He did not say much after that, soon uttering his last words with somnolent inaudibility.

My meditations could not concentrate on anything but home after I had said the Lord's Prayer in French. Thoughts—illogical thoughts, apparently unrelated—drifted into my mind wafting each other gently to and fro. "Perfectionist." "When I was married to your father, he wouldn't even let me kiss my uncle." "He said you children had to eat brown sugar. White sugar is not good for your teeth. We always eat whole wheat bread, since while bread did not contain enough vitamins." "He did not want a commission. He wanted to be a lawyer." "I set too high standards for you children." "The perfectionist exhausts himself and cannot do anything." "I went to a psychiatrist when I was in New Orleans." "Don't disown us when you get to be a millionaire." "I like Lincoln's simple vocabulary."

I began to think of Alice and the last blissful night that we spent on the vessel before debarking at Le Havre. She was part of the paid staff on the boat and had been invited to the captain's party the night before. We were docked and the eight-hundred passengers were filing past the customs agents. It would take a considerable time to check the passports and other credentials, though, so we betook ourselves to the landing between the bridge and the main deck. Alice had brought a blanket with her, since the night air was crisp and biting as small gusts of winds dashed from the side of the vessel through the bodies of the shivering passengers who had become accustomed to the radiant sun during the nine day voyage. She asked me how long it had been since I had seen my folks. I equivocated and we passed on to another subject. "You say that you worked at school during last Christmas vacation?" So that is what had piqued her curiosity. "You must have planned a long time to make this trip. Did it cost you much?" "Yes, I have planned it since the date of graduation from high school." She was tender and knew that either I was much older than the average sophomore or else something unusual had happened in my family. But she did not press the matter once she had seen that I was not being merely modest but really did want to forget this bleak past. And then she told me of the captain's party: "I guess he never had the experience before of having a guest who asked for coke when he served highballs." I loved her for it and worshipped her. "If a woman has enough courage to buck the drinking custom, she is not going to let anyone tempt her into a divorce after once being married."

Jane was the only one in her female group who spoke French all the time, and I and Skip were the only ones who spoke French all the time in our male group. She irritated the others. And I irritated the others.

I wondered why Alice would not drink and why Jane would only speak French. Are they perfectionists also? Was Alice only saying that she did not drink merely because she wanted to please me? Are they to be condemned for not being Babbitts? No, I admire them and admire them more than those who had no individuality. Jane lacked tack and made herself irritating to the others. But she tried. She tried to do something. But did she despise the others in doing it? I did. I despised them, because they were too small and too little. They did not have the intelligence to do what I was doing and I hated them. I learned twice as much French as any of the others, but the suffering and the anguish I went through to learn it. I was adamant and would not flinch. And I would do the same thing again—oh, would I? God help me.

Dick just stepped in the room. "Are you through writing yet?" "Just about. I guess we had better get to bed early tonight. If I get my Classical Civilization assignment done tomorrow morning, I'll go to church with you." "Hell, you're going with me anyway." It will be the first time in about a month that I have darkened the church threshold, but I am looking forward to it. Yes, living with others is the most important thing. Boy, I can hardly wait to get my hands on that turkey sandwich that Dick just made.

December 7, 1952 . . . For three nights now I have been working for one of the school selling agencies, heeling in the competition to become junior manager next year. If I become junior manager of this organization it would be possible to do the things I want. I would be able to attend some of the social functions, have some decent clothes and buy a few things to make life more comfortable. Tonight, too, I was going to work from 7:00 P.M. until midnight. I have sold so far one hundred and fifty dollars worth of material in the college that was assigned to me for the Christmas selling. During the beginning of the year it was I who worked steadily each week and came in third out of six heelers. The one started late and was given a virgin college that had not yet been canvassed but which had a lot of potential purchasing power. The other fellow was given the freshman campus, which contains many more students than the college assigned to me. It was I who worked on Saturday evenings, selling footballs. The college they assigned to me has the record for the lowest donation in a recent charity drive and is acknowledged as one of the poor boys' schools in the residential college system.

The junior manager called me in last night and we had a confabulation about the low sales record. They wanted me to bring in one hundred dollars a night instead of the fifty that I had brought in during the first three nights of this week. The sales were low in all the colleges. I tried to explain to them what my theory was on the situation. I suggested the students become tired of having the same person soliciting at their door all the time. I suggested that they change the salesmen around, putting me in another college and taking that fellow and putting him in my territory. I told him that I thought that some of the students might become jealous seeing another making so much money. In three nights I had made thirty dollars, a commission of twenty percent. He told me that he thought I could do it—that I could raise the total sales for one evening to one-hundred dollars. I told him that I would try.

Tonight the blow came. They want me not to sell this evening. They want to try another person in the college. All that heeling for nothing. They wont be able to get any more money out of that college. Why did I not tell them something else? Why did I not build myself to the sky and tell them something that would have made them believe that I would bring in many more dollars per night? Now there is only one sophomore left in the competition. I asked him if this eliminated me from the competition and he said no. But I could tell that he was only saying that to allay the brutal shock.

For a few moments this news was a mordacious poison to my happiness. But the effect was only fleeting, for after dinner my roommates and I went to the room and instead of studying we began to converse. The conversation turned to the inevitable subject of women and prurient jokes. Al told about a girl he had known in Texas, who was of the most rigid deontological bringing-up. One evening he and one of his friends decided to tell her a joke, which had no meaning, and see what her reaction would be. "There was a little boy who always wanted a bicycle for Christmas. And he waited and waited but Santa Claus never brought him one. Then one Christmas he finally got it and took it out to ride. But he had not been out long when his mother told him to come in." The girl grinned while the others stormed the room with cloudbursts of raucous laughter. After the noise had subsided, she turned to them and very modestly said, "I think that is a little risqué." I told them of some girls I had known in Denver—the girl that had gotten married a month after we had quit going steady and the girl with heart trouble who yearned for a family and told me so. Dick added some more light material to the conversation as we passed from one girl to another, treating them all in a jocular vein. We dissipated about a half hour in this nonintellectual pursuit and vicarious outlet for our pent up emotions before once more going back to the salt mines.

After the others had left, I began to write in response to some ads seen in the Herald Tribune concerning Christmas vacation work and possible work in the Caribbean during the coming summer. And realizing that the chances of being junior manager of the selling agency does not look too feasible at this point, I wrote to an advertising firm that has requested me for part-time work through the employment agency at school:

The Employment Agency at school has referred me to you for securing part-time work while attending school. I would appreciate it if you would outline your plan, stating the financial prospects and the time and nature of the work.

I am a sophomore in college, contemplating a major in French. My present employment is as in-college aide to Mr. . . . , the master of . . . He will be glad, I am sure, to give you such references as might be desired. During the year I have worked for the Sales Agency and the Distributing Agency in my college.

After leaving college at the end of two more years, it is my desire to enter some business firm; especially one where it would be possible to do work with foreign people. If your firm extends that far, perhaps I could also be of some use during the summer.

In addition to the above information concerning your part-time work plan, it would be appreciated if you would supply the names of such firms as would be interested in hiring me after graduation, keeping in mind my special interest in languages. Last summer was spent with a group in France.

Yours truly,
Alexis Evelyn

And so the bastinadoing of spirit received in being virtually fired, had been dissipated to the wild winds as new hopes spring up for making money.

I was just affixing my signature when a light tap came from the living room door. I went to see who was there and found Henry in his polka-dotted pajamas. He wanted to use the telephone to get in contact with another student who is doing a joint physics report with him. I let him in and then began to get ready for bed. I told him to leave the door open when he left, since I would not have a key to open it on returning from the shower. Ten minutes later I returned with large globules of water dripping from my body and the cold air raising large goose pimples on my trembling

torso, and there I found Henry reading a newspaper. I went to my
bedroom and began to dress for bed. As I did so he began to read
an article from the paper describing the recent formation of a
religious group in New York for the amelioration of the slum
conditions and vice that are apparently rampant in the poorer parts
of the city. He told me how he had walked through this district
only last week. He told of the men and women abandoned
completely to debauchery and the satisfactions of the flesh, who
haunt the bars and taverns like flies, leaving their children at home
to wallow in the filth of their unsanitary dwellings. "Yeah, I know
it's terrible," I replied, thinking inwardly, "What do you expect
them to do.? You would do the same if you had to live like that."

I leaped into the top bunk and reclined with a cigarette. "Did
you read this article about crimes in Germany? Says they're on the
decline. There were only seventy-four rapes committed this last
year for every thousand soldiers." "Hey, Henry, what in the heck
are you going to major in, anyway." "Oh, probably religion or
architecture. Dad wants me to major in architecture. You know he
is a lawyer himself and put himself through college. Guess he wants
me to make some money."

Henry left about an half hour later and I began to think how
much different this year has been than last. It was rare that I spent
a half hour or even five minutes discussing irrelevant topics with
my roommates or with those who roomed near us. How much
more fruitful this year is! How much more happier I am to be able
to stop studying for a while and not feel that the world is tumbling
in on me.

December 9, 1952 . . . A letter from Jane arrived a few days ago:

"Dear Alex,

Am really in the doghouse (here she had a diagram). Have been planning to write to tell you what fun it was when you came up . . . but, have been swamped with the bigger than usual work load of this time of year. Today, with two exams and one paper down, two papers to go—my conscience has won out and am finally taking up the quill.

Your trip back sounds like the perfect end to an all-Charles-Adams-type day with the exclusion of a few hours in Northampton, I hope. Am so glad Bill and his girl friend got along.

Had a really good Thanksgiving vacation—what there was of it. Managed to eat lots of Turkey; to see both the French plays of Jean Louis Barrault and "Oedipus Tyrannus" put on by the modern national Greek Theatre on Greek; and get several much-needed hours of work accomplished among other things.

Unfortunately, the disorganized spirit of the group I was with this summer in France reigned supreme—resulting in the fact that not one (she had this underscored) showed up for the reunion planned. I had invited a few other people, so that my Thanksgiving day party went off in fine style—anyway.

Alex, we—of the Smith girls who had gone abroad with the organization that you were with this last summer, are planning a big square dance on the first Saturday after Xmas vacation: January 10th up at Smith. Think you once wrote me you had some sort of group at your college . . . wonder if you'd do us the favor of publishing the fact amongst the people who have been abroad with this organization and those really interested in future participation who haven't yet been "over". Do write me a note, before Xmas if possible, as to how many may be able to make it—were having most of the New England schools come who can possibly make it—but it's essential to know how many will arrive.

Hope you forgive my tardy reply.

Yours,
Jane

I immediately got on the phone and discussed the idea with Tim. "You know my attitude toward Jane. Call Uncle Frank first—he's less emotional about such things." Frank was fairly responsive to the proposal but said that he personally could not go, since his father is to leave the States on that day for England. We decided, though, to have an orientation meeting the Tuesday before Christmas vacation for those who have been abroad with the "X" and those who would be interested in going this next summer. We decided that he would contact as many of the former voyagers and would try to get an article in the school paper about the purpose of the "X." I agreed to secure permission from the master's office to use the Fellows' room of my residential college.

I then wrote Jane the following response:

Dear Jane,

We are planning to have a meeting of the students who might be interested in going abroad next summer. Hope you will send me more definite information about the dance, such as time, what clothes we should wear, how long it will last, if we are expected to stay for the night, etc., etc. Please get this information to me by Tuesday, if possible.

Sincerely,
Alex

The ensuing day I met Tim coming from one of his morning classes. He hailed me and we walked together to the library, where he had a book to pick up. I told him the plans which we had made, expressly neglecting to tell him that Bill would not be able to go that weekend, though I did not doubt the veracity of Frank's statement. The fact that there was already enough confusion of feeling and slight enmity because of a thorough acquaintance with the characters of the people involved in the proposal, I thought it best to remain uncommunicative on that point. Let Frank tell him. "We are planning to have the meeting on Tuesday of next week. We'll need your help at the meeting, but you probably wont want to go to Smith." "Oh, I'll go," he replied in his characteristically aloof but friendly tone. As we parted and he crossed the intersection, he asked jocularly if we were to take our sleeping bags with us. "Hey, that would be great," I responded.

December 11, 1952 . . . Frank and I met last evening to discuss the article that he is writing for the school paper. He had invited me to dine at his college, but on arriving I found that it was Fellows' night and that I could not eat there. We quickly decided to eat at my college instead; and as soon as Frank had finished his game of solitaire we departed for the Hall.

At the table the conversation centered on a rumination of the past summer and the characters of the individuals in the groups which went to Rouen and St. Etienne. He began a systematic catechism as to my personal reactions to the various members in my group and I did the same thing to him. "What do you think of Alison?" he asked. "Personally, I like her very much. After all she is a Byn Mawr girl. She is the kind of girl that one has to know how to treat in order to get along with her. I remember one time on the boat. As I joined the group for a game of bridge (my first game, incidentally) I tapped her lightly on the back. She was indignant. When we went to the Folies in Paris, she declined. On the whole, she was a fairly likeable individual. She and Skip hit it off right away. She was rather hard to make out with. But Skip did tell me that he had succeeded at one of the parties that we had at St. Etienne." I knew why he was quizzing me. I wanted to be as skillful as possible in presenting my sentiments so that he would esteem me rather than disdain me. My initial repugnance for Tim apparently still lingered in his remembrance. He knew that Tim had taken Alison out on a date and he was wondering in this quizzing just what my sentiments were now toward both Tim and Alison. I then began to ask him about the people of his group. "Jane was not very popular, was she?" "No, she had an irritating manner. The way she laughed is unforgivable. She thought that she was unpopular and tried to do little things to make up for it, which were false."

We went to my room to look over the draft he had written for the paper. He wanted me to put the finishing touches on it. "I wont have the time to finish it." he told me. I read it and found no fault in it, though he had omitted to mention the dance at Smith. "It looks all right to me. Better put something in it about the dance. Otherwise it looks great. Why don't you go ahead and finish it." I could see that he was pleased with my reaction, more so than if I had taken the draft and tried to improve on it.

That evening at 7:30 P.M. there was a meeting of the French Club. It was the second time this year that I have been there. I only went one time last year. The president greeted me with all conviviality. I had met him through working with the selling agency and had invited him to dinner just anterior to the Thanksgiving vacation. There were only two or three other members that I knew well. I walked over to one who was engaged in conversation with two other members. One of them was a fellow classmate in Spanish. That gave us something in common to talk about beside the excursion to the Continent this last summer. We smoked and talked and ejected an occasional laugh. After about fifteen minutes refreshments began to be served. "Beer or wine?" cried one of the hierarchy. The wine was from Bordeaux and I was in no mood to pass by such a delicacy. A junior joined this comrade and me and bid me to sing with them in a specialty before the lecture began. I told him that my French fluency was much better than my singing aptitude, though, to evade a possibly embarrassing situation. Between the red wine that warmed our bellies and the stifling fumes that insufflated the small room, we wiled away some pleasant moments in congenial conversation. Just before the speaker began to address the audience, I asked the fellow who is in my Spanish class if he would like to go to Smith after vacation with the members of the "X." Having heard him mention something about his auto, I began to entertain this as a possible means of transportation to the dance. He did not decide definitely but said he would inform me later in the Spanish class.

I left before the lecture was finished, having an English paper to write on Spenser's *Fairy Queen* for the following day. But on the way home, the idea suddenly came to me that it might prove worthwhile to form a French table in the refectory. I had meditated on this idea before, but I could never reconcile the thought with my feelings. Before I have always had a deep resentment to talk to people who thought they knew French yet could talk it only haltingly and with many grammatical errors. But now I am decided to form this table for good friendship one night a week if there are others who would be interested.

Today in returning from class, I chanced upon the Colorado upperclassman who took my girl and me to Central City on the night of the college party. I recognized him and decided not to say anything but could not refrain from glancing at him slightly. There could have been no greater surprise and avatar of spirit when he said "Hi." I replied with the same greeting. Suddenly, my sentiments toward him changed, though I could not help but remember our past experiences and was thus balanced with an ambivalent feeling of antagonism and friendship. I tried to tell myself that it was my immaturity that had caused him to act as he had. But still the past lingered in my mind and did not totally absolve him from the inner chagrin that I had suffered as an uninitiated high school youth. Bottom line: he takes himself too seriously and does not know how to get along with people. Pete says the guy is jealous—green with envy, in fact—whatever! At best, he needs to grow up.

The second meeting of the year was held tonight by the debating club of our college. The president outlined an active schedule for next term and asked the novices to take the debate for the week after vacation. I volunteered.

December 13, 1952 . . . The master of our college is aided by a middle-age secretary and several college aides. The secretary is amiable and good company on a party but she is sometimes rather difficult to understand when giving directions. The day before yesterday I came on duty at 2:0 0 P.M. to put in my two hour stint. She wanted me to go to the Fellows' Commons, remove a blackboard and easel, take the easel to the library and the blackboard to a Fellow's suite, and put the small blackboard that was in the commons room in the television room. The instructions were not too clear to me, but I and another college aide sauntered out of the office in good hope. He had not heard the instructions so I was supposedly directing the operation. We finally ended in putting the easel and the blackboard in the Fellow's suite, going to the library to find the other blackboard and finding nothing, and returning saying the task was complete but that we were not able to find the small blackboard. My spirits sunk to the black dismal depths of despair when I learned that we had done the wrong thing. I felted abashed and a certain unexplainable feeling of ineffable inferiority overcame me. The other aide was not culpable. He had done just what I had told him. The entire blame was on me and I knew that she must have considered me very stupid not to be able to carry out the instructions. We finally rectified the situation by restoring the easel to the library and removing the small blackboard to the television room. But I felt and knew that I would never be chief aide. I tried to reason the situation. One aide says he wants to be in the geology laboratory next year so he will be able to get some additional practice in his major. Another is on the school paper and probably will have a full-time job as one of the board members. There is one aide who is on the varsity football team. He will undoubtedly be the athletic aide. That leaves two positions open; namely, that of chief librarian and chief aide. There would under this plan of elimination, then, only be three left to choose from. The other two were both elected to the student council. One has formed a singing group in our college and the other is a member of one of the literary magazines on the campus and has a personality of pleasant executive suaveness. The lad who organized the singing group rooms by himself on the floor above us in the next entry over the master's house. The other one lives with three other comrades in the other court. There are three aides left to choose from and only two positions to fill. I knew who would be chosen and I felt crestfallen and inferior.

I had another hour to complete when my copemate left. As I marched over to the desk, trying to conceal the dissolution of my spirits, she handed me a dossier and told me to count the number of students who received rebates on their rooms this year. Those who had received refunds had an asterisk to the left of their names. I counted them rapidly by grasping five stars in one eye span. In that way it was sometimes possible to finish one page in three glances, being contingent on the number of stars that were on that particular page. I quickly handed her back the dossier and was immediately penetrated by an exalted feeling that I was worth something after all. Maybe now she would think that I am intelligent, even if the blackboard confusion had disgusted her and disappointed me.

The next day was Friday and I unwittingly arrived an hour late. My schedule had been changed two weeks before and I had confused the Wednesday schedule with that of Friday. In any event, she immediately put me to work with the student who is a member of the university paper. We were to hang Christmas wreathes out of the library windows just over the arch that joins the north and south courts. I did not clearly comprehend her instructions but that the other aide did. She looked at him most of the time while administering the instructions, though she did glance at me occasionally. I looked at the floor or off in the distance, though, feigning that I really did not care whether she looked at me or not in giving the instructions. She provided us with the wherewithal to accomplish the mission—stringed Christmas lights, pliers, and some hanging wire. From the labyrinthal cascade of speeding words that emanated for our enlightenment on how to perform the task, I unconfidently understood that we were to hang the wreaths by the wire. I did not say anything, though, since it seemed apparent that this other aide understood her and that she had full confidence that he would understand her. In the library he commenced the operation by wrapping the lights around the wreath and then dropping it from the window, and fixing it in place by closing the casement window on the light cord that extended from the center of the wreath. I wondered when he would use the wire; but apparently he had forgotten about it or never knew that we had it, until the secretary arrived and asked him how he had hung it. Then I realized, or so tried to tell myself, that maybe I am not so inferior to other people. They also make mistakes. But I was angry—angry at myself and unable to restrain myself from hating the world. I started to think about my naiveness. Why I was naive I did not know—maybe I did not even know what the word meant. But I was decided to assert myself and make people respect me and not think that they could push me around. I was decided that no one was going to look on me with pity. The college aide asked me in the presence of the secretary and the head aide if I were going home. I said I had not decided yet. Certainly, they knew that I had not been home last Christmas. I knew they were pitying me inwardly. What could I say? Suddenly, I felt like running as far as I could forever and fiendishly slaughtering every living or inanimate thing that traversed my path. I felt like crying and was exhausted. Any convention or restraining custom that came into my mind I felt like slaughtering. I no longer carried what people thought of me. I returned to the office and immediately thereafter accompanied the master to one of the guest suites to help him in stocking them with liquor for the arriving guests. He had preceded me into the one suite by a few minutes. "It would be worth it to be a guest just for this stuff," I said rather timidly, attempting to muster some masculine assertiveness in the greeting and hoping that he would not think this aggressive friendliness as unnatural to me. But the attempt was feeble. The first words were weak and lacking in delivering vigor. We stepped up to the liquor cabinet, unlocked it, and found the selves abounding in filth that had resulted from non-use. "God, that's filthy," I asserted with as much vigor and expression as anyone ever did in a rhetorical discourse. It was the first time that I had ever used God's name in order to add force to my personality. My conscience did not trouble me. I thought of my roommate who has no qualms about the vulgarity or quality of his speech yet has enough religious convictions that he goes to church just about every Sunday. I thought of my stepfather and what he had said about a Baptist preacher one time. It was in a sermon that the reverend was discussing the use of God's name in conversation. He asked the congregation if the battle-wearied soldier in a swampy and mephitic foxhole is guilty of sinning when he said "God." No it is the man who believes in God who will say that. That is something that has grown with our Christian heritage. If we had had no God to believe in, we would not say his name. He said this is not using the Lord's name in vain. Then I remembered my mother and the training she had given my brother and me. She had inculcated in us a strict abhorrence of any swearing. She had once given my brother a thrashing when I told her that he had used "fuck" in his conversation with me. Such malversation was never condoned in us. But my stepfather one night told of how my stepbrother had come into his office one evening and said, "God, damn! I'm in trouble again." He told it in such a manner as to make us marvel at my stepbrother's masculinity and make us suffer. Is there nothing that I do that does not recall these dreadful memories of how he humiliated me and broke up our home? But I suppose that it was just as much my mother's fault. And Dad he was not entirely guiltless. Why did he not move to another house when my grandmother became so captious and difficult to live with, as Mother asked him to do?

Before returning to the office to obtain some stationery for the room, I asked the Master to leave the door open when he left. On returning to the office I asked the secretary for the key to the drawer with the postal stamps. She did not think that we had any but gave me the key and followed to help me. We looked in the top drawer. With the celerity and seriousness of a wounded lion, I locked the third drawer from the top, which had been opened to get some material, and opened the top drawer. There was nothing there, so I locked it and immediately opened the second drawer to find nothing there. Finally, I reopened the third drawer and found it locked. I make a few audible sounds, resembling the muttering of an inveterate swearer frustrated to have to retain his modesty in front of a woman. The secretary turned her head slightly to the left and I heard a light laugh. She then turned to me with a serious expression. I could not refrain myself and also began to laugh. We finally retrieved the miscreant stamps, however, in spite of the then mutual laughter.

"Good night," I said five minutes later and proceeded to leave. "You are sure you know your hours now, eh, Alex," she responded. I gave a little laugh and answered, "Yeah, I think so." I had succeeded. The Master had heard me assert myself like a man, and the secretary had seen that I could get angry yet was not beyond laughing at a droll situation. I thought of Dad and felt, indeed, that "like father, like son" and felt proud of my dad and myself.

That evening I felt myself strangely becoming uneasy. The calm after the storm was being dissipated and I was once again beginning to worry. At the table that night I began to feel friendless and sense a consciousness of not being able to mingle into the conversation. As we started from the line toward the dining hall, I saw one of my very good acquaintances and sat down opposite him. There was room for Al and Dick to the right of my commensal and me. Al and Dick began to converse. The tone was so low that I could not clearly hear what they were saying but knew that I was intentionally excluded thereof. I knew that it would happen and therefore made it a point to set opposite to someone else. I have long tried to reason about this situation but have been unable to arrive at a definitive conclusion. The unusual manner in which we became roommates might have something to do with it. It was I who organized the merging of the two doubles into a quadruple. It was I who had known everyone except Tom previously. Generally, when I am alone with either one of them there is no feeling of antagonism. But when we are together it is Dick who makes a very noticeable effort to talk to Al instead of to me. He sometimes goes so far as to remind me of a sycophant. I try sometimes to flatter Al but it seems so insipid and insincere that my conscience rebels against it. The other night he mentioned out of the clear sky that he thought he would take physics next year. He is an English major. I asked him one time what he thought his predicted average is at college. He replied that it is much higher than his average. I knew he was mistaken, because the files that contain his records are easily at my disposal and I have availed myself of them to find out my roommates averages and several other friends in the college. I have not looked at mine. But I intend to next week. This not knowing whether I am of a low or high caliber is unbearable. One of the alumni told me I would have a hard time passing the first year and my freshman counselor said it would be possible to make Phi Beta Kappa.

I did not tell Al his predicted average or even hint that the files are at my disposal. He is not an ignoramus nor is he a genius. According to the files Dick has the greatest God-given portion of intelligence, but even he is not to be classified as a genius. When Al said that he was contemplating taking physics next year, I responded that if he would really take it that I would do the same. This rather squelched him, for he knows that I am not exceptional with mathematics. He knows that I do well in literature courses without too much effort. But this riposte caught him off guard.

Then I wondered if he were jealous of my prowess with women. Generally, I can handle myself fairly well when initially introduced to a woman, though the interest wanes as in all things human. Is Al jealous of that? I told him the other day that I was going to try to join one of the fraternities. Did that antagonize him, since he did not make it the first time? Does he want to be the cynosure in our little clan and think that I might offer him competition? Is Dick just trying to shield Al out of kindness? Is he too insecure? I wish I had the gift of gab.

That evening these feelings were beginning to be uncontrollable. They began to seek an outlet. I began to think of Marguerite. I had talked to her a week before in hopes of securing an engagement with her. She was still sitting at the phonograph recorder when I rose to leave the room and asked her for the first Saturday in vacation. There was a brown hardwood chair in front of me; and looking at it I felt a sudden urge to tear it apart with all the violence that welled up in my chest. (I'll be back in a few minutes. I need a beer now. I am getting a little tired.) She said that I could obtain a definite answer this night. But it was still rather early in the evening and I did not think she would be ready yet. At 7:30 I went to the rehearsal for the French play *Topaze*, which the French Club is going to perform the month after Christmas vacation. It was just an organizational meeting for the distribution of roles. The drama teacher gave me the role of the policeman, since my Belgium accent would be very appropriate for it. He wondered where I had acquired this Belgium accent. He asked me if I had ever been with a Belgian. I told him no except for a few moments in the Folies-Bergère at Paris. He asked me if it was with a girl and I told him no. We then began to discuss where it would be possible to secure some girls for the feminine parts. One student suggested getting a French immigrant who had tried to play the part of Suzy Courtois last year before enthusiasm waned to such an extent that it was necessary to call the whole project off. Pete's last year roommate who failed out had gone around with her quite a bit. He related the story to Pete how that she propositioned him. When they wanted to buy a car, the only way to do it and avoid trouble with the Dean's office, it being forbidden for freshmen to have cars, was to register it in her name. I did not tell the group at first that I knew this girl rather indirectly and would be glad to get in touch with her. But I was charmed to hear one of them say that she is a "demi-prostituée." The way I was feeling now enhanced the beauty of being able to have an opportunity to talk to her and, of course, get a date with her. They then discussed asking Marguerite. I remained silent, thinking it best thus far to conceal the small relationship that we had had, since it might prove to be embarrassing to her if the others knew that she was considering going out with a student much younger than she.

After the role had been assigned, we spread through the building, through the exit, and started toward one of the town bars. The fellow whom I asked to accompany us to Smith next week was in the middle of myself and another student. We walked before the professor and the others. During the auditions this fellow and I sat together. He had no cigarettes so I loaned him mine. Once when the professor remarked that only freshmen and seniors work and sometimes juniors they generally go to the Continent, this fellow quickly clapped his right arm about my shoulder in recognition of the fact that we are both sophomores. I felt a little embarrassed, thinking that perhaps this was too much of a display of friendship under the circumstances, though I was rejoiced that our recent friendship is perhaps a real one. As we walked down the steps after the meeting, I asked him the name of one of the members. He remained silent so that it was necessary to ask him a second time. He hesitated a few moments before showing any signs of hearing me while I practically begged him. Finally, he answered me.

As we walked along in front of the others, he talked to the fellow on his left and not to me. I hoped this was not because I had not knocked when the fellow on the left was trying out for a burglar's role as I had for his competitor. We entered the bar and we all separated and began to converse with different members of the group. I kept a well-trained eye on the group to notice just who was talking to whom and how long they continued to do so. There was one fellow who had been abroad last summer with some other students from our university, but he was lacking in fluency compared to the other members. I talked to him for about ten minutes, found out his history and his opinion on a few items of controversy. Then I began to listen to the professor, who was humorously expounding on the idiosyncrasies of the head of the French Department. To the right of him was the student with whom I had just been talking and across from him and to my left was the fellow for whom I had not knocked. (I later thought that it would have been better to have knocked for the last person to try out for the role of the burglar, since no one would have expected it and I would not have been obliged to knock again if I did not want to offend the last one playing it. I thought it would have been rather trite to repeat the same action twice, though; and that is why I did not knock for the last auditioned.) To the left of the professor were two proficient Francophiles who had spent last year in France.

Everyone was smoking except the fellow across from me. As he turned from the conversation to his right to our little parody, he stared at the professor for sometime and then asked me if he were about to become the head of the French Department. I dryly added a "yes" without looking at him. I then forgot the group to the right and began solely to observe our group. The fellow to the left of me was not saying much to me, but neither was he saying much to any of his other equals in the group. Nobody was paying too much attention to anybody but the professor whose witty remarks sliced the smoky air with mental keenness. The fellow across the table from me tried to get a remark in. The professor very kindly turned his head and condescendingly smiled at the fellow and answered his rather insipid question as the former stared him in the eyes like an admiring youngster. As the conversation lulled he placed a couple packs of cigarettes on the table and told everyone to help themselves. He turned once again to the lad at his right and told him in a jovial tone to enjoy himself and have a cigarette. He declined and nothing was said. I then broached a question to him and determined not to let him think I had to be subservient to him in order to be popular, I looked at him once in the eyes. And then as he began to explain his question, I turned my head first to the clock on the wall, then took a puff on my cigarette and then a swig of beer, and finally looked at him again to let him know that I was still with him but that he had to keep working and that he had to treat me as an equal and not smile at me condescendingly as he had the lad across from me. He said something rather humorous and we both laughed as did the others who had been listening to the conversation. I then grew weary of his jokes and turned to talk to someone else. And I enjoyed every moment of it and liked everyone of those members.

Before the evening was finished I had been asked to see this "demi-prostituée" and arrange for her to be in the play. I called Pete that evening and he said he would have her telephone number sometime this weekend. I called Marguerite and she explained that her schedule is complete until after Christmas. After then, though, she would be glad to go out with me. Al heard the conversation and muttered a sound of amusement, which made me laugh also.

As I lay in bed that night reading a gazette and puffing on a cigarette, Dick returned from the library. He walked in without a word being said between him and Al, who was engrossed in a science-fiction magazine. He walked into the bedroom and I continued to read. After a silence of several minutes he said something to which I responded without raising my head from the journal.

Vacation is only one week distant. The early part of the day was spent in a wild race to do the domestic chores of the week and to get Christmas greetings on the way. I sent out cards to just about everyone of my close friends for whom I had addresses. Some of them I was rather hesitant to send for reasons of remembered unpleasantness. I saved the card for the assistant girl leader of our group until last. I remember how caustic she had often been with Skip and me and how her characteristic cynical indulgence and jealousy had caused great discomfort. I remembered that in Paris one time she asked me why I wanted to learn French, doubting the worth of my efforts. I remembered how she had called me an egotist to one of the French girls when she was certainly by no means free of this vice. But I conquered my personal enmity and tried to reconcile myself to the fact that we all are human and not perfect. I remembered that the last night before the male leader of our group departed for the States to resume his teaching position, that really presented a pitiful sight full of cynicism. She told how the organization that we were with boasted in its brochures that a summer abroad changes one. It had changed her into a cynic. I began to address one to Mae and found that she had skillfully given me the wrong address. From the small piece of paper on which she had written the address, she had taken one item from each of the preceding addresses and incorporated those into one to give to me as her address. I opened up one of the suitcases, though, and got the true address that the "X" had sent before embarking for this trip. I still was not decided to send the card, though, until I had reflected more on the events of the summer. I first thought of this skillful deceit she had employed in giving me her address.

Then I thought of her first offering to give me a ride from Canada to the States after returning, and then afterwards asking another boy to go with her and expressing surprise that I wanted to go with her. I thought of the night at the party when she broke into English to say that she was so tired of speaking French that she did not care if she ever did again. I grabbed her by the arm, for it was quite obvious what she was doing. But my childhood inhibition held me back and I merely twisted her arm gently. And I remembered that on the boat how she and Alison came down in the men's dormitory to see me one night after I had been in long hibernation, pondering in cynical terms on mankind and on the group and on myself. And I remembered the last night on the boat when she came and sat down close to me during the party on the upper deck. I did nothing that night. I lay down on the floor with a blanket and neither did nor said anything, so torn was I by the fact that the world is not what everyone had been telling me. After about fifteen minutes, she moved to the other side of the party with this exclamation to Alison, "Let's get out of this dreary atmosphere." It cut like a rusty knife. During the summer the group had come to associate me with the Charleston, knowing that I like the dance and could perform it fairly efficiently. Someone suggested that the group do the Charleston. Mae quickly jumped up. But there was no partner and I remained wrapped in my blanket. I wondered what her feelings are toward me now and could not help thinking that she did like me and still does. I addressed the card—with a little sentimentality, I guess, and some admiration for her finesse. I even thought of asking her to come to the campus for a date. I also sent a card to Alice, hoping that this might give her the opportunity to write if she will.

Before going to the history class this morning I wrote a letter to the folks, telling them I would be home for Christmas and asking them to arrange me some dates and permission to use the camp swimming pool. I did not mention the dispute we had had the last time. This afternoon a letter came through the mail from them. It was in Dad's handwriting. The first one had been in Sandra's handwriting.

"I am sending this (a check for $25.00) in advance in the event you may need it or should care to use it for a trip here.

We have had no word from you since you left here Thanksgiving. So we have no idea what your plans are.

Hope our heated discussion did not make you angry—but if they did I hope you are over them by now—and remember that it would be a dull world if everybody agreed on everything and very disagreeable and unpleasant if they agreed on everything."

Sandra, Betty, and Daddy

After coming from the short worship service at the chapel with Dick, I immediately sped myself around town to get myself out of debt and to by some beer and cigarettes.

December 15, 1952 . . . This evening has been spent in utter dissipation; that is, if a complete social evening can be termed a dissipation. It first started this morning when the school newspaper did not publish the article that Frank had written about the "X" in which the orientation meeting scheduled for this evening was to be announced. Yesterday I had posted a notice announcing the meeting in the post office, but it was an improvised bit of work done Saturday night when I realized that I had forgotten to ask the Master for permission to use the office materials to make a good one. Therefore when I read the newspaper and saw the article missing, I knew that there could be no meeting this evening. I called Frank and in the most invective and vulgar language lambasted the student who had apparently forgotten to publish the article. Frank said he would immediately get in touch with this student to determine what the cause was for this irritating situation. We concluded to meet this evening and discuss the matter further; and, depending on the reason for the article not appearing, revise the article. Another alumnus of the "X" had phoned during the later part of the afternoon. I told him the situation and we decided to eat dinner together for discussion of the situation.

When I arrived in the latter's room there was no one present except him, though he had invited two other members of the "X." We briefly discoursed on his trip to South America this year to write a special research paper on the relationship between church and state in general and particularly in Ecuador. After waiting for about fifteen minutes, we finally decided that the other two friends had not received his invitation. So he broke the label on a bottle of Scotch that he had been given by some marines in Ecuador and we eagerly poured a quantity into some glasses and began to drink and talk. From what he said I learned that the alumni group of the "X" at school is fairly well organized already among the juniors and seniors and that they eat together each Wednesday evening. He thought that it would be best to attend this assembling this week and broach the Smith dance to them so that they would be able to inform prospective students among their friends. This he thought would probably produce more men for the dance than anything else. Of course, we still contemplated having an article in the paper after I had talked to Frank and learned what the difficulty had been that the article was not printed today.

After draining the last drops of the Scotch, we went to the dining hall, where we continued the conversation about his voyage to South America and the means for organizing the trek to Smith. He then introduced some material into the conversation that was not anticipated about a lucrative endeavor, which he had commenced while in Ecuador. At first he said that he was the representative of some import-export company which operated between Ecuador and the United States. He said it first merely to liven up the conversation, it being his turn to say something since I had been the voluble one thus far. But when he saw that I expressed a more than unusual interest in the project, he attempted to shy away from the subject. Then something Professor Smith (the man that I told you I visited several months ago and in whose presence I thought I had been slighted because of being a teetotaler—however wrong the impression might have been—and then decided to join a fraternity) had told me last year about a businessman, came to my mind. Mr. Smith had worked in New York several years ago for this man and marveled at his pretended ignorance in the company of other businessmen. He would never commit himself. He would act as though his knowledge was extremely limited on this other businessman's specialty, though he had spent days previous to the invitation in studying everything that concerned this opponent's line of business. He would invite the rival to eat with him and then would use the social friendship thus created to pry information from him. He would just ask questions, but when the meal was through a great deal of the opponent's vulnerable spots had been exposed. And this is just what I began to do on this student with whom I was eating. He tried to back away from the question, but I would not let him to so. We drifted shortly to another subject, not entirely against his will. Then suddenly I asked, in manner solely indicative of my concern for his progress, what was the name of the company for which he is working. He then began to equivocate and say that he was working for many companies, that he was working for himself with others under him, and finally that he was an entrepreneur working entirely for and by himself and would be able to net 100 or 200 thousand dollars a year if he gave the enterprise full time. "How does the operation work?" I asked him. Finally, he explained to me that he was selling curios from Ecuador, taking previous orders for them, and then sending them to the companies. I did not succeed in obtaining the name of the company for which he is working, but I am sure that he is not doing this enterprise by himself.

As we walked out of the Hall, he stopped to hear a debate scheduled to commence in a few minutes and I went to the Fellows' Lounge, to attend any students who might have seen the sign that I put in the post office. No one came but it gave me time to think, to think about this summer, to think of the things I regretted and the things of which I was proud. I was proud that I had learned so much and was sorry that I had caused so much antagonism by showing myself so superior to the others. And I wondered if it would not be possible, if I were to ever go overseas with a similar group, to learn as much French yet to do it without offending the others. It is not good to yield to everybody and be a wishy-washy individual without any fortitude whatsoever. Maybe if I had shown more personal attention to the girls in our group individually they would not have been so antagonistic toward me. True they did what I said when we were in Paris. Skip and I could plan the operations without any worries there, for the girls did not want to be let alone. But why did they choose that other fellow to represent the group at the annual meeting? Is it because he was so neutral all the time and never was amorously liked by the girls and never showed any real perseverance in learning French yet was generally active with the zest of a young boy? Maybe I should not have flouted the girl leadership that we had forced on us when the leader had to return to the States to reopen his school. Maybe I should have swallowed my pride and succumbed to her dainty discussions every afternoon. I would never again commit myself to a situation like that in which the leader of a co-educational group is a girl. Maybe I am too proud. But are not men made to be the leaders and women made to help them lead? Is that not the arrangement that nature has made? Is not the woman the weaker of the sexes and to be protected by the man who, in turn, derives from her certain physical and spiritual satisfactions? I do not mean that a woman should be a slave, for none of us are made for bondage, either to man or animal. Here is the report that I wrote to the "X" in returning from the trip. It was written in a spirit to defend myself from any claim to unpopularity that either the girl or the male leader might have written. The girl leader is only two years my senior, whereas the man is of middle age. If I am going to take them on, I want to do it in the best light possible. All is fair in love and war, though this is probably neither. If nothing else, we will have a little fun with them—a little warm and cuddly blood sport—nothing serious.

INTRODUCTORY REMARKS

As 1952 courses neared completion and college students began their annual trek to the home stomping ground, I found myself on the threshold of a somewhat Pollyannish excursion in distant Europe. To me Europe was unreal— more like an Alice-in-Wonderland creation. France meant little more than perhaps what the "Place of Pigalle" means to all American tourists.

In any event, my two main objectives were to learn to speak French fluently and to become familiar with the home life of the typical French family. Both of these goals were realized to my satisfaction. But there was a crescive realization from the day that we left New York that the "X" consists of much more than one can possibly incorporate into publicity brochures. The people in this group were human regardless of how idealistic an organization they were traveling with. And this was good. But there are still some problems that the organization could have discussed and did not. On the other hand, I suppose that the problems are the same year in and year out. Nevertheless it is my purpose to discuss these same problems while proposing suggestions that would probably have been feasible in our particular group.

At this point I wish to thank the "X" for the $100.00 scholarship to make this trip. Though your organization is not heavily endowed, you will find that one of the best means of advertisement is through scholarships. It is generally true that prospective and former scholarship "X'ers" give people a sense of confidence in the organization, since they know that there would not be any scholarships if it were not functioning well. Also it is the prospective scholarship student who will seek out the organization and pass on the enthusiasm to the more wealthy classmates. This is said in all frankness, since I have already received my scholarship and have no reason to cajole you.

CHANGE IN ATTITUDE

While returning on the ship the group had the opportunity to mingle with students who had traveled with other organizations and others who were free-lance tourists. After this stint of three months in Europe, it is amazing that individual attitudes and observation were so dictated by the manner in which they saw the Continent.

On sailing to Europe there was a certain envy which I could not conceal for the Americans who had sufficient money to travel luxuriously through Europe, seeing the Olympics, the music festivals of all the countries, and most of the historic Mecca's of the Old World. On their return voyage the majority of the free-lance tourists could gain nothing but my pity. The superficiality of their analysis of European problems was redolent with naïveté. They could have analyzed many of the problems much better if they had never made the journey. What they saw of Europe could be seen on post cards. And that is the depth of their experiences. They could talk with authority on no country, since they had seen much and yet nothing.

My French mother was the only one at the station to extend the happy greetings to their new French son. She was small and plump and had a smile that could light up in the most embarrassing moments to save this awkward stranger from chagrin. At home we were greeted by a noisy but well disciplined group of youngsters. Through the summer Robert became my closest copemate, though the two older brothers are not passing friends. But one was sick and in the infirmary part of the time, while the other was working in a factory.

It was the friendship of this family that created in me a warmth for France. The local excursion, the days spent in hunting and swimming, all coupled with their hospitality and painstaking devotion to teach me French, cannot but bind me closer to this nation. When the head of the central organization visited our city and only two groups of parents showed up, you can imagine the joy it gave me when one of these families was mine. They had come not because I had used any great personality projecting; but because they were essentially a family that would go to the ends of the earth to make a congenial atmosphere, they put forth this extra energy.

If you could possibly find the means to help send one of their sons to the States for a short time, I think the effort would be rewarding. The one brother Robert never spoke a word to me in English, though he could speak the language and would have been glad to practice it. Such unselfishness should not go unrecognized. I have suggested that he write my university for information regarding a scholarship here when he is ready in a year or two. Whether he will be responsive to the idea is hard to say at this point.

COMPLAINTS AND RECTIFICATIONS

Whenever a group of college students are assembled for any kind of work or recreation, there always seems to arise certain psychological and social difficulties. Though such problems should not be shunned by any individual, since they form an integral part of life, they should nevertheless not be forced on anyone. Especially, is this true in something like the "X", where all possible elements contrary to good harmony should be eliminated. In this connection my observation was that the girls is our group were not going to France to learn French and the customs of the French, as much as they were going to find a suitable companion among the American boys. (When I wrote this I had in mind the occasion when our male leader remarked to someone that the girls were easily made to like me. I hoped that this would get to the "X" before they read this and thus give my opinion more consideration.) And on the other side of the fence there were one or two trouble-shooting French girls who were eager to create some atmosphere of affection with the American boys also. Of course, the American girls could offer little competition with the French girls in such a situation as we had during the camping trip. Consequently, they formed a rather small clique in which they were liberally using the English language. One girl did achieve in attracting a Frenchman and thereby succeeded to a certain extent in breaking this clique. But this was not until the end of the camping trip. The girls therefore became irritable, presumably thinking that they were not liked when every boy did not show them affection. This was followed by a loss in enthusiasm to make great strides in the language.

The boys, especially the French boys, were particularly harassed by the girls who were continually complaining of their fatigue. And though the boys had their shortcomings also, you will find that they seldom complained of being tired and made the greatest strides in the language.

Certainly, I profited from having the girls to talk to. But even that lagged in some places. I have perhaps more respect for a woman as a woman because of this experience. But with this understanding has come the realization that when a woman oversteps her position and ability she becomes a burden and instead of a joy, a sorrow. For this reason I would strongly suggest that the girls and the boys make separate camps, that the girls make a rather nonfatiguing camping trip or whatever they would so desire and that the boys make a trip or whatever they should so desire and that the boys make a trip that is longer and perhaps more strenuous. I would not suggest separating the groups from the beginning, because that is really a big calling card of the "X" to be able to offer coed accommodations. The group should function as one just before and after the camping trip but not during it.

This report is not to be considered as a discussion of the personalities of our two leaders, since this is not for me to judge. Without any attempt at vilification, though, I wish to say that there is generally a certain dissatisfaction when men are placed under the leadership of a girl of the same age. For an all girls' group perhaps a girl leader is the ideal thing, but in a group with boys it is a detriment to the "X." There are a large number of college students whom I know personally who refuse to try the "X" simply for the fact that they believe that there is too much regimentation. And certainly regimentation by a woman is much worse than regimentation by a man, especially when the reputation of the organization depends on the type, maturity, and sex of the leader. I have attempted to discuss only the latter.

For real success while living with a foreigner one must have a fair command of the language before even attempting it. The argument is how can your officials determine who has a sufficient speaking ability. I do not really see how your selection of applicants can be any better in this respect than it already is. One suggestion, however, is that you group students very closely according to their previously demonstrated language aptitudes. In this way those students who are not linguistically inclined are not embarrassed by the more precocious ones. Also, linguistically the talented students are not held back by the fear of creating petty jealousies through the demonstration of too much ability.

The student probably is more richly rewarded in visiting a foreign country after his freshman year or his sophomore year. This is especially true of those who are interested in pursuing a French or other foreign language major. This plan should be for the individual to make. But it would be very helpful to bring this item to the prospective candidate's attention.

BENEFITS

Certainly, one reward that we all reaped from this summer was an increased fluency in French and a better accent. It is quite astonishing to reflect on the results that can be obtained with a little work. My personal layman's opinion is that one can increase his ability in the language much more than the equivalent one year's college credit that the "X" boasts. That of course depends on the ability and desire of the individual to learn the language. How much French I learned is hard to say. In any case, it was worth the investment.

The friends that we acquired in France are permanent. Each one of us has undoubtedly found a Jonathan in his family whom he considers as his second brother.

I hope, dear friends, that this lengthy report has not bored you. I know that it is not interesting as a report. But I merely wanted to show you that through your kindness in listening to my past and present conflicts you have helped me overcome many difficulties. You can determine for yourself how this same report might sound if I were to go through the same experience again. You know that I am not saying that a woman cannot be a leader, but that I think that this particular girl was not fit to be the leader of our group at that particular time. Maybe next year she will be prepared, for perhaps she also has learned some of the same things that I have learned—that the main thing in life is to live happily with yourself and with the rest of the world without jealousy and petty prejudices while realizing that man is not perfect and was not meant to be perfect. I do not care if I become a great linguist or a great leader if I can let my fellow man live n peace and be loved by my family.

Now that you have received the daily philosophical discourse, let me tell you what happened when I went to see Frank this evening about the newspaper article. He was friendly as usual but even a little more this evening. He even said he might go to Smith for the dance, but we debated the question and finally decided that it would be more important to see his folks off for England, since this might be the last time that he would see them in a long time. The article cannot be published, since its nature is too much like direct advertising. So we decided to have the meeting the first Monday after vacation. I promised to compose some signs for the post office. The signs for the other colleges could be made by other members after we have asked them at the meeting tomorrow.

Earlier this evening when I was writing to you, Al entered the room just about ready to bursts into tears. "Damn it, you could at least have told me that my mother called yesterday evening when I was at Smith." I had completely forgotten about the telephone call and immediately replied, "God, I'm sorry, Al." He broke down a little bit then and said that was all right but that it had got him into hot water with his folks. They had thought that he had not called them purposely. And to make things doubly worse the girl that he had gone to see at Smith is not liked by his mother, since she considers this young fille as a gold digger. Al began to get talkative and I really felt glad that something had happened to him to cause him to confide in me and really think that he has a roommate who is human. With a rather blurry pair of eyes but with his typical Texan grin, he began: "I've got a guilty conscience about this whole thing. Mother demands that I send her my grades with the exactitude of a numerical statement from the Dean. She doesn't like the idea of my not being at school on Sunday night." My heart too sunk with a chilled heaviness, because it was I who had told his mother where he was. I could not say too much to him, though, to atone for this lack of foresight on my part. All I could do was talk. And we did. We talked about our parents. I told him Sandra (I called her mother to him. He does not know that my folks are divorced. Neither does Dick) said that men who go to all men's schools do not understand women and that I would be a baby in their eyes no matter what age I attain. I told him that I sometimes think that the Epicureans had the right idea to a certain extent. I tried to console him, though I could not really feel the impact of this dispute with the force that it tore him. But I knew that it must be great, even though the incident might be small, for I remembered my last trip home. "You can imagine what my attitude toward life has become," I told him. "When you have to start calling up prostitutes." He laughed a little and neither of us took each other too seriously and he went back to his studies a little consoled; and I began to write, much consoled, for my roommate had truly confided in me something that he felt deeply— not something just to make conversation but something that he felt and needed someone to tell it to.

A few moments later Dick's folks called. Al dispatched speedily to the library to alert him. As Dick talked on the phone, I noticed that his language was much more minced than in ordinary conversation with us. Yep, there's a time and a place for everything. "In Rome, do as the Romans do." After the conversation, he invited me to spend sometime in his home before departing to my abode in Indiana. He promised a date and I replied, "She has to make out." "Oh, no, I'm going to get you a nice girl, damn it all anyway. Does she have to be pretty?" "No, Dick."

December 18, 1952 . . . Tuesday was a general party night on the campus. As a college aide it was my duty to help set up the dining hall for the caroling and drinking that we were to do later on in the evening. Before starting to work, though, I paid a visit to Mr. Smith. He was the professor whom I thought had ignored me when I visited him during the early part of the year and found that he had several students already as company. He had said something disparaging in regard to the radical opinions that some of the chairmen of our college newspaper often expound. I thought that he was probably thinking of a graduate who was chairman of the paper some years heretofore and had written a book attacking religion on the campus, claiming that it was not too existent. But I thought more specifically that he had heard of the report that I had sent to the "X" at the beginning of school. "What good is the opinion of a nineteen year old?" he said. He told us something of a scandal some years back when the paper had written a story that gave the general public a rather low opinion of the mores of the college. The consequence was that it was quite difficult for the students to secure dates for the big weekends and it took some time before the effect wore off. But I was sure that he was aiming the conversation at me. And I felt hurt and chagrined, for I had tried. He was in the process of making up an itinerary for his next trip to the West to interview prospective applicants for matriculation next fall. He seemed glad to see me and extended a warm greeting. There was no one else visiting him, so the whole evening was mine to talk as I pleased. He began to ask questions about my activities this year. I did not want to seem like a braggart and thus concentrated on one activity of fairly minor importance that carries with it no prestige. I did not tell him of the impending French play, nor of the two selling agencies I have been heeling, or my other projects. Instead, we started on the "X" and spent the whole evening thereon with few divagations. I did not want to seem too sentimental in the dealing of the subject but at the same time tried to tell him objectively of the conflicts which arose in the group, especially on the camping trip in Brittany. He then told me of his intended trip to the West. And then asked me my plans for the holiday. I knew that he was about to ask me to spend some of it with him. I knew by the pleasant way he asked and the rather well concealed disappointment that he showed on learning that I would not be here. But he seemed to be glad that I was going to be able to go home. I told him that my roommate also had invited me to pass a few days with him. Before I went to visit him, there were secret fears in my heart that the same cold reception of the time before might be reenacted. But it was not. And as I went to the dining hall to set up the party, a certain feeling of beneficence toward everyone lulled my mind into a sweet calm of happiness and joy.

During the party there arose a minor difficulty with Al. After he had been at the party for a few minutes, I approached him and found him talking with one of the freshmen waiters who had been invited to the party. Several of the other students were having their roommates save seats for them together. I asked Al if he would do the same for me. I knew that Dick would be singing with the college glee club and thus did not trouble him. Al responded that he would. About a half hour later, when the drinks had been served and the singing leader was getting poised to commence the songfest, I proceeded to the aisle where Al was seated and hoped he had reserved the seat as requested. The chair on his left was taken, though unoccupied, as was the chair in front of him. The chair to his right was occupied by the freshman waiter. I finally secured a seat to the right of the freshman, no thanks to Al's efforts. They pursued a rather unanimated conversation in which Al talked of his being the first one to graduate from a certain preparatory school and attend Yale. The freshman talked of a friend of his. His phrasing was as follows and was said in a very sneering manner to impugn the motives of the friend: "I have a friend and he doesn't think it is good to drink." Al at this time arose to fetch another eggnog. In the ensuing minutes the singing began and continued the gamut of Christmas carols until about a half hour later my throat became dry and I asked Al if he would like to have another drink. His answer was no. I then asked him if he would mind getting me one. "I'm not too enthusiastic over it, no," he riposted with a wry and somewhat irritated grimace. I said nothing further, merely turning my head and ignoring him for the rest of the evening. I wanted the drink but found it rather embarrassing to have to make my way through the aisle and disturb the others. He, however, was one seat from the end of the row and could have easily obtained the drink. He left early in the program without saying anything and I made no effort either.

The caroling continued and I began to be more and more angry at this haughtily childish deportment of my roommate. He never does mention doing anything together, whereas Dick and I have proposed doing things together many times, both among ourselves and with him. I grew more and more angry as the party continued. He always wants attention and is never willing to let anyone else have attention. Before dinner this evening, one of the other students came to our room to ask Dick about an assignment in Classical Civilization. As he was about to leave I came in and we began to joke a little bit. The friend remarked what a terrible fellow I am to have as a roommate—doing all kinds of mean things. Of course, I replied with some gentle counters. Al, who was reading a magazine, then got up and meekly said in an asserting manner: "And I never do anything." He was trying to be friendly and felt uneasy. But doesn't he realize that it is not necessary to be the cynosure of attention all the time.

After returning from the Colorado Yale Club, I went first to see if the debris of the college party had been taken care of and then went to the dormitory. Al was the only one there. I walked in and made it a point to ignore him in immediately going to my bedroom and getting ready for bed. I went into the living room some minutes later to get the paper. He said something and I tried to reply as decently as possible; that is, until his manner became too irritating. He was talking of the examination he was to have the next day and the effect of studying on his precocious mind, "It has a very stultifying effect." "What?" I asked with no attempt either at friendliness or antagonism. He repeated the sententious statement two times and then I asked him, "What does that mean?" He told me. I turned and walked away with an unenthusiastic "Oh."

The next day, yesterday, I had dinner with the members of the "X." John, the fellow who has just returned from Ecuador, and I went to pick up Frank and a senior by the name of Bart. Both Bart and John were active in the organization on the campus last year and when John left for South America he left Bart with the responsibilities of official representative. It was very amusing for me to note a certain petty rivalry between them. During the earlier part of the year Bart had sent to the headquarters and requested an official list of the names of students who had been overseas. This automatically made him official representative. John returned just a few weeks ago and neglecting to contact Bart to see if he had already secured the name list, and he sent to the home office for his copy. He did ask me if I had sent for the list, though; and finding that I had not, he skillfully withdrew the question, intimating that Bart would already have a list. I supposed his conscience was bothering his equilibrium, though, for he managed to introduce that into the conversation at the table in the bar. Bart had not thus far this year done anything to organize the members, though he has been, and will probably continue to be, the official representative, unless John is also declared representative by the home office on receipt of a response to the letter requesting names.

There were five of us when we had finally assembled at Mory's around one of the wooden tables of the bar, which table showed the remnants of past gatherings in the carvings that embellished its beaten face. Across from me Bart seated himself. And one of the graduate students' wives warmed my right side. Frank sat across from this young lady and on his left was John. At the right end of the table was another graduate student and to the right of the young lady was her reticent husband, who had just recently been selected to lead a group to Holland this coming summer. In a few moments a young creature of muliebrity joined the clan to add her multiplicity of charms to the ebullience on travel that was evolving before us. She sat down at the left end of the table with Bart and me on either side. Bart immediately slinked down into his chair and turned his small figure toward her and began in very low and jovially excluding tones to converse with this new mistress of enchanted travel. I could see that these two were going to occupy the evening together and that I had better seek someone else to converse with.

As the feast of beer and chicken à la king approached its last burning flame, I broached the subject of the dance. Two minutes later, Bart suggested in a very hurried flash of jumbled words, that Frank take over. I then continued: "Frank and I have received an invitation from Smith to attend a square dance the weekend after Christmas vacation." I then continued to explain what had happened to the fiasco of a meeting that we had attempted to have this Monday and the plans to have one the Monday after vacation instead. Polly volunteered to write the members about the event, Bill said he would make the posters and I promised to write the freshmen counselors. The couple, Mr. and Mrs. Jackson, invited John and me to a party tomorrow, since we will be the only ones who remain here during part of the vacation. Polly promised to come by to pick us up about 7:00 P.M. Mr. and Mrs. Jackson were the local representatives for the "X" in reverse, which brings foreign students to this country for the summer. Last summer there was a girl from St. Etienne in their group for whom the leader of our group secured a job in Boston after he arrived home at the end of the summer. Her sister was in our camping group, so it will be a happy party to be able to meet someone from my second hometown.

Last night Dick's parents came to take him back home. I had promised to be in the dormitory at 7:00 P.M. but was detained because of the meeting with the "X'ers." So when I finally arrived about twenty minutes later than promised, they were just about ready to commence the homeward trek for the holiday. Dick's mother was seated in the fauteuil and her husband was relaxed on the sofa, which was stacked high with impedimenta that was about ready to be embarked into the automobile. Dick was gathering a few final necessities in the bedroom preparatory to leaving and Al was packing in the midst of the front room. Dick's parents extended me a cordial greeting and we exchanged a few pleasant remarks before Dick told them that I would be visiting him during part of the vacation. I could tell that Al was a little ill at ease as the conversation tended to exclude him, not out of rudeness but merely because the topic centered about my impending visit. Al seemed to feel that he was being left out of the act and immediately tried to counteract that by interspersing at the right moment that he certainly was interested in going skiing with Dick and that he had asked him before. True, Dick had asked him during the early part of the week whether or not he would like to return early and go skiing with him. Al was rather unreceptive at first, saying that he would have to wait and see. But now he sensed rather disconcerting uneasiness that he was not included in the friendship that was permeating the room cluttered with baggage. Al has a lot to learn and I think he and I will have to learn it together. But I am confident that both he and I will learn it and be the better of friends for it.

I accompanied them half way to their car and then bid them goodbye in returning to the library. The au revoir was unpretentious and unsentimental yet I felt a warmth in my heart that is often rare in telling people goodbye. And I realized that it is not in effusive sentimentality and overfriendliness that friends are made but through an intangible feeling of confidence that develops through a demonstrated friendliness, which is not false. It is difficult to explain, for it is difficult to learn; but learning it brings happiness. The next morning Al departed. My eight o'clock class was dismissed after about twenty minutes in recognition of the holiday and the exuberance so nonconducive to study that the students demonstrated. I returned to the dormitory and lay down for about a half hour before Al also returned. In about ten minutes I was again obliged to go to class. This would also be dismissed after being there for about ten minutes—time enough to take the attendance and give the assignment for the next session after vacation, but before going I bid a merry Christmas to Al. It too was unsentimental yet I think it was sincere. I know it was on my part and I think it was on Al's part. "Merry Christmas, God bless you, etc., etc.," were the words that I made reverberate on leaving. I did not take his hand and shake it with tears in my eyes and express a profound sorrow to have to part. Our relation is above that. Our friendship is and is going to be a demonstrated one void of meaningless sentimentality. I hope Al will want to do things with us on returning from vacation, not solely with Dick but with me also. And I think he will.

I called Dad this evening. Dick's and Al's folks had called them, so I thought that a telephone call to my folks might add to the cheer also. That is what I thought in a moment of lonely sentimentality now that my roommates are gone. But it is sad how wrong people can sometimes be. I put the phone call through collect. Sandra answered the telephoned and disgustedly asked Dad if he wanted to accept it—if he wanted to accept it . . . What am I—a pariah dog that should be treated with scorn and distrust by his family? Who can I trust or confide in if it is not my family? Dad answered the phone with some exuberance but even that soon dwindled. I told him the plans for the vacation—that I would arrive home on Wednesday after spending some time working at the art gallery and a weekend with Dick. I told him that it would be necessary to have some money to make the trip. "What happened to the $25.00 that I sent you?" he snarled. I then knew that it would be impossible to get any more money out of him and said it would be sufficient. Maybe I should have told him that it would be necessary to send some more if he wanted me to make the trip but that seemed too dishonest and besides that I did not care. My voice lessened in warmth and finally ended by conducting the rest of the conversation in a mechanical monologue from which I could not remove myself. It felt as though I were chained in fetters and after many hours of trying to free myself realized the task as an impossible one and hung my head unable to fight the pain. Why can I not have a family like everyone else has? Why can I not have a mother and a father who would welcome me home in joy because of me and my meager achievements? It has been a year now since I have told anybody that my parents are separated. Oh, how blood and sweating agony flow from the heart when people ask me where I am going for Christmas when they know that my folks are divorced. If I had the money to stay here, I would. If someone would only invite me to stay with them. Four people have but that is not Christmas when one is not with his family. I keep thinking

that things will be better next time but they are always the same.
I do not want pity but what is there to be done? Maybe Dick will
invite me to stay with him and I will be able to send Dad a
telegram, telling him that I have broken my leg in skiing. I wish
Mother and Dad were not divorced. But what do I care? That is
the way it is and no one can change it. I know what is going to
happen when I get home and there is nothing to be done to rectify
it. And if it is the same, I promise to myself and God that this will
be absolutely the last time that such a trip will be made. If they
want to see me, let them come here. If they do not want to see me,
that is up to them. The confusion of divorce and hatred in our
family has continued long enough. I am through with it. Let them
straighten the situation out themselves. And when they have done
that and realized that I am not a poor helpless creature that can be
battered around and considered too immature to have any ideas or
happiness of its own, then let them come to me. The situation
cannot be altered. What time has done cannot be effaced. The
memories still linger and will forever. As I said before I can forgive
but I cannot forget. And it is for them to realize that two enemies
cannot live together. Someday maybe I will attain happiness, but
it will not be through this confusion and hatred and distrust that
exists in these families who have never been free from divorce for
three generations now. My son shall not go through this agony
that I have. I hope this will be the last time that I have to go home.

I finally secured an engagement with Françoise, the French
girl who has been termed as a "demi-prostituée sans classe" by the
director of the play we are to perform next month. I received
permission from the Master to have her in my room from 9:00
P.M. to 11.00 P.M. this evening. I am to meet her near the cemetery
at 10:00 P.M. and we are then planning to return to the room. I
do not care what happens now but do not let them condemn
either of us, for it is only a god who can live through the hatred I
have for my family. Maybe she too has suffered much and maybe
she is not what the men who know her seem to think she is. And if
she is, let someone else condemn her, for who has made her what
she is if it was not those who speak disparagingly of her. Those

who have an easy life with freedom from the debilitating effects of vice may condemn in others the flaws that they do not find in themselves. But I, I would rather live and be happy. God knows I am not perfect, but I am sure he has compassion on those who suffer though they may transgress his laws and not wish to. All I want is someone whom I can love and trust and in whom I can confide. I do not care what she is, for she is no worse or any better than I.

December 19, 1952 . . . I met Françoise at the street corner near
the cemetery last night. There was no moon, merely a heavy
blackness that loomed over the whole town and made more
insufferable by the damp air that clung to my body. I had brought
a newspaper as a shibboleth to Françoise, who did not want to
meet the wrong person. She crossed the street at about 10:00 P.M.
I could not see her very well at first, but as she approached nearer
her face appeared through a fur coat, which covered her figure. I
looked at her face and saw in it nothing but the decaying of an old
woman of thirty years. Her colorless face was carved with small
furrows that were filled with the fearful darkness of the night. I
was repulsed and ashamed of myself, knowing the heinousness of
what I was contemplating. I wanted to leave but it was too late.
There was nothing I could do but see the evening out with her
and hope that this would not be an evening that I would later
regret. I told her that the Master had given permission for her to
stay in my room to 11:00 P.M. She was reluctant and mentioned
that last year certain rumors had spread around the campus because
she had been seen frequently in a certain freshman's room. She
wanted to go to a bar or restaurant instead, but I persuaded her
that there was nothing to fear. We walked as far as the entrance to
the college and before she could refuse she was registered with the
guard and quickly whisked away to my room.

On entering the room, I immediately began to play French
records that might have produced some passion. I kept thinking of
what I would do. I gave her some wine and we began to drink and
smoke. She looked at the Figaro (a Paris newspaper) and then at
some of my pictures from France. We were both seated on the sofa
with little space between us. I felt so much repugnance in looking
at her and thinking what she represented that I did not even want
to touch her. But I had brought her there for one thing, and I was
not going to be frustrated again. And yet I knew throughout the
whole evening that nothing would happen even if she wanted it
too. But something seemed to say that I had to go through with
what I had planned. I slowly moved my arm to the back of the sofa
where she was sitting. We were then reading from a French play. I

then clasped my hand on her shoulder and pulled her back. She balked and moved forward again with great rigidity. I looked at her in the eyes, detesting every moment of what I was doing, and repeated the French word for "no" several times. She got up and went into the bedroom to fetch her coat, for it was time to leave the dormitory. I quickly followed in her wake. As she finished adjusting her coat to her loathsome body, I grabbed her by the shoulders and stood at a distance from her. Once again she was adamant and accused me of having evil intentions in bringing her to the dormitory. Going down the stairs I made the remark that she would think me too brash. Her answer was a betraying "no" and I could see much that I could not see before. On her porch she remarked that there are many young students in town who want to make natural love to an old lady. I asked her if she thought the same of me. Her initial response was "yes" and then when she saw the growing stern coldness on my face, she changed the answer in a feigned sweetness to a subtle "no."

After I had been home for five minutes she called and asked if I were angry with her and that she would like to listen to my records and talk again some other time. I told her that the incident had provoked no anger in me and bid her a speedy but kindly "bonne nuit." I began to bite my fingernails and breathe rapidly and pace the floor. Small globules of sweat began to pour from my face and evaporate into the stifling hotness of the room. I began to pity her and then I became afraid. I do not know why. But I became afraid—afraid of her. My heart trembled as I held a cigarette in my unstable fingers. One cigarette after another disintegrated in my fingers until I could no longer contain myself. I ran to the coffee table, seized some object and crashed it against the burning fireplace. What if I had done what she had accused me of? How could I have ever face my friends, my God and myself. I threw myself on the bed and there remained until the cooling breeze from the casement window dried the sweat from my guilty brow and my body lay limp as one who has just been hurled from a bicycle without injury, full of fear and thankfulness. If she calls again, I will not be home.

December 21, 1952 . . . Friday I went to work with my ambivalent feelings of hatred and love bringing havoc on any equilibrium that I might have had. As the dust rag wiped clean the volumes, my mind regurgitated on the telephone call and alternatives to rectify this situation that has plagued everyone's happiness since I was nine and the divorce struck our home brought by the filthy carrier who later espoused my mother and brought into the family his degeneracy. I would think of the telephone call and the part of it where Dad was fairly generous with his enthusiasm at having me home. And then I would think of Sandra and the way she answered it initially. Dick would listen to me. I would tell him and no one else the reason why this Christmas trip would not be made. And even then I would not tell him too much. I would let him infer the reasons, merely informing him that he is not to tell anybody that I did not go home. Then I thought of Sandra and the pies she made especially for me during vacation. She was so meticulous that one, which was slightly burnt, had to be thrown out. Nothing was too good for a son returning from college. And I decided to go home. But the argument—would that be repeated again, would she again belittle me and call me a poor judge of men and women? And I decided again to send the telegram telling them of some minor accident that had precluded the voyage home.

It was with the latter resolution in mind that I conducted myself for the rest of the day. About an hour before quitting time, the girls invited us to drink some cider and eat some popcorn with them. The conversation soon centered on frivolous topics between two of the girls and myself, with the others contributing interspersed comments? Then one of the girls (they were both married) looked at me with a sorrowful compassion of eyes and affirmatively asked if I were not going home. Never before had I concealed the truth. But this time I did. "I'm leaving next Tuesday on the plane for Indiana," I quickly retorted with all the nonchalantness possible to dispense with any pity she might have held for me. My stepbrother's former escapades were swiftly recalled as I remembered that he was never trusted because he lied all the time. But is it not better to lie or to equivocate than to introduce unhappiness into the conversation and cause the others to feel pity? The others do not have to lie, for they do not have a broken family.

That evening I went to the party given by the alumni of the "X." There was a girl from Germany who is living with one of the big men in the organizational headquarters of the "X." One of the students whom I had known previously introduced me to her initially before we went to the other side of the room and began talking with some of the men. The dinner was a buffet one and we soon went into the dining room to take from the cornucopia of nourishment that the various individuals had brought to this festive potluck. In the center of the front room was one card table at which I seated myself beside Polly, the girl from Smith who is doing some secretarial work for us now. Soon others joined us. At my left was a French girl of no beauty and to the left of Polly was one of my copemates at school. Across from us were seated two individuals whom I had not known previously. The one turned out to be a very humorous individual in that he began to vie in all earnestness for the attention of the young girl from Germany, who was seated at this time by herself on the side of a large arm chair to the left of the card table. I could see at first that he thought himself a natural leader and thus displayed an unusual amount of effusiveness to convey his points. He would talk to one individual and if it were a girl he would stare her in the eyes with the most agonizing expression of pity. He was on leave from a naval base, having received his commission from Harvard, and had been in France with the "X" for one summer. After dinner I arose from the table, while he and some of the others wrote letters to a group of French people who had been here last summer. I tried to disperse myself as much as possible among the people, hoping to meet as many of them as possible. After an hour we cleared the rugs from the floor and piled records on the phonograph that played for the rest of the night. I asked the German girl to dance. She was not essentially shy but her language barrier did present some trouble in trying to be as voluble as she might have been in German. After she explained the difference between the old fashion and the modern waltz, we requested the Blue Danube first and then others. We

were the only ones to dance the European way—twirling wildly around
the room with our eyes locked on each other's eyes to keep from
getting dizzy—the way I had learned it that summer in France. But
as the vertigo of dizziness twirled us around in a lightness of smiles
and laughter, I knew that she felt at home and was glad to be able to
do the waltz in America and to find someone who was as interested in
it as she. The people she had come with promised to drive me home
with the good-natured stipulation that I help with the readjusting of
this now cluttered house, now showing the signs of having been the
site a party. They knew that the opportunity would give me pleasure
to be able to go partly home with my new acquaintance. Everyone
else left except two married couples and my competitor, who had just
started competing toward the end of the evening. He had had the
opportunity to speak to her once before after one of the waltzes when
I had gone to get some eggnog. I returned to find him, the German
girl, two other married women, and a French girl conversing. I secured
a chair and to begin conversation asked the French girl if her sister
who is going to college in town, might want to act in *Topaze*, the play
that we are planning for next month. That had been the only time
during the evening that he had been able to talk with her. And I did
not care, for I was not trying to compete in love but merely to give her
an enjoyable evening and to have one myself. While the women were
washing the dishes and the males were conversing in the living room
about the profession of the host, the young naval man was busily
engaged in securing the address of the German girl. On the porch he
bid everyone goodbye except me. As he turned and walked away, I
bid him a merry Christmas. While we were going home, the couple
asked me when I was planning to go home. I told them I would be
leaving on the train the following Tuesday and I felt secure.

Saturday night Dick and I double-dated with some girls from
Skidmore and from Smith. Dick had gone steady with the girl
from Skidmore during his high school years and knew my girl very
well. It was no more than a half hour after Dick and I had entered
his girl's house that her parents asked me in the course of
conversation whether or not my folks had seen me last Christmas.
Without any qualms of conscience I replied with utmost mendacity

that I had gone home last Christmas. Dick knew differently but had enough common sense to realize that it was only a strategy to make the evening a success and banish any pity that might be inspired in anyone's heart. After the cinema we went to one of the girls' houses and danced and talked until late that morning. Hunger began to conquer our stomachs, so Dick and I drove into town for some sandwiches after the girls had been safely returned home. While going to the restaurant Dick asked for a cigarette. I had just lit one and thus gave it to him while lighting another one for me. We were buddies, I thought. I had succumbed to his liberal use of the English language and he had begun to do some smoking.

As a keener knowledge of Dick's family presented itself, I began to change my mind about not returning home. Dick was not intending to stay with his folks all the time. Half of the vacation he will be away skiing and for the week preceding Christmas he is working all day for the post office. Sunday Dick's paternal grandmother visited for a few minutes. Her husband is dead. She was not given an overly abundant portion of attention, yet I knew that she was liked. And she left without too much ado as Dick's mother took her to another old lady's house to visit for the afternoon before returning to her home in some other northern state. I noticed, though, that there was no heated arguing in the family while I was there. On the way home, one of the men who gave me a ride explained how inconsiderate he thought it was of the Americans to not live with their mothers-in-law. I thought of the German girl and how she said her family always argued. I thought of the man who had employed me for two years in Denver and how he had said that he would never allow his mother to live with him and his wife, though he would be willing to pay for an apartment for her near them. I thought of Sandra and how she said that after her mother had been with them on a vacation for more than two or three days, they began to get on each other's nerves. The words of a girl with whom I talked this evening came to mind. "Oh, I've been sulking all day. You know we all get on each other's nerves before Christmas," she said, not too bitter yet with some truth

I have decided to go home. I realize now that my situation as the result of a divorce may not be ideal but that I cannot run away from it. The main thing is to live and it is not living unless there is resistance. This resistance sometimes becomes too strong and then it is not living to try to resist it. Dad is married again and there is nothing that can be done about it. Mother made a mistake and has thus separated herself from me through the years. I love her but no longer have any fear of her. I no longer care whether she tries to visit me or hunt me down. I prefer that she would not, for it appears that the best solution to our troubles is to stay completely estranged and let me try to give my devotion to one family, though that family may not be the desirable one. People will ask me if my family is divorced, and I will answer "no," but I will not have any fear of their learning the truth if there are those hateful enough to reveal the stinging truth. In every way and means I shall henceforth try to give everyone the impression that I too come from a family like every other happy person. My family shall not house any of my relatives. If my wife does not have the foresight to see the disasters of such a plight or is forced to do it beyond her will, there will be nothing to do but wait and try to avert an inevitable tragedy. I am going to visit Dad and Sandra and try to be happy with them. The visit will be short and I will try as best as possible not to be angry when he talks of an unpleasant past and his love for Mother. I will try to subordinate myself to them and try not to be haughty when they flout my opinions. I cannot feel that their home is mine, never have been able to and never will be able to. But I will try to make the best of the situation to secure all of our happiness. Their happiness must not be sacrificed for mine and neither must mine be sacrificed for theirs. I am of a new generation, Dad, a generation that is separated from you by thoughts and time. You have your life to live and I have mine to live. It is going to be hard to teach you that—to teach you that I am happy and that I do not hate you because I do not want to be with you all the time but would rather be with people of my own age. Maybe if the situation were different our closeness might be better preserved during the coming years. But you know as I know, Dad, that when I see you all the miseries of the past become real. I wish that a part of the family really belonged to me. But we must not be sentimental about it, for Mother has her family and you have your family. And neither one of them have a place for me. There was a time when I wished that I was a part of the family. I no longer suffer, though, for I have learned to tell people what is not true and thus banish the feelings of inferiority that have developed. The past does not look so hard in perspective as long as it can be kept at a reasonable distance. I am going to try to keep our relation a good one and rectify the evils of the last trip, yet I am going to attempt to keep you far enough from me and in great enough fear of me to refrain from telling my friends about this disgusting past.

December 27, 1952 . . . On Wednesday evening December 23 at 4:00 I took to the road to return home by hitchhiking in my Air Force uniform. Dad would not send any more money to make the trip. He said I should have enough left from the Thanksgiving vacation, since they had sent a check for seventy dollars and I had hitchhiked back and they had given me some more money to buy a return ticket. I have not told them that I am trying to save enough money to make a trip to Cuba this summer, for I know that they would disagree or something else. I decided therefore to hitchhike and to tell them that I had taken the train. It was not too difficult an ordeal, for it was interesting to compare the response of the public to a student and to a member of the armed services. I found that most of the people who gave me rides had themselves been in the service and were glad to share their experiences. I was fortunate in not having many delays and thus reached home on the next day December 24 at 4:00 P.M. for Christmas Eve.

There was such little time to start traveling before it turned dark on Wednesday that I completely forgot buying the folks something for Christmas. I was thinking about purchasing a record with all the school songs; but on reaching Indianapolis, the previous discussion about my college with Sandra placed a certain repugnance on this idea and so I purchased Albert Schweitzer's record of Bach's "Chorale Preludes." It seemed like a good compromise and might possibly stimulate some interest in them for classical music, which Dad has always said he does not like. Sandra has generally displayed a certain penchant toward classical music, but she has not developed it too thoroughly.

It was with a sickening fear of heart that my feet scuffled along the floor of the veranda. My uniform made an imposing sight and struck the folks with surprise when they saw me. Sandra was sitting on the divan with her lips puckered and her eyes directed in an angry contemplation of the coffee table. I was afraid—afraid that this trip would not be any different than the last one. I was afraid that Sandra would be as self-asserting and always right as ever. But that made no difference. I was determined to make this vacation a success, even at the expense of my pride. As I opened the door Dad arose from his swivel chair and Sandra from the divan. I placed a gentle osculation on Betty's cheek and then kissed Sandra and shook hands with Dad. They were not mad and it appeared that they too would make some effort to create a warm atmosphere. The conversation centered on my trip by train and nothing was said of our previous disagreements, for it was this evening that we were to open the Christmas presents.

The cadeaux were to be opened at 9:00 P.M. and it was with this happy anticipation that we received friends and sent them away. One young girl who had lost her husband about a year ago in a plane accident paid us a visit. She tottered and the alcoholic odor was profuse. She had been invited to dine with us about two hours earlier but mustered some feeble excuse to exculpate herself from this breach of hospitality. She sprawled into a chair, spreading her jeans-covered legs out widely and resting her black and gray frowsy hair on the back of the chair, as though our home would offer her a few moments of friendly relaxation from the fiendish life she has had to lead since the death of her husband. She brought some unwrapped Christmas gifts with her which she had bought during the day for her two small children. Sandra wrapped them as this young but unhappy relict masculinely pushed food into a living and suffering machine, which wants security and feeds on alcohol. Dad looked at her sometimes with disgust and at other times he would attempt to be friendly. The whole evening was a joyous one for us and probably not too different than that of any other happy family. Dad was Santa Claus and, of course, Betty received most of the presents. The room was tenebrous except for the one corner of it where we all hovered around the Christmas tree as Dad gaily called the names on the packages. The purple and red and green lights shown as bubbles rising and dispersing in the water and so our hearts grew light and felt the oblivion-giving light penetrate into our bodies and give a medium to the rising cheer that flowed from our body and soul. Betty received two games called "cootie" and said I could have one to play at school. And Sandra took a couple pictures as I held my ten-dollar check for cigarettes.

It all ended the next day and we once more returned to reality. Reality had returned and there was nothing to do but face it. We all revived rather late from the cheer of the previous night but were ready to depart for the special Christmas dinner at the post by noon. Since Dad is on patient status it was only through invitation that we were able to eat there. The Commanding Officer of the base is a close friend of the family and made it possible for us to eat there and afterwards invited us to a small party at his house. It is Colonel Ticen who has been instrumental is making it possible for Dad to stay at home rather than be confined in a hospital. It was this same Colonel who sent several recommendations to the Commanding Officer of the American section in Germany, telling of Dad's ability, his past service rendered so efficiently both in Denver and here and requesting a direct commission as a captain for him. But Dad did not bother to visit the officer while overseas. By the time the Colonel had sent a second recommendation urging the German commander to get in touch with Dad if Dad were not inclined to take the initiative himself, one of the hospitals was tending to a man confused and unwilling to do anything. The Army sent him back to the States, placing him in an Eastern mental hospital. It was only through the influence of Colonel Ticen that Sandra finally succeeded in having Dad brought home and given treatment here. Dad had missed any opportunity he might have had to secure a direct commission as a captain. He had been accepted into OCS during World War II, when he was thirty-six years old, but his feet gave out during a long march at Fort Riley, Kansas, where he was in training to become a Ninety-Day Wonder (a shavetail—the product of OCS)—so here we go again. Just after World War II a new mayor (a Yalie) was elected in Denver, and he offered him the position of chief aide to the mayor. This was an incredible springboard position, but he turned it down. At least he seems to have a talent for turning things down. He who hesitates is lost forever and he has hesitated too long to now seize the opportunities that had presented themselves to him, and is passing by the single best opportunity that lies before him—to complete his career with the U.S. Army, to which he really is attached emotionally. The way is now open for him to advance through the commissioned officer ranks. Familiarity breeds contempt and that is how he views this opportunity. But with his stubbornness, he will succeed in getting his discharge and later regret it. I guarantee it. He recently mentioned out of the blue, that we have different backgrounds, which tell me a lot—he just doesn't get it. This incipient role reversal is not pleasant.

There were three officers at the party, Dad, and their respective wives and myself. Dad felt uneasy, for he knew that everyone in the room knew of his mental condition. Yet he tried to mix with them. I did not feel ill at ease but enjoyed their company and knew that in two years those bars would be on my shoulders also. Colonel Ticen asked the crowd if they would like to have a drink. The women graciously refused or asked for an innocuous beverage perhaps more apropos to their sex. The three officers and I asked for bourbon on ice. Dad said he did not want anything. The Colonel departed to the kitchen and I followed in a few minutes. He gave me some Drambuie and said understandingly, "Here, take this to your Dad." I did but he would not drink it. I asked him for a light and he harshly replied, "You smoke all the time, don't you?" I did not make any effort to reply and felt no antagonism, merely resignation to the undeniable fact that nothing can be done at the present—that he is the only one who can help himself and maybe in time he will. But it will take a long time. On the way home in the car, Dad had to stop and make his daily report to the doctor. While we waited in the car, Sandra told me that the Colonel had given her three choices to choose from. Either they could retire, return to the Army base at Denver or remain in the Army here. The day Sandra went to the Colonel to make the final decision, Dad said to her as she left, "Don't betray me." He wants to retire. He hates the Army and everything connected with the Army. He wants to go to law school or start a business. Sandra knows as I do, though, that he does not have the drive to do either. And why should he want to do either? He does not have to be a great man to have the affection of his wife and his children. I would rather have a father that amounted to nothing financially or intellectually, if he would take an interest in me and not try to hold me back. But he is holding on to Sandra with one hand and to me and his past experiences with the other. He is dangling in the air trying to hold on to his loved ones by tying them to him with a heavy iron chain. He is afraid to let me drive the car, for fear that this accomplishment might make me more skilled than he and thus able to flee his encompassing chain. When I went from Denver to college in the East and passed two weeks here in the journey, he became angry when I asked him to teach me to drive. He would never let Mother drive the car. He would not use reason and move away from an antagonizing in-law when Mother asked him to. Well I remembered how Mother told me this with nostalgic love for Dad. "We would still have been married if he had moved." But he was afraid—afraid that if he moved he would lose everything. This gnawing disease of insecurity bred by an unconventional union between a girl of eighteen and a drunken father of thirty-three, has made him so jealous that he wants the world to stop so he can always watch them and make sure they are not betraying him. He does not want to do anything but sit in a swivel chair and read psychology books and philosophize and tell everyone and me about him how to live.

We drove home and Dad continued a philosophizing tirade against drinking, stressing how ridiculous it is. Sandra had cited the meritorious abstinence of General Marshall while we waited in the car for Dad. And thus they lambasted drinkers of all degrees as insecure. I did not argue with them but deeply wished that they could see that it is merely an excess in anything that makes it evil and then it generally causes other people unhappiness. I could not speak for teetotalers, especially women, because it seems admirable that a person can refrain from drinking. But if one is in a crowd that does drink, why should he buck their conventions and think his morals better than theirs? And on the other hand, would it not be just as ridiculous for a person to take a bottle of whiskey with him to a party where he knew no one would be drinking? But neither Dad nor Sandra can see this. Dad has at times during his life been the most devout follower of Ingersoll and has at times become drunk. I remembered Sandra telling me that he got drunk one time shortly after they were married. That was the last time, though. All he does now is read and philosophize. He is even becoming a little more than religious. He is becoming rabid about his ideas. When he was an atheist he was fanatic and now he is becoming fanatic at the opposite extreme. He has no pastime—no hobby. All he thinks of, is becoming a great man. He wants to be a lawyer or a prosperous business man. He knows he has an intelligence quotient approaching that of a genius. But he is not the only person that ever lived who had the natural gifts of a genius but never became rich or famous or distinguished. When Dad was married to Mother, she tried to encourage him to take the examinations to become an officer. But he would not. He was going to become a lawyer. He had to gain recognition by himself. He did not want to gain recognition in an organization that he had not founded or in which there could not be enough individualism. He was insecure, wanting something that would be his and his alone. And he has not changed. He is unhappy and thinks that everyone else is also. He sulks when another man talks to Sandra at a dance. He is afraid that the man is trying to steal her from him. Now I can see more clearly why Mother divorced him—not that she did not love him, but that it is impossible to live with a man that wants to be as perfect as he wants to be. Mother once said that someday I might be able to understand the situation. And now it seems clear, for there could be no greater agony for me than to have to live with Dad all the time. If I did and he had his way, I would sit at home, go to the theater when he did, and maybe have a few dates when he decided to drive me to the girl's house. He visited his father a few years ago, but the father did not recognize him. His mother did not send him a birthday card this year, though Sandra's mother did. But he cannot realize that this is passed— that this same thing is not going to happen again. He can analyze other people but he does not realize that humans are not like machines—that they must live—that they are not going to hurt him. Certainly, there are those who themselves are so confused that they will try to deliberately hurt another. But this is passed,

Dad. You are no longer living with a fanatic mother or an insane mother-in-law. I can think of my stepfather with a certain love and respect that was not possible before and I can hope for reconciliation. Common sense tells me, though, that as long as my grandmother is living this is impossible, for such a move would only plunge us once again into a terrible havoc from which it would be impossible to arise. Mother will not lose her love for me in the meantime, for as it has taken time for me to understand the situation so it will take time for her to understand the situation. Oh, Dad, how can I help you to realize this?

During the afternoon I wrote to Dick and Al and the roommate that quit school. It has sometimes seemed a hypocritical thing to me to write letters to people—as though one were writing in competition with the rest of this person's friends. But people are glad to hear from another and feel slighted if one does not write. The little things count A GREAT DEAL and the big things count as much. When I get back to college the folks are going to start receiving a letter once a week from me.

Yesterday I tried to get Dad to let me use the car for a date with Martha Griffin, the daughter of the leading surgeon on the post. She is a freshman at Stephens College, an all-girls school in Columbia, Missouri, and home on vacation. Of course, he refused. "You don't have a driver's license." "Well, let's go downtown and try to get one." But he did not want to. Then I asked him if he would like to play some pool. "With that bunch of bums?" he retorted. After about three hours of persuasion, I succeeded. On returning he remarked that they were not a bad group of fellows after all. That evening I played bridge with Martha and two nurses and got the booby prize. Mrs. Griffin played my hand most of the time, though. I think that by the end of the vacation bridge will be second nature with me. Dad was going to come after me. But it was so late when Martha and I decided to put an end to the evening that her mother gave me permission to stay at their house. It was too late to phone home. Today the phone rang early with a worried father on the other end. I told him we had tried to call him and he seemed somewhat reassured.

After Martha and I had passed the day looking at television and dancing in the Officers' Club, she and her mother took me home in their English sports car. Martha only has a beginner's permit, so her mother had to accompany her when driving off the base. They visited for a few minutes and we arranged for another bridge game next week. They had been gone only a few minutes when company stopped in. I waited till they had gone and them began to write to you. Betty had showed me a little story she had written during the day. And as I sat down to write, there came to mind the memory of the pride it gave me when Dad typed a Superman story I had written in third grade. I picked up the story without Betty's knowing it and typed it:

The CAT
by Betty

One day I was walking along the street and I saw a cat. He had a sore eye and a sore leg. I took him home with me. We took care of him. We took him to the doctor's. He took care of him. I asked Mother if I could keep him. She said I could keep him. He followed me to school this day and yesterday. Then he got run over. Then I couldn't have any more cats, because we might move away. Mary Lou has a cat but I don't.

I gave it to her cautiously, not knowing what her reaction would be. She looked at it and not knowing what to do laughed a little. Then when she saw that it was something she had written, her eyes grew bright and she ran into the living room to show it to the folks. Sandra guessed she had written it along time ago, since she had since acquired a new cat. The rest of the evening she spent in writing short stories; that is, when she was not trying to have me teach her how to dance. I was drinking some coffee while writing and so Betty asked her mother for something to drink while she worked. She even began to smoke on her yellow crayon. Here are two of the stories that she wrote and which I will have to type tomorrow:

THE FAT MAN

My Daddy is a fat man. He is a funny little fellow. But I love him. He makes fun of me. He makes people happy. He loves my kitten. He plays with it. Are you glad you have a daddy?

THE THINGS

I have a kitten. He is nice, and he can jump up. He is sleeping. Now he woke up. My brother Alex is here. He came on Christmas Eve.

December 27, 1952 . . . Early this morning the sun rose and sprinkled its warmth through the white clouds and over the frozen earth and we slept peacefully on until the resounding chimes told us that it was time to go to church. Sandra prepared the breakfast with eggs, sausage, toast, and coffee. We all came to the table in our pajamas and dined in the harmonious splendor of the morning. Sandra did not have to ask Dad to go with us, for it was apparent that he had been accompanying her for many months now. The preacher has one year to finish in the graduate school at my university. I had met him during the Thanksgiving vacation and discussed existentialism with him and Sandra. Sandra had asked him about how well he thought the students at the all-boys university could come to understand women. This was the morning after the heated argument that we had engaged in. He told her that he was of the personal opinion that the weekends are long enough to learn to understand the muliebrity of the Eastern schools. Sandra seemed temporarily assured by that and when I arose from bed after he had been there for an hour she had a little more confidence in my ability to understand humans.

When the preacher ascended the rostrum, I was glad to see that he had not brought back with him the sophistication of the East to this small town but that he had assumed their clothing and their manner of thinking. It was difficult to refrain from laughing, though, when he made a parable out of a temporary power failure in the lighting system at school. Dad greeted the people jovially and we joined Sandra and an elderly lady in the front part of the church. Dad enjoyed the service and sang and read the responsive readings with assertiveness. But half way through the first prayer, I raised my head and saw Dad arrogantly aloof to praying. As the service came to an end, I watched him surreptitiously out of the corner of my eye. Never once did he bow his head to pray. He was afraid of what the other people would think of him. He did not want them to think that he is a fanatic like his mother was. He did not want them to think that he is so confused that he has to have some object to retrieve him from a state of despair. He was afraid and yet he has admired the Catholic Church because of its extremely religious atmosphere. He has always admired it because the people knelt and prayed to God and confessed their sorrows to a priest. After the service Dad lingered to talk to the members and proudly introduced me to some of them. The parson was glad to see me and extended a friendly hand. He laughed heartily when, trying to refrain from laughing myself, I told him that I liked his comparison of the university without lights to a soul without any divine worship. It was two years ago when a small hurricane caused the power plant to fail. "We roamed the streets until the live wires which were strewn on the ground caused us to fear and we returned to the dormitory, hovering in darkness for seven hours until illumination once again filled the campus." The point he was trying to illustrate would have been brought out very forcefully for one who does not know the character and actions of college students. He could not refrain himself from laughing, though, when I mentioned the comparison on leaving. The people behind us heard little of what was said and I could see that they too were enjoying the joke as much as he and I.

A lady, who lives across the street with her son and his wife, accompanied us home and spent an hour discussing philosophy and the evils of the world with Dad and some with Sandra. Dad concentrated mainly on analyzing people and receiving with the greatest of pride the blandishment of this lady that he would have no difficulty whatsoever in securing a good executive position in civilian life. "You know," he expostulated with pedantic authority, "you have to understand people to work with them and sometimes one uses wrongly the same means to correct something which was caused by this action originally. And you know, etc., etc." The lady explained how the young people of today have no values in life and do not look forward to the future. They tried to arrive at a definition of intelligence and Dad quoted Webster's Dictionary. The lady bade us goodbye and remarked that this is the only family with whom she can discuss her troubles. Sandra answered that she would have to accompany us to Denver when Dad retires in a few months. "I suppose your daughter-in-law would miss you, though?" Sandra asked with a pleasant smile and yet some curiosity. "No, she wouldn't miss me."

Dad and I soon rode out to the post so he could check in with the psychiatrist. Going through the east gate he neglected to wait for the guard to signal him through and we soon found a patrol car beckoning for us to pull over to the curb. We returned to the gate. Dad parked the car and entered the shelter where they issued him a ticket—the first ticket he has ever received on an Army base. At least that is what he replied when I asked him. When he returned to the car, he turned the music off and I could see in his eyes the repressed tears of a man too sensible to affronts and too logical to understand either himself or others.

At the dinner table Sandra began harping about the girl she called to secure an engagement for me. She goes with the same crowd as does Martha and I have therefore been hesitating through the day whether it would be possible to have a date with her without creating some embarrassment for Martha, since she did introduce me to quite a number of her friends during Saturday. Sandra said she should not have called until after I had had an engagement with Martha, and began worrying that I was going to cause everyone in town to be mad at her. "We were good friends of the Griffin's before you came and we want to remain like that." Then I mentioned a need for some money and immediately the thunderbolt struck and everyone spewed forth bitter invectives. Dad started his philosophy of life and Sandra gave him assistance. "Listen, let me take care of this will you. What kind of a guy do you think I am?" I disgustedly said to Sandra. Then they started condemning me for not riding on the train when returning from college during the Thanksgiving vacation and not bringing enough with me for a return ticket. They lambasted me for not being prompt enough in telling them that money had arrived when they sent any. "If you can't recognize this little favor, then I wont send you any." Dad growled as he told me how much he thought he knew at nineteen. This gave me the opportunity that I had been half-heartedly anticipating to try to tell Dad that his son does not despise him or think him the less for not being a general or a president of some firm. "Don't swear at me. You think you can insult me. And you think I am stupid," he said as his anger increased.

"Gee wiz, Dad, you think I don't appreciate anything. If you were not so damn sensitive, maybe you would realize that I do appreciate you. Now don't start your philosophizing with me. I don't want your advice. If you had some good advice and would follow it yourself then maybe I would do the same. I don't mind taking good advice. And I don't think that you are stupid. You are a much more intelligent man that I am." I did not think that this last remark would have any bearing on the winning of the present argument but hoped that in reflecting on it he might later realize I love him for what he is and not for what he might have been or for the hardships he has endured. He tried then to tell me what a difficult life I have had and how I should live to be happy. He walked out to the kitchen to fetch some water. As he did so, I motioned gently to Sandra to keep the argument down. I know that she really did not want to become involved in an argument that would leave hatred in the atmosphere for the rest of the vacation. At least that is what I hoped. I tried to forget our other disputes and remembered that on returning from Colonel Ticen's on Christmas day she asked me for a puff of my cigarette as I shucked my coat and prepared to take it to my room. She assuaged the discussion to a certain extent but was still determined that I would not come out favorable. Then Dad came back and began to analyze why I delayed in acknowledging the receipt of the money he had sent. "You were trying to escape authority and thought that you could do it by slighting me. Everybody does it. Everybody wants to escape authority. That is why you started smoking. You think that you can get away from authority by smoking." I thought quietly to myself: What Peter says about Paul, tells more about Peter than it does Paul. "Dad, people are not machines. You have a very good mind for analyzing people logically, but we are not made to be analyzed logically." I tried to explain and then admitted to him that it was impossible to explain to him what I meant, because it is something that cannot be explained rationally according to some pedantic system. I told him that I had never thought of why I had not written him sooner in acknowledgement of receiving his money in the light that he had presented it, but that he might be right. I conceded defeat to them and tried not to look angry. In fact, I was not angry and strangely enough did not really feel as though the argument had been against me.

After leaving the dinner table, I went to my bedroom to begin to write. A half hour later I walked into the front room, doubled my fist, aimed it at him and winked. He laughed heartily and it gave me courage that perhaps this argument will do him some good. Maybe he will listen to me—maybe. Then I sat down and thought—about Mother and the events of the past and how Dad has influenced them and how he has been changed by them. I began to think of my maternal grandmother and that her remarks were sometimes just as cutting as Dad's. One time when Mother came home late from a date, my grandmother accused her of being a prostitute and she did it in front of the neighbors. She used to live on the unhappiness of others and tell them how to live. At times she has been an atheist and at other times she has been a religious fanatic. She used to blast my stepfather as being a degenerate until I began to believe he was. Dad has termed him a neurotic. She never wanted Mother to do anything. She wanted to keep her tied in a corner and subjected to agony. Oh, how Mother must have suffered during those days when the three of them— Mother, Dad, and Grandmother—lived in the same house. I remember how she said that Dad did not even kiss her on the day of their wedding. I remember one night when Mother went into the bathroom and cried for a half hour. I put my arms around her and the tears ran from both of our cheeks. Those times were many and Mother was unhappy and suffering and yet trying to salvage her marriage and the lives of her children. One night she took my brother and me to the movies in Dad's old Ford and cried when we had to go home. I won a watermelon that evening when they drew our ticket during intermission. I remember when Grandmother testified against my stepfather in the trial of his cruelty toward me. And I remember that she testified against Dad in the divorce action. He did not go to the trial. Why did he not go to the trial? Why did he not fight? But no, he chose to do nothing but to think about his miseries. After the divorce, we became adjusted into the new family. There was strictness but there we were living. My stepfather used to play with us, to tickle us at night before we went to bed. Even if he did do certain disgusting things, such as placing his hand underneath Mother's dress when she served him coffee, he was living. He was usually partial to my younger brother, but it was my younger brother who had been only three years old at the time of the divorce and did not remember the troubles of the past. I was insecure and unhappy. But I really did not become so until we moved back to Denver, where Dad was living with Sandra and their young daughter in base housing at Fitzsimons Army Hospital. We had always written him, because Mother made us and we were really glad to see what our father was like. But then the trouble recommenced. We started visiting Dad on the weekends and I came back hating Mother more and more as the reality of the situation became impressed on my mind. I was about twelve when we all returned to Denver—he from duty in the Pacific Theater of Operations with an appointment as head of the OP Mess (Officer Patients' Mess) at Fitzsimons Army Hospital and the rest of us from Nashville, Tennessee, where my stepfather had been on assignment as Post Exchange Manager at the local Air Force Base, and I was just entering the adolescent stage of my life which is hard enough without having to combat an ambivalent feeling of hate and love toward my parents and my step-parents. Every time that I went to visit Dad he would tell me how Mother had tried to turn me against him and that he had never said anything against her. There were good times—he was a master sergeant then and took me to the NCO Club, gave me a tour of the OPMess where I remember the Italian prisoners who were working there under him as cooks; there was a base theater, and the atmosphere was always friendly as he was greeted by the nickname Johnny, a picnic in the mountains where one master sergeant jovially and with great respect greeted him by saying "there's the smartest man on the base"—it was a great life. I remember going with him to his favorite bookstore. Across from the Loop in downtown Denver, it was huge with dusty and dark shelves of used books to the ceiling with the rows that lined the

entire store. As we entered the owner greeted him: "Hi, Johnny."
Here he fed his insatiable passion for books as well as at the Denver
Public Library in Denver Civic Center. I remembered this when I
took the entrance examination for the U.S. Air Force ROTC, for it
had the question: "Should commissioned officers fraternize with
the ranks?" I knew the answer they wanted and answered it correctly,
but it is the only question that I remember to this day—it bothered
me. Everything now had the potential of Plato's good life, if he
would just leave it alone. Yet it was he who spent one evening
reading a Sherlock Holmes' mystery about a wicked stepfather, to
my brother and me, in the company of his wife and young daughter
as we sat in the livingroom—nothing like having an intelligent
and well-read bibliophile for a father doing his thing. During the
war when we were in Palm Springs, California, I used to swim and
play with the other youngsters. We three brothers used to play
together. For two years this bliss continued until my stepbrother
began to become intractable. He developed a deep hatred and
resentment for me, which eventually caused my brother to do the
same, since the former was the idol of his life, being fairly popular
with other children. But this development of estrangement between
my family and me might never have matured if we had not returned
to Denver. I retired from the world and became belligerent toward
other children. There was very seldom a week, which passed that I
did not have a fight with someone. In the sixth grade I became
known as the bully. Then in junior high school there were several
boys much larger and more powerful than I. One gang became
belligerent toward me and harassed and picked on me so, that I
withdrew myself into a world of my own with no friends. I never
went swimming. I never played football. All I did was to commute
to and from Dad's house to Mother's and develop hatred in my
heart. I tried to commit suicide when I was twelve years old—at
least that is how it appeared on the surface, though that was not
my thought as such, but rather my mother's characterization and
interpretation and I went along with it since it sounded very daring.
When my mother decided to take me in the car to my father's and
let him have custody—not as a reward but as punishment for my

normal teenager moodiness—I jumped from the moving car and cut my chin. I was just trying to survive. It apparently worked its desired effect and she relented after having taken me to have my chin sown up. I thought Mother did not love me or understand me and I feared Dad's unsympathetic sternness and self-pity. But it worked—I pitied him and tried to please him and yet loved my mother and stepfather too much to hurt either of them. I then placed my affections on a dog that we had. After a year it was stolen. And everyone accused everyone else of doing it until I was hating everyone. I even went to a detective bureau in Denver to see if they could help me find my little dog. But the jump from the running car started a series of events that resulted in my stepfather's selling his roofing business and the family home and moving the family to New Orleans, Louisiana. My paternal uncle, a Denver chiropractor, had filed a dependency action against my mother and when it was dismissed after hearing, we left. I told the judge I wanted to stay with my mother. This is how I ended up in New Orleans. My father had played his role well—they both did—tit for tat. My father had read to my brother and me one evening a mystery from Sherlock Holmes (The Adventure of the Speckled Band) about a wicked stepfather and it took, though this was just the tip of the iceberg. Oh, the joys of having well-read and intelligent parents! I was the jury and they were trying to sway me—they tore me apart. I was the prize. They were evenly matched—two very strong egos with all the instincts of a feisty Pit Bull, though they both had their own distinctive brand of subtlety. These two soul mates—strong and stubborn—would not let go. And to fuel the fire my stepmother informed me that my father loved my mother and always would, as she still loved her former fiancé—the Columbia man—theirs was a marriage of friendship. Her intentions in telling me this were good—but hell is paved with good intentions. When we were on the road from Palm Springs, California, to Nashville, Tennessee, my mother asked me if she should go back to my father. The moment is burned in my mind. We were on the road and it was at a rest stop. I said "no." Why I said that I do not consciously remember now, but I know that there was a feeling of protection for her in that answer—she had made her bed and should make the most of it. My father had written her from the Pacific and asked her to come back, but when he did so he was remarried and had a daughter. Whether her asking me my opinion was just a mood swing or not, I do not know. But I wonder what would have been her response if I had said "yes." The response that I gave was the right one. Sometimes I think of King Solomon and his manner of determining who was the true mother—stating that he would have the baby killed and at that point the true mother backed off and he knew then who was the true mother. So this is how we all came together—my stepfather who was born in 1900, my mother who was born in 1914, my father who was born in 1907 and my stepmother who was born in 1913. My father's daughter was born in 1944. My mother's son was born in 1949 at Denver, Colorado, and his brother was born in 1949 at New Orleans, Louisiana, just before I came to Denver, Colorado, to spend the summer with my father before going out on my own at sixteen years old.

This is all passed. And it is ridiculous to brood on it and to condemn all humanity as being the same. It is impossible to change the past. But there is a future. It is my duty to try to help Dad. How I am going to do it, I do not know. I do not really think it is within my power to help him. He, and he alone, has the power to help himself. Only he can change this negative attitude he holds toward life. As long as he sits in his chair and philosophizes about life, surrounded by books, and dreams about being a rich millionaire of a large firm and never makes any attempt to live with the rest of the world, there will be nothing that either I or anyone else will be able to do. And he is not to be pitied. He has given himself enough of that already.

December 30, 1952 . . . Yesterday Martha and I spent the afternoon ensemble riding in her English sport car. We were supposed to stay on the post, since she only has a beginner's license and her mother is afraid that she might have an accident in town and cause trouble with the authorities. They are personal friends of the Provost Marshal, so that it really does not make as much difference if something happens on the post. She is a fairly good driver, though, and there is not much danger that she will have an accident. We therefore drove off the post and made a short peregrination to the downtown drugstore where all the high school and college people spend their afternoons and evenings. As we sat in one of the booths, drinking coke and a malted milk, she would introduce me to her incoming friends. My contretemps came, though, when the girl that Sandra had called came in and Martha began to introduce her. "Oh, you are the fellow that I am supposed to meet." I rose timidly and shook her hand and then reseated myself as my heart sank in embarrassment and I found myself unable to say anything. Martha became sarcastic and so did the other girl as they conversed and gave sour replies to anything I could muster to say. As they extended friendly gossip and news, I looked between them with nonchalant unconcern at the wall and sipped on my malted milk. I did not want to offend either of them and neither did I think that it was my place to explain the fact that neither one knew that they were in competition with each other. Sandra called the other girl during the day while I was with Martha but after this untimely rendezvous. She was busy that evening but might be free some other time during the week if I should care to call.

Martha is the only child of a medical colonel and is still treated like a small youngster despite her resentment and protests. That evening they were to go to a dinner given by the Commanding Officer of the base. All persuasion and arguing was in vain. Her parents were determined to bring her, though. They knew that she would enjoy it. They left me at the swimming pool on their way to the Commanding Officer's residence. The swimming pool was closed, though, so I returned home, ate supper with the folks and retired early. But I could not sleep. For hours and hours, I

twisted and turned in agony and unrest, trying to think of some
way to pull myself from this confused situation which involves
both the past and the present clinging to the past, plus the inevitable
problems which arise in spite of one's past. Dad spent the evening
reading philosophy. He is now trying to analyze why people
apologize for what they have done.

I decided not to write Dad. I decided to write him. I decided
to write him infrequently. And I decided to write him frequently.
I hoped that Martha and I could go to a young people's party on
New Year's Eve instead of being forced to go either to the Officers'
Club with her folks or the country club with my folks. I did not
want to offend the folks and did not want to offend Martha parents.
I knew that Dad could not go to the club, even though he is
entitled to do so. And I knew Martha's parents would resent her
going to the country club and I knew that neither one of us would
like doing either one. I thought of going into business with a close
colleague of mine at school. I thought of Martha when she remarked
that my memory is not too good. I laughed then. Next time I
would look at her in a disgusted manner. I thought of writing
Martha when she returns to school and hoped she would not sign
her letters "love." And I thought of Dad and Sandra and then
decided not to write her. I thought of going to Smith the weekend
after vacation for a date with Jane and then I thought of her tactless
remarks and friendliness only towards me and decided not to. I
thought of how I hated the Army and how I hated being with the
folks and wished that they could understand the situation and
knew they never would. I thought of telling Martha that I could
not write her and that I thought she would understand. I thought
of Professor Smith. I thought of telling him that Dad is being
discharged from the Army because of psychological troubles. And
then I thought of my grandmother when she lied and said that I
had received my scholarship by saying that I was an orphan—the
aphorism that anyone who does something has those who talk
about him, did little to assuage this insult. I decided to tell him
the following and no more if he asked me how the vacation has
been in relation to my parents, "Oh, Dad has his troubles." I

thought of returning to the dormitory and hoped that Al would feel like really getting boozed with me. I thought of calling the girl Sandra had called for me, apologizing for not calling her earlier for a date. And then I decided not to. I thought of Martha and wished she had many boy friends. I thought of how I hated the Army and how I hated being with the folks and wished that they could understand the situation and knew that they never would. I thought of the bridge game with Martha and went to sleep, determined to buy a book on bridge tomorrow and to be more attentive to keeping score in ping-pong rather than forcing Martha to have to keep it.

Today I wakened late and since have been reading some and looking at television. About 12:00 o'clock noon went to town and, not finding a book on bridge, sauntered through town for an hour, merely thinking—thinking about my future and the future of my parents and the people with whom I have had contact, thinking how I could get myself out of this situation without either humiliating myself or hurting my parents or causing Martha any chagrin or heartaches. And I decided.

January 3, 1953 . . .

"Dear Folks

Arrived home safely this afternoon after not a too tiring
journey. Got a ride to Fort Wayne with a young soldier and
his wife. They had had to borrow money for the trip, but
insisted on buying me a meal.

Tomorrow evening I will get back in the saddle again
and buckle down to some direly needed study. Since finals
will be commencing in another two weeks, I guess I had
better start studying harder than during the first of the
semester. Sophomore slump, you know. I think the grades
will be all right, though, if the finals don't stump me. History
will be probably the hardest. French will be no trouble.
Have a seminar in Classical Civilization, so it will be a little
harder. And, of course, history will be hardest, since it requires
a review of just about half a text book plus a book of old
documents.

Thanks for your hospitality. Hope you did not think I
was slighting you when I spent so much time dating. But I
really think I would have gone nuts doing nothing. Here at
school one is so busy—not with studies, except for finals—
with extra-curricular activities that it is hard to stop the
pace. I know that it is hard for parents to realize this. I think
Martha's folks have the same trouble realizing that you can't
just stop and do nothing for a few weeks. I really had a lot of
fun and enjoyed seeing you all. But you know that after one
has once made the initial break with his family—by going
to college, or in my case by going to work in high school—
it is rather hard to come back to the old stomping grounds
and consider oneself as one of the children and accept the
obligations that a son or daughter has to when living with
his family. And I just can't help resenting authority. And
whether you realize it or not, I'll probably be having a family
and be a father myself in two or three years. So, gee, I hope
you understand. (No immediate prospects right now. But

it's possible just the same.) I think you do. For if you will remember your early married years, you will remember that much unhappiness was caused by a well-meaning mother who did not realize that her daughter was no longer a child but a mother herself. (This involves perhaps not exactly the same thing in my case, since I am perhaps more fortunate and have more understanding parents.) When I was being interviewed for a Yale scholarship in Denver, I met a certain bachelor who had been in the Marines during the war. His father is a millionaire and owns a large beet concern in Denver. He sent his son to a wealthy preparatory school in the East and finally to Yale, where his son made Phi Beta Kappa in a B.A. course, though he just about failed physics. The son had had a very happy childhood, but when he returned to Denver to set himself up in business he refused to live with his folks. But rather did he choose to live in a one room cubicle in a small rooming house across from East High School. This last year he married a girl from a middle-class family in Denver and now has a child of his own. Of course, he is no longer living in the cubicle.

What I am trying to point out to you, Dad, is that no matter what background an individual has had sooner or later he makes a certain break with his family and from that time on he can no longer consider himself under the authority of his parents because he himself is preparing to become the head of a family entity. The argument during Thanksgiving did not arise, because you did not like or agree with what I was expounding. Nor do I really think that you do not think Yalies capable of understanding women. Nor do you think that we have long debauched parties in which we flout society. But you were trying to make me realize that in your home I must accept the obligations which are implied. And I was trying to tell you that I am trying to break away from authority and profit from the mistakes of the past. But that would have happened in practically any family. Both of my roommates have been having an increasing amount of this kind of trouble. There is not one girl in the last month whom I have dated who does not find herself having an increasing amount of this trouble. It is hard for you to realize this, because my break started earlier than that of other students and has thus reached a more matured state now than that of most sophomores, though sometimes I even doubt that.

I hope, therefore, that you will respect my judgment and not try to make me live a life that I do not want to live and which it is not necessary to live. And remember that whatsoever I am or ever will be, I am not going to hurt either you or Sandra either through words or other means. Friends that you have had before I met them will always remain your friends. I'm not out to tear apart anyone's happiness. But I'm out to build a small world of my friends in which the future will be lived and the past rather honored.

If circumstances permit I will probably see you sometime next Christmas, depending on a multitude of things.

Your loving son,
Alex.

P.S. Hope the Christmas spirit has not carried me a way with sentimentality. Let's try not to discuss it anymore. It becomes tiresome after a while. Right? Unless you really want to and should think it best to add something to what I have already said.

"Dear Martha

Arrived yesterday afternoon after an interesting trip by auto. Left the big city for Indianapolis about 3:00 P.M. Friday afternoon and was fortunate in having a private and his wife pick me up for a ride into Schenectady, New York. They had borrowed the money to make this trip but insisted on buying me food in spite of the fact that I had told them that I had sufficient money. My final ride was into New

Haven by some colored people who were fairly intoxicated with something other than the scenery. They told me their troubles and, of course, I cried with them, trying in the interim to get some sleep. Incidentally, don't tell anybody that I hitchhiked back. If anybody found out about it, there would be many hurt feelings and I would never live through the shame of it. The folks worry a lot about those little things. God bless'm.

Today I slept until about 1:00 P.M., trying to recuperate from the journey. Was blissfully awakened though, about 12:00 by a young voice, which sweetly asked if this were the train depot, as I cursed and howled at the bruise I had gotten in jumping from the top bunk to the desk to the telephone.

Started today reading Kenneth Harkness' *Invitation to Bridge*. Not too many students play it, but there are probably three amateurs interested enough to have the patience to learn. Of course, I am not really that interested in it myself. But I suppose it is enjoyable when one knows what is going on. I don't.

Finals start in two weeks and I'll have to start studying more than usual if I'm to keep the average of last year. There is a old saying here that only freshmen and seniors work, that sophomores take it easy and that some juniors work, though they then generally take off for the Continent. I don't think there is really anything to worry about with the finals. But there is always the pre-exam scare. After the finals we have a three day vacation in which to get drunk, so that is worth looking forward to and studying for.

Hope your folks were not too annoyed at our escapades. I still can't help laughing at your mother when we were at the party. I can see that under certain circumstances it could be very annoying but I guess parents never realize that their children grow up and want to live a life of their own with their own values and their own friends. I keep trying to explain this to Dad, but he thinks I don't appreciate him because of certain things. I think, though, that this vacation has shown him that he is not so really despised after all. After arriving from vacation, I visited the Dean of Freshmen. He and I have become fairly close friends—not through what you might think—and we were discussing this situation. It was his wife—a graduate from some southern university in Georgia—who introduced the topic. And I thought he hit the nail on the head when he said that once the initial break has been made by going to college that it is never the same when one returns home. He went on to explain that a stint of three years in Syria teaching economics, more or less made the break final—final in the sense that his family no longer considered him a child. Both of my roommates are having the same troubles at home. You remember the girl I told you about who had broken off with her fiancé because of a common cause. Well, I was talking to her the week before vacation. And she too is having this trouble. So I guess we are not really so unique after all.

Don't drink too much Champaign. Gee, that Champaign was good! Incidentally, who ever paid for the reservations.? I didn't. Wish you would find out."

Yours,
Alex

January 6, 1952 . . . Al arrived home Saturday after a short flight from his Texas habitat. He and I were really glad to be back together and to tell each other about the escapades of the vacation. He told me of the New Year's Eve party that his parents had given and then we began to talk about parents after I told him a partial amount of my difficulty in trying to shuck a burdensome load of authority. "I can either kill him or leave home," was Al's expressed sentiment after he explained how his father becomes very irascible during the vacation. "My Dad thinks that I consider him stupid," I told him. "Oh, so you're having that same trouble, eh," he retorted rather disgustedly. Dick came home the next day. And before many hours had elapsed, his mother called to remind him of something he might have forgotten. "Yes, mother, the little boy has finally developed a memory." Al asked him something that escaped my hearing and Dick responded in his nonchalant yet serious manner, "Yeah, it's a little disconcerting." Within the next five minutes he asked Al for a cigarette.

Today when working in the office, the secretary, a lady of about fifty, and I began to discuss this relation also. She is living with her aged mother now, and though she has been married her husband is now dead. "If she would only forget sometime that I am her little daughter!"

Al and I have been doing quite a good deal of talking together since we returned from the vacation. It really has not been anything too pedantic, just small talk and small philosophy of our own. This evening at the dinner table we talked about how everything is so organized already in this school and that it is practically impossible to do something original or start something new. Then we talked about the fellow next to him who had fired me from the sales agency. He could remember some literary passages fairly well, but then told me that his prep school teacher had told him his I.Q. over the vacation and it is not too high—high enough but not too high. Then we discoursed on the learning of plays and how well each of us can recall lines from old plays we have been in. Then we both talked about our dislike for ambitious people and how the ambition of the freshman year soon wanes. We talked for a good while, but having other friends and interest to care to, we parted from the first meal we have eaten together in the refectory since returning from vacation and he went to a sports car club meeting and I went to a debate. Tomorrow will be my first intramural swimming meet and, boy, am I looking forward to it. I do not supposed there will be too much recognition, but there will be other things that I would hate to measure in terms of glory.

January 7, 1953

I swam in the first intra-mural meet today and was victorious. I beat that fellow from Colorado who rather looked down on me when we were dating in Central City. Maybe now he will not think he is so good even though he does have more brains than most people. The school does not produce aristocratic half-wits— he came here with that attitude—all neatly packaged and delivered, like a fish out of water.

Al and I are planning to go to Greenwich Village after finals.

Oh, God help me.

*   *   *

FIFTY YEARS LATER

Eventually, I made the right decision and it was then that I became a man. It seems so long ago—so distant, yet so real. And over the next several years it became the great American dream. The best advice that I ever heard was at law school from a psychiatrist lecturing in Medical Evidence: To stay healthy, make a lot of love and get a lot of exercise. My younger brother went to Rice University and became an architect—his daughter followed there in his footsteps. My one half brother became a medical doctor (internist) and retired as a bird colonel from the United States Air Force; and another half brother is a clinical psychologist—both are well-known writers in their respective fields. All are well-integrated persons, high achievers, leaders in their communities, committed to "giving back" and making a difference, trying hard to give others a better life—kind and loving grandparents with no divorces. Every tub must stand on its own bottom. The psychologist at Fitzsimons Army Hospital, who administered the I.Q. test to me when I was twelve years old, later became a leading trial lawyer in Denver, Colorado. We were partners for many years until he was elevated to the bench. He always kept on the top of the judge's bench toward the front for all to see, a copy of my treatise *Matrimonial Practice in Colorado Courts*, then used as a text by all the law schools. At the same time my mother's brother was Head Captain of the Denver County Jail. And my wife and I were enjoying doing research with Dr. Raymond Bell on the line of President Richard Milhous Nixon, who shared with me our common Quaker ancestors William Griffith (died at 105 years old in York County, Pennsylvania) and Gayen Miller (died 1742 East Caln, Chester County, Pennsylvania) through my maternal line. This dovetailed with the research on United States President Millard Fillmore and the first Surgeon General of the United Army James Tilton, M.D., both descendants of immigrant William Tilton of Lynn, Massachusetts, in 1638. My graduation from the College of Law of the University of Denver was enriched by my knowledge that James Henry Causey, was a direct descendant (as was my father) of the Norman line from England of Captain James Fowkes (mariner and shipbuilder) and his son Dr. Thomas Fookes (chirurgeon) of Accomack County, in colonial Virginia, and that he had made the gift that established the Social Science Foundation, now known as the Graduate School of International Studies at the University of Denver. Vide *Fooks Family* by Major Herbert C. Fooks, Esq. A plaque in his honor is in the foyer of the Ben M. Cherrington Hall. It reads:

Ben M. Cherrington Hall
Dedicated November 14, 1966

James H. Causey, Founder, Social Science Foundation,
University of Denver President of Its Board of Trustees
1926-1943

> My desire is that the students of the University of Denver
> have an altogether unusual opportunity to be well-informed
> upon the major aspects of the great social, industrial, and
> international problems of the present and future, and that
> as a result the University may be the means of training
> leaders in these fields."

Dr. Ben M. Cherrington was the first to assist me during the summer after my graduation from high school, in my desire to spend the summer after my first year at Yale, in France. He gave me the name of the organization that sent me there and wrote a recommendation for me.

Pete became a lawyer in the Midwest; Dick became a neurologist in the Northeast; Al became a yacht salesman in California after a divorce (his son was a legacy admission to Yale); and Jabe fulfilled his potential by becoming a low-level, obsessive-compulsive bureaucrat with a god complex.

Life can be beautiful!

APPENDIX

The following paper was done in the senior year for Speech 2 at East High School, Denver, Colorado. The class was taught by Genevieve Kreiner, who also taught Shakespeare. She wrote at the top of the page: My veteran cherub, you're making me proud of you. She graded the paper A. In the graduation year book she wrote:

To Bob

"A combination and form indeed.
Where every god did seem to set his seal
To give the world assurance of a man."

Affectionately, Genevieve Kreiner

Robert L. Johnson
Speech 2
Period 2

SEMANTICS

One not too infrequently finds that the semanticist is correct in stating his theory that the words do not match the facts and that words govern our thoughts rather than our thoughts governing our words. For example, confer the word "marine" in its literal meaning to its connotative meaning expressed in the term "Marine Corps." Many people have no idea as to the true meaning of "marine" as defined in Webster's New International Dictionary (Second Edition), but upon hearing this word they immediately think of a strong, brutal, and rugged individual with a physically and mentally perfect body. This same thing is true of numerous other words contained in phrases and appellations that have acquired a common usage among the populace. To perhaps the majority of people the title "New Testament" means no more than a new "book" in which are recorded the acts of Christ and his apostles. However, the true literal meaning of testament is covenant.

According to the semanticist our evaluations of some things are prejudiced by words. The present trend among officials to require educators to pledge their loyalty to America and their help to rid America of subversives, does not necessarily mean that any one of these educators cannot turn traitor whenever he thus chooses. But by the means of offering a few words of loyalty he has assured the public of a deep devotion to his country, and thus the fears of many people have been quelled. At the end of World War I the United States, together with our allies, signed a peace treaty with Germany in which Germany agreed to never create destructive weapons or arsenals of defense. How woefully wrong was our evaluation of Germany's peaceful intention because of the superfluous words uttered with great finesse by her diplomatic representatives! Likewise, men lost money because of an improper evaluation at the beginning of the last depression when the Stock Exchange went broke.

To adjust to life one must be able to predict happenings accurately, and to do this one must have a sense of proper evaluation. Some individuals have found, through actual experience, that certain rules can be applied very successfully in most situations about which one is forming an evaluation. In view of the fact that these rules are quite numerous and that different people have different ideas concerning these rules, I shall attempt to discuss only those rules that I consider of foremost importance: (1) "An evaluation which is good in one situation may not be good in another, or even good the day after." For example, a student may act in a way that is entirely satisfactory in a certain class to a particular teacher, yet his same behavior may be thoroughly revolting to another teacher in a different class. (2) "Adequate evaluation adjusts to the situation as it is, uncolored by desires or prejudices." For example, one must not belittle a race or underestimate its average intelligence because of a certain prejudice for this race. Many people malign the Negro race and brand it as being intellectually inferior, but could Dr. Ralph Bunche be the man he is today were he intellectually inferior. (3) "Proper evaluation prevents argument." For example, bitter arguments of little actual importance have risen over such trivial items as the meaning of a word. (4) "Proper evaluation prevents the nervous system from shock." For example, one may consider himself to be very intelligent when in reality he is only average. Perhaps his superiority complex would lead him to attempt to attain many scholastic honors, only to find that he inevitably failed. If a careful and unbiased evaluation of himself had been allowed perhaps not such a severe spiritual defeat would have been sustained. (5) "Proper evaluation recognizes similarities as well as differences." For example, individuals may have aversions to certain types of foods, certain types of people, or certain types of cars, because sometime during their lives they had an unpleasant experience with that with which they are now antipathetic toward; and they have failed to recognize the difference in what exists at the present time and what existed in the past. (6) "Proper evaluation distinguishes the world of things from the world of words—the extensional world from the intensional world." For example, because of the failure of the U.N. interpreters to interpret the connotative meaning of words from American into other languages several misunderstandings have been created regarding American foreign policy.

Indeed, the whole world could be brought closer together if we were all to follow the teachings of the semanticist. Oh, that we could adopt a universal language!

We're wide open for
D I S A S T E R

By FLETCHER KNEBEL
LOOK Washington Bureau

The country has come to grips at last with the stark necessities of preparation against a sneak attack by atom bomb, gas or germs, but we have dawdled too long over organizing the defenses that can save John Doe and his family

FOR FIVE AND A HALF YEARS, a sluggish and timid administration in Washington hesitated to trust the American people with the facts of life and death in this gruesome age of scientific destruction. As a result, thousands of lives would be stupidly sacrificed should an enemy attack us tomorrow with any of the hideous weapons of modern warfare.

SPECIFIC EXAMPLES
OF SEMANTIC
TEACHING

At the end of the war with Germany and Japan, our leaders fervently believed that peace had come at last to a country that had known the ravages of two world wars. Yes, Russia had succeeded in duping our leaders into believing that she would go to all extremes for peace. As a result, the instruction of the public in atomic warfare was an unheard of thing for five and a half years. Now that war with Russia seems so imminent, the American people are faced with the problem of familiarizing themselves in a short time with measures to be taken in case of an atomic attack. To the semanticist this mistake would be an improper evaluation that could have been prevented if our leaders had not taken the words for the facts.

Chinese Reds Laud 'Virtues' of Invaders

SAN FRANCISCO, Feb. 11.— (AP) — To hear the Chinese Communists tell it, their troops are paragons of virtue in Korea, winning friends and influencing people all over the place.

That was the idea they tried to put across in a propaganda broadcast from Peiping today, lauding the behavior of the Chinese troops.

The broadcast, heard by the Associated Press in San Francisco, quoted a "special correspondent" as saying these troops "have voluntarily imposed upon themselves" the following rules of conduct:

Return what is borrowed; dig your own latrines when billeting in a village; sweep all floors before you leave; take off your shoes on entering any civilian house, in conformity with Korean custom; do not accept even so much as a needle and thread from the civilian population.

Was the individual who delivered the address described in the above article making his words match the facts? From all the evidence that our soldiers bring from the battlefield, I hardly think so. Yet, the fact must not escape one that this speech was absorbed by thousands of unenlightened Communists who failed to realize that their rulers employed the science of prevarication and mendacity to control their subjects. A semanticist among these suppressed people would be quick to realize the falsity contained in this speech.

British Let Us Down

BRITISH SHIPMENTS of iron and steel to Red China last December alone were almost as much as her total shipments for 12 months of 1949.

British woolen goods exports to Red China shot up from $2000 in December, 1949, to $300,000 in December, 1950. And in the same related periods, British shipments of assorted machinery, also vehicles of various kinds, rose from a few thousand dollars to hundreds of thousands.

Britain in 1950 sold 20 times as much raw rubber to the Soviet Union as in 1949.

Right now two shiploads of rubber totaling 10,000 tons are at sea between Singapore and Hong Kong, destined for a Communist enemy which British troops are fighting on two fronts.

And the Socialistic British government says it has no intention of stopping these shipments.

A Conservative member of Commons got a brush-off this week when he asked Prime Minister Attlee whether he was aware that British rubber was moving to Hong Kong and what he proposed to do to prevent the loss of this strategic material. An undersecretary merely confirmed that the rubber, worth 10 million dollars, was on the way and said the government intended to do nothing about it.

No British paper printed the story, or mentioned the huge rubber shipments, according to a London dispatch.

Small wonder. Reports from Korea said that Red tanks and self-propelled guns spearheaded a drive which threatentd to cut off 100,000 Allied troops including British around Seoul. If those tanks weren't made of British steel, if those self-propelled guns weren't moving on British rubber, they could have been—or more like them will be.

How can we win a war when an ally—which we are banking—persists in selling much-needed raw materials to the enemy?

Senator O'Conor of Maryland repeatedly has called attention to the "alarming proportions" of strategic materials exports from Britain to the Iron Curtain countries. In the first 10 months of 1950 these exports have aggregated 68 million dollars.

His subcommittee on export controls and policies is doing valuable work in disclosing Britain's trade with the enemy. Its findings should get closest attention as Congress looks into the foreign aid proposals in the Truman budget.

What fallacious reasoning is contained in this article! It sounds more like a Russian sophism than the cry of a true-blooded American interested in the welfare of his homeland. Before one condemns the British for trading with the Russians, he must first investigate the facts to find out why the British continue to trade with Russia during the present tense international situation. By doing this he will find that the Britains could not survive for long if foreign trade were abandoned; and secondly, Britain is not technically at war with Russia; thus, the chances are that this article would not have been written if the author had first made a proper and unbiased evaluation of the subject under discussion.

The above caption reminds one of the fatal decision that the U.N. made last summer regarding the crossing of the 38th parallel in Korea. Though the 38th parallel is only a line on the map, it has ignited a fire that may in a few months become a world conflagration. To the whole world the term 38th parallel represents an extremely improper evaluation. U.N. delegates believed that the Chinese Communists' threat to enter the Korean Conflict if foreign troops crossed the parallel, was just so much buncombe. This instance is an excellent example of "not" taking the words for the fact.

700 on CU Faculty Sign Loyalty Oaths Under Law

Special to The Rocky Mountain News

BOULDER, Feb. 13.—More than 700 Colorado University faculty members now have signed the state's loyalty oath for teachers, but it will be several weeks before all the signatures are obtained, a university spokesman said today.

He expressed belief the oaths are "coming in faster than in any other state educational institution."

The 700 signatures include about 100 from faculty members at the CU Medical Center in Denver and a sprinkling of non-teaching employes of the university who asked to be permitted to sign although not required to by law.

There are about 500 teaching faculty members in Boulder, the spokesman said, and tabulations are expected to be completed tomorrow on those who have not yet signed. President Robert L. Stearns then will dispatch "reminder notes" to those not accounted for.

The university has about 70 employes scattered about the state in its extension division, and some 300 part-time physicians on its medical faculty in Denver.

Oath forms have been sent by mail to them, and the spokesman said it may be several weeks before they are returned for counting in Boulder.

Some state institutions are not requiring that the oaths be executed immediately and are waiting until the end of the school year, when teaching contracts are renewed.

What a farce an oath is! Because a certain professor at the University of Colorado was at one time affiliated with the Communist Party in American, his colleagues have been aroused to defend their country verbally, by an oath. No doubt, this same instructor, who is now repeating a loyalty oath to defend his country against its enemies, also at sometime during his Communist affiliation repeated a Communist oath. How deceptive are words!

The following paper was done in the senior year for College Preparation at East High School, Denver, Colorado. The class was taught by Lawrence Garrett, a Harvard man, whose son graduated the same year from South High School and went to Harvard College. He graded the paper A+20 and wrote on the front in the typical red pencil used by teachers in those days: "With a dictionary in one hand, I enjoyed this very much."

THE ORIGIN AND DEVELOPMENT OF HERMETIC PHILOSOPHY

Robert Leland Johnson
College Preparation
Period 4

THE ORIGIN AND DEVELOPMENT OF
HERMETIC PHILOSOPHY

BY

ROBERT LELAND JOHNSON

EAST HIGH SCHOOL
DENVER, COLORADO
1950

THE ORIGIN AND DEVELOPMENT OF HERMETIC PHILOSOPHY

I. EARLY TRACES OF APPLIED CHEMISTRY

    A. In general
    B. In Particular
       1. Babylonians
       2. Jews
       3. Egyptians

II. ORIGIN OF HERMETIC PHILOSOPHY

    A. Chaldeans
    B. Egyptians
    C. Grecians

III. DEVELOPMENT OF ALCHEMY AMONG THE GRECIANS

    A. Thales
    B. Democritus
    C. Aristotle

IV. THE DECLINE OF ALCHEMY

V. THE RETURN OF ALCHEMY

VI. ALCHEMY AFTER THE CRUSADES

VII. THE THEORY OF TRANSMUTATION

VIII. Summary: A PLEA FOR THE ALCHEMIST

PREFACE

The research that is represented in the following pages of this report has greatly enlightened me as to the important role that alchemy has played in the progress of pure science. Before doing this research, I, like many other people, could only adumbrate the history of alchemy; and because of this fact I have underestimated the true meaning of this art.

To me the word alchemy has always presented a mental picture of unlearned and unintelligent individuals pursuing a pointless course. Quite the contrary, however; the alchemist was a hard-working man of great genius and high learning—I do not say that he did not pursue a fanciful course in trying to perfect the philosopher's stone—paved the way for modern chemistry.

To the reader I wish to express my sincere desire that he may find the following pages both interesting and educational. And to my family I wish to express my personal thanks for the kind consideration that they have shown me while I have been preparing this paper.

Robert Leland Johnson
Denver, Colo.
December 1950

THE ORIGIN
AND
DEVELOPMENT OF
HERMETIC PHILOSOPHY

Though the ancients applied many elementary principles of modern chemistry in their lives, they were unable to explain them or unveil the mysticism that enveloped the chemical and physical changes, such as the rusting of iron or the melting of ice, that nature wrought day by day. In time, as a consequence of the people's utter ignorance of the true causes of various phenomena, they began to believe that the gods (in most instances the sun or the moon) controlled all natural phenomena and would punish evil men by inducing a long period of dearth or by some other equally feared means. Thus ridiculous superstitions thrived on the ignorance of the time and retarded to a large extent the growth and development of chemistry as an exact science.

Amazing, as it may seem, though, scientific achievements are recorded very early in the history of Palestine, Babylonia, and Egypt. Historians have recorded the following as examples of outstanding accomplishments of the three nations just mentioned: the production of imitation pearls and an imitation dye resembling Tyrian purple; the preparation of soaps, dyes, pigments, medicines, and perfumes; and the use of fermentation—a process later used by the alchemists in their chimerical attempts to transmute metals. [1]

---

[1] See p. 10.

In spite of the fact that authentic records of applied chemistry among the Babylonians are not so copious as among the neighboring peoples of Palestine and Egypt, W. Libby asserts that applied chemistry flourished on a considerable scale among dyers, cutters, solders, shoemakers, architects, painters, and sculptors. [2]

Many pertinent facts which merit attention at this point regarding applied chemistry are contained in the Bible. So fond were the Jews of their delicacies that it may truly be said that to peruse the Biblical accounts of the ancient Jews is to read of their lavish indulgences in good wine and wide use of choice condiments consisting mainly of salt and vinegar. The artificial beautification of the face is not a practice confined to the ladies of our era—as some moralists would have us believe, for many centuries heretofore the women of the East employed the use of cosmetics, such as antimony trisulfide, to enhance their beauty. [3] Having thus exposed the innocence of the female sex in ancient Bible times, I might further add that the angel Azazel is reputed to have imparted a knowledge of the application of rouge and the making of jewelry to the Jewish women.

Even more advanced than either of the two neighboring countries of Babylonia and Palestine that I have just discussed was the small North African kingdom of Egypt. As a matter of fact, Egypt is the matrix of both alchemy and applied chemistry. At the present, however, I will concern myself solely with applied chemistry and relegate the discussion of Egyptian alchemy to a latter portion of this treatise. [1] Present-day historians are very fortunate in having at their disposal unlimited numbers of Egyptian writings describing the latter's achievements in the field of applied chemistry. Perhaps one of the most universally known Egyptian writings is the Ebers papyrus, which is largely a collection of prescriptions. In addition to its seven hundred prescriptions

---

[2]   Foster, *Introduction to General Chemistry*, Vol. 2, p. 4.

[3]   Bible, 2 Kings 1X.30 and Ezekiel XX111.40.

[1]   See p. 4.

recognized by contemporary medical authorities, the papyrus contains numerous supposititious prescriptions, such as one recommending the use of the fats of various animals combined in equal proportions for baldness. Two thousand years before the Christian era, the Egyptians showed a great proficiency in making glass, and they were not unacquainted with the working of gold, silver, copper, lead, iron, alloys, and enamels. The influence of Egyptian science upon the world during the ensuing years cannot be too strongly emphasized. To impress this fact more thoroughly, I wish to point out that the word chemistry itself refers to the land of Chemi (Egypt). [2]

In the foregoing paragraphs, I have endeavored to trace the origin and development of applied chemistry in order that the reader might, by realizing the limitations of ancient chemical knowledge, understand why such a pseudo-science as alchemy could impose its doctrines first upon the priests and they upon the masses of the people.

As far back as history can be traced, there are evidences of alchemy being pursued by the Chaldeans and the Egyptians. Because, however, this art was considered sacred, it was confined to the priests and also, in Egypt, to the heir-apparent to the throne. This explains why there are few written records of alchemical accomplishments antedating the third century A.D. among the Egyptians and the Chaldeans.

Though the Greeks did not take up the pursuit of alchemy before the fifth century B.C., their savants of later centuries attributed the founding of this art to their own god of science, Hermes; hence, the phrase "Hermetic philosophy." Many and varied theories have been propounded by great Grecian philosophers as to the nature of the universe and the chemical changes that could be wrought by the alchemist through the application of these respective theories. Thales of Miletus (600 B.C.) considered water to be the only element; Democritus of Abdera believed all chemical

---

[2]   Foster, *Introduction to General Chemistry*, Vol. 2, p. 3.

changes to be the direct result of the separation and recombination of atoms. To one who is somewhat acquainted with chemistry, the two latter theories of the construction of matter are recognizably similar to the modern theory of atoms and molecules. Yet these theories faded into oblivion and in their stead arose the hypothetical doctrine of Aristotle.

To Aristotle the universe seemed to be composed of five elements—water, air, earth, fire, and quintessence, which when mixed in varying proportions constituted the formation of different substances. As a corollary to the above theory, Aristotle stated that an element can more easily change into one with which it has one property in common, such as cold water to cold air and hot fire to hot air, than one that is completely its opposite. While most Greek philosophers held aloof from observation and practice of chemical observation, Aristotle experimented to no small degree. Yet in spite of this fact, he allowed his philosophical mind to deviate into channels of deductive reasoning (applying the general to the particular), and thus fallacious theories came into being that proved to be great hindrances in the development of chemistry as an exact and true science. Alexander the Great, who was himself keenly interested in the furtherance of science, provided Aristotle with such equipment and man power as was necessary to carry on experimentation on a large and diversified scale. The munificence of this powerful emperor is illustrated by an instance in which he allocated one hundred thousand men to Aristotle to help in scientific investigation. However, Aristotle was an exception in that most Greek philosophers contributed just theory to the art of alchemy and did not often attempt the transmutation of metals.

Under Roman rule, the world saw alchemy ruthlessly crushed, as the Romans were an extremely practical and matter-of-fact people. After the conquest of Greece, the Roman scholars aggregated all available Grecian learning of pure science and destroyed most treatises on spagyrism. The Romans had living standards, as the result of their singular interest in pure science and the application of it, that far surpassed all other nations at that time. Sanitation was a feature in the Roman life. In Rome, for example, fourteen aqueducts were constructed that had the capacity for supplying the city with 300,000,000 gallons of potable water daily. Remains of Roman plumbing are contained in the British Museum. True it is that applied science among the Romans reached a peak not paralleled by any other people before that time; yet it must be acknowledged that the Romans themselves contributed little to applied science. Their knowledge of the subject was the aggregation of knowledge acquired by several nations who were forerunners in the field.

After the fall of the Roman Empire (476 A.D.) the barbaric hoards from the North, learning gradually declined until ignorance prevailed throughout the whole Western world. Were it not for the fact that the Arabs overran Egypt about the middle of the seventh century, it is very likely to assume that alchemy would have become extinct long before it did and that modern chemical knowledge would be considerably restricted to elementary theories. Instead of allowing alchemy to perish, though, the Arabs were quick to avail themselves of the alchemical writings that the Romans had not destroyed and offered liberal rewards to individuals who would undertake the translation of Grecian and Egyptian works into Arabian. The Saracen caliphs established academies all the way from Spain to Egypt. A very large university was founded at Baghdad by Al-Mansee to which Greek, Persian, and Indian philosophers flocked to present their theories. Possessing a lust for gold, the Saracen caliphs avidly pursued the art of alchemy until the fall of their empire to the Moslems.

One of the first prominent Arabian scholars to expound upon the subject of alchemy was Era-Zosminus, who lived during the fourth century A.D. In his "Manipulations" (a book widely referred to by the medieval alchemists), Zosimus proclaims mercury to have the power of transmutation.

Geber, the first so called "alchemical adept," is said to be to alchemy as Hippocrates is to medicine. [1] Devoted to the

---

[1]   The Outline of Knowledge, Vol. V11, p. 415.

advancement of spagyrism, he spent the greater part of his life performing experiments rather than philosophizing. His theories received great attention by the medieval alchemist. And though his efforts were chiefly directed toward producing the philosopher's stone, he acquainted himself with the properties and possibilities of such elements as sulfur and arsenic.

Two other Arabian scholars who also influenced to a great extent the art of alchemy are Rhazes and Avicenna. The former, a disciple of Geber, writes of the influence of the stars upon the earth's formation of metals, a supposition first recorded by the Chaldeans. Avicenna, a supposedly more prosperous scientist than the one just discussed, is credited with the development of the Philosopher's stone, from which he received the power to enjoy the bliss of eternal life. He regarded mercury as the universal and vivific spirit, and he mentioned in his writings sulfur, saltpeter, sulfur, orpiment, vitriol, and salt ammoniac.

Alchemy was the universal science until the fall of the Saracen empire to the Turks about the middle of the eleventh century. After the fall of Constantinople to the Turkish invaders (1451), Egypto-Greek and Arabian doctrine was brought to Italy. Much alchemical knowledge was transmitted to the European peoples by the returning Crusaders, and the nobles, being eager to replenish their depleted treasuries, began to employ alchemical adepts in their services in a mad quest for the secret of artificially producing gold. Under the pressing demands of their rulers, those scholars who were not laboriously searching the ancient writings for new knowledge to aid in the quest for gold were ever experimenting with weird concoctions that they hoped would prove to have the power of transmutation. Alchemy, having been officially sanctioned by the church since the beginning of the Christian era, found many followers among the European monks, some of whom devoted their entire lives to the cause of this art.

But in spite of their earnest efforts to produce the philosopher's stone (the material reputed to have the power to transmute base metals into gold or silver and to give perpetual life), the medieval alchemists miserably failed. They failed mainly because no such thing as the philosopher's stone existed; yet if perchance the philosopher's stone did exist, no man, following the unscientific methods of research employed by the spagyrist, could possibly have produced it. Paracelsus describes the alchemist's laboratory very vividly in the following quotation:

> "A gloomy, dimly lighted place, full of strange vessels and furnaces, melting pots, spheres, and portions of skeletons hanging from the ceiling, the floor littered with stone bottles, alembics, great parchment books covered with hieroglyphics; the bellows with its motto, spira spera (breathe and hope); the hour glass, the astrolabe, over all cobwebs, dust and ashes. The walls are covered with various aphorisms of the brotherhood, legends and memorials in many tongues." [1]

The mysticism that shrouded all their writings is illustrated by the following excerpt taken from an American translation of a writing attributed to Hermes:

> True it is without a lie, sure and most true; what is below is like that which is above. And what is above is like that which is below, of one substance to perform miracles.
>
> And as all things have come from one being, the meditation of one, so all things have been generated from this one thing by adoption.
>
> Its father is the sun, its mother is the moon. The wind has carried it in its womb. Its nurse is the earth. The father of every talisman of the whole world is this. Its power is unimpaired when it is turned upon the earth.
>
> Separate the earth from the fire, the subtle from the material, gently, with great cleverness. It rises from the earth to heaven and again descends upon earth, and receives the force of those above and those below.

---

[1] Darrow, *Story of Chemistry*, p. 4.

Thus thou wilt have the glory of the whole world. All
obscurity, therefore, will leave thee.

This is of all strength the strong strength, because it
will subdue every subtle thing and penetrate every solid. [1]

It is interesting to note the various methods of procedure used
by the medieval scientists—if they may thus be named—to perfect
the philosopher's stone and the theories that formed a basis to
these methods. Most metals, according to the Aristotelian theory,
were threefold in nature; namely, they were composed of principles
(sulfur, mercury, and salt), peculiar to all metals; elements (air,
earth, fire, and water), characteristic of many metals; and, essence
(an ethereal substance), common to all metals. To transmute a
base metal into gold, which was thought to be pure essence, it was
necessary to remove all impurities (principles and elements) by
heating or by some similar means. Another widely used theory
stated that the same law of growth and decay that takes place in
the organic world applies to the inorganic kingdom of ores. From
this latter theory the alchemist developed the following intricate
procedure for the transmutation of metals: calcination, dissolution,
separation, conjunction, putrefication, congelation, sublimation,
fermentation, exaltation, multiplication, and projection. A slight
mistake in any one of these steps would have resulted in failure.
Using this latter theory, Trevison tried to prepare gold. His recipe
was thus: Harden one-thousand hen's eggs in boiling water; remove
the shells; separate the white from the yoke; putrefy the yokes in
white horse manure; and, distill for a white liquid and a red oil.
After countless years of continued failure, he relinquished all hope
for success and announced to the world the utter preposterousness
of the theory of transmutation.

If, in presenting the ideals and aspirations of the alchemist, I
have been unjustifiably caustic, I wish to make amends for it, lest
the reader should form a wrong impression of the alchemist. The

---

[1]   *The Outline of Knowledge*, Vol. V11, p. 412.

alchemist was a man of the highest type of integrity and a man of deep religious convictions who strived for the betterment of mankind. Admittedly, he labored under delusions and, therefore, did not make any remarkable progress. But let us carefully view the reasoning that led him to believe in the transmutation of metals. First there are the theories formulated by Aristotle.[1] Then there are certain natural phenomena that tended to confirm the suppositions of Aristotle. Near the small Hungarian town of Herrngrund is a spring "pure and clear" which has a high content of copper mineral. An iron vessel placed in this solution soon is covered with a layer of copper. To the alchemist (and how was he to know that this reaction was one of displacement?) this was transmutation. When heated crude lead yields a powder and a small button of silver. The alchemist thought of this as the transmutation of lead into silver. Therefore I wish to give to the alchemist the respect that he duly has earned, for, indeed, he undertook a monstrous task and diligently pursued it.

---

[1]   See p. 5.

BIBLIOGRAPHY

1 Books:

Arrhenius, Svante August and Leonard, Clifford Shattuck
Chemistry in Modern Life
New York, D. Van Nostrand Company, 1926
2 vols. rev. ed. pp. 6, 7, 11, 31, 32, 65

Biddle, Harry C. and Bush, George L. *Dynamic Chemistry* ed.
by William L. Connor
New York, Rand McNally and Co. 1936 pp. 730, 16,
107, 108-109, 752

Darrow, Floyd L. *The Story of Chemistry*
New York, Blue Ribbon Books, Inc. 1930
2 vols. rev. ed. pp. 1-13, 109

Findlay, Alexander. *Chemistry in the Service of Man*
New York, Longmans, Green and Co. 1920 p. 5

Foster, W. and Alyea, Hybert N. *An Introduction to General
Chemistry*
New York, D. Van Nostrand Co., Inc. 1941 pp. 6-9

Jaffe, Bernard, *Crucibles*
New York, Tudor Publishing Co. 1934
3 vols. rev. ed. pp. 9-15

Weeks, Mary Elvira. *The Discovery of the Elements*
Easton, Pa. Mack Printing Co. 1935
3 vols. rev. ed. pp. 9-19

11 Encyclopedias:

The Outline of Knowledge. "Alchemy"
Vol. V11, pp. 411-422

ALCHEMICAL SYMBOLS*

Silver ☽	-Air	-Retort	-Hour
Gold ☉	-Water	-Alembic	-Bricks
Iron	-Fire	-Filter	-Powder
Copper ♀	-Element	-Bath	-Talc
Sulphur	-Earth	-To Purify	-Phlogiston
Lead	-Acid	-Soap	-Sand
Tin	-Aqua Regia	-Glass	-Borax
Platinum	-Oil	-Crucible	-Spirit
Bismuth	-Vinegar	-Wax	-Spirit of Wine
Carbon	-Saltpeter	-Kaolin	-Ashes
Cobalt	-Vitriol	-Quicklime	-Gum
Antimony	-Iron Oxide	-Alum	-Sublimate
Arsenic	-Mercury	-Nickel	-Acetic Acid

1540 Tamarac Street
Denver, Colorado
May 11, 1951

Dean N. S. Buck
Chairman, Freshman Scholarship Committee
Yale University
1003A, Yale Station
New Haven, Connecticut

Dear Dean Buck

You have no idea how proud and happy I am to be able to accept the honor which you have conferred on me by your grant of a Yale scholarship.

During my high school years I have always aspired to be able to acquire a college education, but because of my financial status I often wondered how and whether such an undertaking would be possible. Now that this extraordinary opportunity for an education has been given me, you may be sure that I will exert every effort to profit from it, to serve Yale well, and to be an asset to my community and my country.

It is with keen pleasure that I recall our meeting at East High School during the earlier part of this year; I look forward to being with you at Yale next fall.

Particularly, do I thank you personally for the splendid consideration which you have given me.

Sincerely

Robert Leland Johnson

1540 Tamarac Street
Denver, Colorado
May 10, 1951

Mr. Harry B. Combs
Chairman of the Colorado Yale Association
127 Vine Street
Denver, Colorado

Dear Mr. Combs

It is with a great sense of pride that I write to express my thanks and sincere appreciation for being awarded one of the coveted Colorado Yale scholarships. Through this scholarship an opportunity, which I had often dreamed of but never expected to realize, is made available to me.

Of course, I am fully aware of the fact that in accepting this scholarship certain responsibilities are assumed by me. To these responsibilities I shall give the most punctilious attention. I shall strive in every way to avail myself of the opportunities which have been made possible, and I shall exert every effort so that neither you nor any member of the Yale scholarship committee will ever regret having bestowed this great honor on me.

Again, let me thank you and your committee for making it possible for me to attend Yale University.

Sincerely

Robert Leland Johnson

YALE UNIVERSITY
NEW HAVEN · CONNECTICUT

BOARD OF ADMISSIONS
WELCH HALL
EDWARD S. NOYES, CHAIRMAN

MAILING ADDRESS: 1502A YALE STATION

May 1951

Dear Sir:

It gives me pleasure to report that you have been voted tentative membership in the Freshman class entering Yale University in September 1951. This action of the Board of Admissions will become final, without further notice, when your principal or headmaster informs us that you have satisfactorily completed your school work and are entitled to honorable dismissal. We shall inform your school of the action of the Board of Admissions and send for your final record.

Should the final report be unfavorable, it will be necessary to reconsider your application. In this event, the Board of Admissions will notify you promptly of its action.

Please return as promptly as possible the enclosed postcard, indicating whether or not you intend to matriculate in September. As soon as we know that you plan to enter, we shall send a program blank for your election of Freshman courses and a Planning A Course of Study bulletin. You are urged to read the bulletin carefully and to fill out and return the program blank before the date given on it. A dormitory application blank and other pertinent forms will be forwarded to you by the Freshman Office during the summer.

Yours sincerely,

Edward S. Noyes
Chairman

Mr. Robert Leland Johnson

THE COLORADO YALE ASSOCIATION

Denver, Colorado
June 12, 1951

Robert Leland Johnson
1540 Tamarac St.
Denver, Colorado

Dear Bob:

I have been out of town for almost a month but returned to find your letter accepting the Yale Scholarship.

I am very pleased that you received this award and know that you will do well with your opportunity. You can be sure that the Members of the Committee will be watching your progress at Yale with interest and they will be counting on you to fulfill all of the hopes and ambitions of which you seem capable. This is a real turning point in your life and we all know that you have the stuff to come through with flying colors.

Best wishes for a fine Freshman Year at Yale.

Sincerely yours

Harry B. Combs, Chairman
Scholarship and Enrollment Committee

HBC:hh

FRESHMAN
MATRICULATION DINNER

Y 5 5

UNIVERSITY DINING HALL
September 17, 1951

MENU

❦

Fruit Cup

Celery Hearts   Olives

Broiled Chicken - Currant Jelly

Whipped Potatoes   Fresh Green Beans

Rolls

Vanilla Ice Cream   Chocolate Squares

Milk   Coffee

Speakers

Norman S. Buck
Dean of Freshmen

Herman Hickman
University Football Coach

The Reverend Sidney Lovett
University Chaplain

Edmund W. Sinnott
Dean of the Graduate School

∽⫯⫯∾

The University Glee Club
Marshall Bartholomew, Director

SONGS OF YALE

Eli Yale

As Freshmen first we came to Yale,
Chorus:
Fol de rol de rol rol rol!

Examinations made us pale.

Chorus:

Fol de rol de rol rol rol!
Eli, Eli, Eli Yale,
Fol de rol de rol rol rol!

As Sophomores we have a task:
'Tis best performed by torch and mask.

In Junior year we take our ease,
We smoke our pipes and sing our glees.

In Senior year we act our parts
In Making love and breaking hearts.

And then into the world we come,
We've made good friends, and studied—some.

The saddest tale we have to tell
Is when we bid old Yale farewell.

Aura Lee

As the blackbird in the Spring,
'Neath the willow tree,
Sat and piped, I heard him sing,
Singing Aura Lee.
Aura Lee, Maid with golden hair,
Sunshine came along with thee,
And swallows in the air.

In thy blush the rose was born;
Music, when you spake;
Thro' thine azure eyes the morn
Sparkling seem'd to break.
Aura Lee, Birds of crimson wing
Never song have sung to me
As in that bright, sweet spring.

Wake, Freshmen, Wake

The stars brightly glancing,
Behold us advancing,
And kindly smile upon us from on high;
Our summons awaiting,
With hearts loudly beating,
The Freshmen trembling on their couches lie.

Chorus:

Wake! Wake! Freshmen, Wake!
Wake while our song smites the sky,
For now, ere we leave you,
We heartily give you
A welcome into Delta Beta Xi.

While some sadly ponder,
Still others will wonder
Why we their doors in silence dead pass by;
But, O fortunati!
O, terque beati!
Who hear the mystic call of Beta Xi.

Bright College Years

Bright college years, with pleasure rife,
The shortest gladdest years of life;
How swiftly are ye gliding by!
Oh, why doth time so quickly fly?
The seasons come, the seasons go,
The earth is green, or white with snow,
But time and change shall nought avail
To break the friendships formed at Yale.

In after years, should troubles rise,
To cloud the blue of sunny skies,
How bright will seem thru mem'ry haze,
Those happy, golden, bygone days!
Oh, let us strive that ever we
May let these words our watchcry be,
Wher-e'er upon life's sea we sail:
"For God, for Country, and for Yale!"

This paper was written early in the freshman year at Yale College in the class of Cleanth Brooks. It was a very selective group of students with advanced English skills; and to be selected for it without even trying attests in some degree to Yale's view of where my talents might lie. Later in the year we studied poetry, using the text that he and Robert Penn Warren had authored, which bore the title *Understanding Poetry—An Anthology For College Students* (1938). This very same book still remains a part of my library with my notes and those of others from his class. Robert Penn Warren was also the author of *All the King's Men* (1946), based on the life of Huey P. Long, a southern politician from Louisiana.

His corrections were:

1. "Great Expectations" changed to *Great Expectations.*
2. paragon in second paragraph—comment: look up this word.
3. old man in second paragraph—comment: or matured.
4. Pip is telling his story as he felt as a young boy . . . comment: Pip is telling his story as he felt it as a young boy . . . (Second paragraph).
5. Let us examine some more characters first and answer this question later. comment: Let us examine some more characters first before trying to answer this question. (Second paragraph).
6. In the margin at the last half of the fifth paragraph, he wrote in red pencil: Good insight, but perhaps here carried too far.

VERISIMILITUDE
AND CARICATURE
IN "GREAT EXPECTATIONS"

Through the whole of Charles Dickens' "Great Expectations" there are characters that seem grotesquely out of proportion with the rest of humanity. Primarily, these characters are Miss Havisham, Mr. Jaggers, Mrs. Joe, and Mr. Wemmick. Though some of the other characters also possess certain rather unusual features, I believe that a discussion of these four will be sufficient to afford an understanding of the manner in which Charles Dickens has employed verisimilitude and caricature in this illustrious novel.

Miss Havisham is one of the queerest characters that have ever been described in literature. A woman who carries the burden of a heart shattered to pieces by unrequited love, she sought to wreak her wanton revenge on the whole world. Her spacious manor was the paragon of deep inscrutability and vengeful mysteriousness. It seemed to Pip as though her house was somehow the second abode of the devil. On the surface, this certainly appears that Charles Dickens was enjoying himself caricaturing those miserable souls who hold onto the memory of a loved one until death ends all. But consider for a moment who is supposed to be telling this story. It is not the author but Pip as an old man recalling earlier experiences with all their original vividness. Pip is telling his story as he felt as a young boy, occasionally inserting sententious remarks which reflect the perspective of an older man. Because of this it is imperative that one consider the caricature in this novel in somewhat of a different light. Is it not possible that this caricature was introduced for some reason other than solely for the sake of caricature itself? Let us examine some more characters first and answer this question later.

Quite obviously the adult world appears rather inscrutable to the young child. The ominously towering height and considerably greater strength of a grown man as compared to the small stature and comparative weakness of a child, are sufficient to create a gap between the two which is to the youth an extremely awesome thing. This situation is not at all dissimilar to the one in which Pip found himself on being introduced to the isolated and morose Miss Havisham. To Pip she seemed to be an inscrutable and ominous creature thoroughly devoid of any human warmth. What would the adult have seen, though? Would he have seen that same monster? No, the grown man would have seen a pitiful and suffering woman who had been through the agonies of unrequited love and needed consolation. Her manor would have appeared far less mysterious to the adult. Because the house was dimly lighted, an occurrence not uncommon where old people live, Pip conceived of it as being completely dark and thoroughly morbid. It is as the old Pip says, "The child is small and its world is small, and its rocking-horse stands as many hands high, according to scale, as a big-boned Irish hunter."

Mr. Jaggers is another intriguing character who was to Pip as mysterious as Miss Havisham. But it is again well to notice how a child regards a lawyer and how differently an adult thinks of a lawyer. The universal theory among youngsters is that a lawyer is an omniscient and omnipotent being who can free anybody from jail and to whom everybody renders reverence. On the other hand, the adult regards the lawyer as just another individual struggling for a living.

Perhaps the most readily understood exaggeration is that of Mrs. Joe. It is very hard for children to understand that discipline is employed for their betterment. As a result, most children regard their parents as extremely dreadful beings when punishment is being administered. When they reach maturity, however, reflection reveals the wisdom and splendid guidance of their loving and devoted parents. From this it might easily be inferred that Mrs.

Joe did truly love Pip and, accordingly, meted out severe discipline that he might in his maturity be a credit to himself and to his family. Concerning the rather harsh manner in which Mrs. Joes is reputed to have treated Joe, it need only be pointed out that a wife and husband often show their mutual affection by jocularly and paradoxically asserting their fear of each other. This is especial true of the man, who knowing himself the stronger, finds a pleasant bit of irony in asserting his wife's dominance over him. To Pip, who could not properly evaluate such a situation, this might seem the very antithesis of jesting.

Though the comparison may at first seem rather absurd, Mr. Wemmick is the stage and screen star of the present era. The glittering world of popularity encompasses the actor throughout his professional life as people view him on the screen or applaud him on stage. But returning to his private life at night, the glitter of the outside is forgotten and he becomes just another family man. Therefore, why would not Wemmick also be in perfect character when returning after office hours to the homely atmosphere of Walworth and pushing into oblivion the affairs of the business realm? Of course, to Pip this seemed rather incongruous, just as it would seem incongruous to a young child if he were to learn that his favorite cowboy star had never chased real Indians and did not ride horses all the time.

It may be said, therefore, that Charles Dickens has not employed caricature for the sake of caricature but rather to forcefully portray the reaction of a young child to the adult realm. He expects the reader to be able to see through Pip's exaggerations and thereby realize that these characters were not merely grotesque segments of human society.

This was written for Philosophy 12b at the end of the first term of the freshman year—I had hit my stride. At the beginning of the course, he gave me the only failing grade I ever received on a paper at Yale. I had visions of losing my scholarship and so contacted him and asked for help. We spent many challenging hours talking about philosophy in his book-filled cubicle of an office. This final paper had no grammatical corrections—just three marginal notations in red pencil: good, good, good statement. And at the end was a note from him written in black ink, reproduced at the end of this paper. George Alfred Schrader, Jr., Ph.D., who taught the course was at the time a thirty-four year old Assistant Professor of Philosophy. He became in later years a full professor, Chairman of the Department of Philosophy and Master of Branford College (one of the residential colleges composing Yale College)—vide *Who's Who In America.*

IDEAS:
HOW THEY ARE RELATED

IDEAS:
HOW THEY ARE RELATED

Wherein lies the cause of the orderliness by which the mind functions? No one can truthfully deny that the human mind has a certain distinct orderliness of thought intrinsic to it, which enables man to think rationally and intelligently. This has never been in question, but the problem which has always drawn considerable attention is that of the cause of this orderliness. Some dismiss the question as being totally unfathomable, while others have developed very elaborate explanations. Some of these explanations were given little attention, whereas others have been meticulously scrutinized and studied down through the ages to the present era. All have been unanimous, though, in conceding that the mind is orderly and does operate systematically. The explanation of this orderliness is what has been and is sought for.

On the other hand, some might claim it equally logical to assert that the mind will not in the future conduct itself orderly and systematically, as it has always been known to do in the past, though perhaps to a lesser degree in demented than in normal persons, but will relinquish itself to the caprice and freak of chance or of its own cause, assuming that it has one. This proposal might be called for convenience in dealing with it the principle of illimitable transformation. Common sense tells one that this cannot be so. Yet this assertion cannot be refuted on the grounds of common sense, for philosophy then becomes only an ad hominem argument and any enquiry endeavoring to reach beyond our immediate experience is rendered useless. An undeniable and fundamental truth is therefore needed to bring the philosopher out of the quandary to which this situation subjects him. To this end, I now postulate an elementary principle on which both animate and inanimate objects depend for their existence. This principle states that all objects, whatever their nature may be, must have unity to retain identity and must have identity to exist. Certain unity is present in the most complexly unorganized substance, and it is the persistence of this unity which gives this object identity. The identity will be retained as long as the object exists; and when the identity ceases, the object also ceases to be. In response to those who might project the theory of illimitable transformation, it is evident that a change in the orderliness of the mind to an absolute disorderliness is impossible. For when this happens, the mind ceases to be, and how could the body operate without a mind? It would be impossible, just as it is impossible for a stapler to staple papers without an actuating force.

An explanation as to why the mind cannot function in any way other than in orderliness does not, however, afford an answer to the original question of how unity is effected. To account for this there is another principle, not so closely related to life in general as the principle of unity but still intrinsic to the existence of the human. It states that man, from his conception in the womb, is endowed with an idea of unity. At first, this a priori knowledge of unity is latent and unknown to the individual. Through experience only is this innate idea aroused and is man able to relate his ideas systematically so that he can reason and think and live rationally and intelligently. Were this idea lacking, the other subordinate ideas of the mind would mix in confusion and man would be unable to think clearly. Similar ideas could only be related if by chance it occurred that they conjoined themselves together as they wandered among other ideas. A man might observe an automobile as it sped down the boulevard, but as the same vehicle returned the man would be unable to relate the idea of his original viewing of the car to the idea of the second viewing unless, as I have just stated, the two ideas conjoined themselves by chance. He would be unable to know that he had seen the same object twice. This, of course, cannot be possible, since it is an undeniable contradiction of the principle of unity.

Without a doubt the assertion of an idea of unity binding ideas together systematically, raises the question of how man can know this to be true. This requires the explanation of a new and very different kind of knowledge than man has of the immediate world by experience. This knowledge does not have to transcend all human knowledge, but it must exceed knowledge based on contingent particularities of experience. The constitution of the mind requires that transcendental knowledge be an intrinsic part of it. Transcendentalism causes man to consider himself as an organism composed of a mind whose ideas are systemized by a more powerful idea of unity and with a body actuated by a mind.

As the child is conceived the idea of unity and transcendental knowledge are latent and completely unknown to him. The idea of unity is latent because the mind has not had any impressions which would cause subordinate ideas (i.g., ideas formed from impressions), and there is therefore nothing to be organized. The transcendental knowledge is latent because there is no idea of unity or an orderly system of ideas to be considered. When experience introduces ideas into this tabula rasa (mind without impressions), the idea of unity is immediately aroused and begins its function; and when this happens, the transcendental knowledge also responds to its function.

To recapitulate, all objects or substances, living or inanimate, are what they are only so long as each retains its essential and peculiar order. This is the principle of unity. The human mind exists on the principle of unity, but it is a more complex item, possessing a priori an idea of unity and a transcendental knowledge which enables man to determine how this unity functions in regard to ideas and how it originates.

Excellent. You've written a paper which seems to me to have been worth the time & thought which went into it. Your work has improved so much that this can hardly even be compared to your earlier papers. Congratulations.

I recommend a study of Kant sometime. I think you would find it interesting & profitable.

SAYBROOK COLLEGE •
YALE UNIVERSITY •
NEW HAVEN

May 13, 1952

Dear Bob:

I am happy to inform you that the Bursary Committee has just notified me that they have approved our request for you as an in-College aide. I trust that you will find your work on the College staff interesting and profitable.

Could you join me and the present staff next Monday, May 19th? We will meet for cocktails in Hall and hold a very short meeting immediately thereafter, so that it should not take you away from your studies.

I would appreciate it if you would let me know if you can attend.

Sincerely yours,
Basil D Henning

THE EXPERIMENT

IN INTERNATIONAL LIVING

GORDON BOYCE,
Director Phone Putney
119 PUTNEY, VERMONT, U. S. A.

March 26, 1952

Dear Robert Johnson:

I am delighted to notify you of your acceptance as a member of an Experiment group to France. Also I am glad to be able to tell you that you have been selected to receive an Experiment scholarship of $100. This will be applied to the fee of the group in which you will be a member this summer.

Experience tells us that you're in for a challenging summer. You will have a chance to make warm and lasting friendships, gain an appreciation of another culture in human terms and get a clearer understanding of international problems. You will also have one of the best times in your life.

I hope you will work hard on your French and will spend at least three or four hours a week increasing your fluency and understanding of the *spoken* language. The best method is to converse daily with a person who speaks it fluently and with a *good accent*, preferably a native of the country. Listening to French records and attending French movies are also helpful. Whatever work you do now will make your first weeks in your home abroad much easier and more enjoyable.

You will soon be receiving information about preparatory reading, what to take with you and how to get ready for the summer. We will also submit a bill to you with an understanding of the conditions under which The Experiment operates.

This acceptance is testimony to our belief that you are an open-minded, tolerant person capable of making a personal contribution to international understanding.

Faithfully yours,

Gordon Boyce
Director

GP:PC

Mr. Robert Leland Johnson
1135 Yale Station
New Haven, Connecticut

ARTICLE # 1

The tenth of this month will probably not have any special importance for most of the people at home. But for those students and teachers who spent nine days of warm friendship aboard the M/S Nelly, it marks the first month of being physically separated from the homeland.

We were the first students of an expected several thousand to leave for Europe this summer. Most of us are members of some organization, such as the IRC, The Experiment in International Living, the IRYE and others. Of course, some of the passengers are traveling independently. But all of us have one goal in mind; namely, to gain a true picture of Europe and to perhaps give Europe a better picture of the U.S.

It was a clear Thursday night when the captain put us safely in port at Le Havre. Since then a new Europe has been unfolding for me. The process has been slow and gradual, but always presenting something new from the European standpoint rather than that of an American.

There were two days to be spent in Paris before our group of twelve had to take the train for St. Etienne, an industrial city in south-central France. The first problem that confronted me was what should be seen and done in those two days. There were two alternatives. Either I could tread the beaten paths of the never ceasing tourist trade, or I could embark on an adventure in which France would present itself apart from the tourists. I chose the latter as we had all vowed to do on the boat.

Instead of going to a tourist agency I set out alone. First on the itinerary was a trip to the Garden of Luxembourg, where I basked in the sun and watched little children play hide-and-go-seek (in French it is "cache-cache"), while the old men of the neighborhood were engaged in croquet. Some of the men bade me to sit down and began to converse. In a little while the game of croquet became familiar. Then we began to talk of nothing—just to satisfy a human desire to be friends. It was getting dark by now, so I told the gentlemen goodbye and began walking back to my hotel. As I stopped for a moment and watched the park fade in the twilight, it suddenly came to my mind that the day had been a Parisian one yet void of any wild and naughty gaiety or filching vendors.

That night was spent in an unknown part of the Latin Quarter talking to a small restaurant owner and the next day talking to a young Parisian of Italian descent. The Latin Quarter is on the Left Bank along the south bank of the Seine River in the area of a part of the University of Paris (Sorbonne). This is where the building Sorbonne is located, but the name Sorbonne is also popularly used to designate the entire University of Paris. Just northwest of it along the Seine River is located another part of the University of Paris. Just south of these two adjoining quarters is the Jardin du Luxembourg and just south of that is Boulevard du Montparnassse ("The Quarter") where Ernest Hemingway lived, played, drank and wrote. As for nostalgia, I do not think it could have felt more like home. There were the large buildings and crazed traffic of New York, the historic atmosphere of New Orleans, a winding river running through the city remindful of Denver, and above all people.

ARTICLE #2

After a few hours' trip through the undulating verdure of the terrain lying between Paris and St. Etienne, the group alighted at the train terminal. We were all a little frightened. Would our French be ridiculed? What questions would be asked concerning the States? Would the cuisine be difficult to become accustomed to? Yes, and what about the communists? In the lectures on the M/S Nelly, we were told that St. Etienne is a typical unattractive industrial city. And to climax that we were rather disheartened to learn that this city where we were to spend several weeks and the faubourgs of Paris are the two strongest communist centers of all France.

Most of these questions resolved themselves. The families are kind and sympathetic—always painstakingly trying to better our French, refraining from asking delicate points concerning the political, and serving an excellent cuisine. But the problem of the communists has not been quite the same.

It truly made me feel unwelcome in France when flagrant insults appeared at every turn in the road. Some of these communist slogans were rudely inscribed on walls and stone fences, while others were well-worded placards appearing in no special place. Whatever their form, however, the slogans all delivered the same unpleasant message—"U.S., GO HOME"; "RIDGWAY, PORTEUR OF MICROBES"; "LA GUERRE APPORTERA LA CHOMAGE" (War will bring unemployment).

Thanks to the majority of the Frenchmen in St. Etienne the posters began to have a diminishing effect on my morale. The posters, I found, are not representative of France or of St. Etienne. However, this industrial city proper and the environs number an estimated 24 thousand people; this same area is populated with about 575 people who are not communists.

Facing "La Place de Waldeck Rousseau" in the heart of St. Etienne, there is a modern building which resembles one of the several traveling agencies in Denver. Tickets are sold in this building also. There is a difference, though, for behind the vituperative posters displayed in the window, there sits a man who directs the communist party in this region. He does not have a long tapering mustache, dark piercing eyes, nor a mysterious lurching gait. But inside his mind writhes in a peculiar sort of confusion. He has certain ideas concerning the U.S. and certain ideas concerning Russia. And no amount of logical discussion can change these ideas.

Here then are some of the ideas and ideals of a communist chief as he related them to me on July 3. His first tenet maintains that the United States wants a war with Russia and needs one to sustain the capitalistic system. It was in vain to try to explain that there is nothing worse that the U.S. would like to avoid than a war with Russia or any other nation. Asked whether the communists of France are for France or international communism as directed and propagated by Russia, he said the latter.

It is important to realize that the nucleus of the French communist party consists mostly of the peasant segment of the population. In this period so close to the end of WWII, the European standard of living still reflects the unhealed wounds of the past war. The richest French families would probably be classed by most American tourists as corresponding to our middle-class family. The peasant standard of living is basic. It is the aspiration of every peasant, bourgeois, and aristocrat, whether communist or not, that conditions will be bettered as this last war is put more and more in the past. Russia has taken advantage of the low living standards, seizing every opportunity to blame the U.S. for these conditions. And some people have been duped—unable to grasp the significance of suppressed thought that exists with the hardships behind the Iron Curtain. But I believe that as conditions improve, the communist movement in France will diminish. The communist leader did not say anything regarding the failure of the recent strike called to protest the arrival of General Ridgway. And I did not ask him to.

ARTICLE #3

It is not hard to believe that every French city, village, or hamlet is redolent, in one form or another, of some act which forms a part of the French historic drama. To think of Chartres, is to think of the famous cathedral it has sheltered against time and war. One cannot mention Rouen without recalling the heartwarming story of Joan of Arc. Then there is sentinel Paris who has watched some of her protégés rise to renown through an unforgettable work of genius and seen others die in despair because of failure or an unsuccessful love. And there are other cities and other heritages. They are all over France.

In St. Etienne there are the cobblestone streets flanked by tiled buildings on each side which seem to bend over to greet each other, so narrow are the passages. As one walks toward the outskirts, the town seems to cease lending its histrionic gesture to history. But there between the hill and the town lies the bread of this city. It is here, and in similar nearby areas, that the majority of the workers spend their day. It is a coalmine, dirty, filthy, and repugnant for the tourist. It is not here that the tourist thinks he will find French culture. But he is mistaken, for down in the mine there are men working—Frenchmen who are inheritors of a long tradition. We read chef-d'oeuvres of French literature and enjoy their paintings. But remember that the greatest heritage France has is that which each man carries with him—the desire to better himself and the will to work in order to accomplish this end—the same intangible that has made America. Yes, the mines date back to a time when the Romans were conquerors here and so does French culture.

If France is propelled by the same initiative that has created America, why is it that she is not as powerful as we? One reason is that she lacks the necessary raw material. After the last war, a certain American expert was sent over to study the mining methods and the quality of the coal. He hoped to be able to give some assistance. But he found that the reserves are so situated in the ground that the modern methods used by the U.S. could not be employed.

The coal beds of our Pennsylvanian mines lie in a plane parallel to the surface. Because the beds were discovered close to the surface, it has been possible to mine the upper part over a wide area and gradually work down. Not so in France. Here the beds lie pressed between hills into the shape of a bowl. These beds are separated by layers of hard rock which are also pressed into the shape of a bowl. This means that only a limited area can be mined before penetrating deeper into the interior where the beds assume an increasing concavity. To reach this coal it is necessary to construct two tunnels, one on each side of the bed, in the hard rock lining. One tunnel is used for bring in supplies and the other for transporting the coal to the surface. Explosives or powerful machines cannot be used, because the resulting force would cause the surrounding rock to cave in. The American expert was frank with his consultants. Our technology is developed for an entirely different type of mining. U.S. mines comparable to those of France are left unexploited.

ARTICLE #4

One of America's greatest pastimes and lucrative enterprise is the movie industry. It is a rare American who does not see at least one film a month. And for the majority, especially the youngsters, one film a week is not sufficient. We never tire of the grimaces of Bob Hope, the winning glances of Elizabeth Taylor, or the daring audacity of our cowboy stars. Sometimes an imported foreign picture is shown to add to the variety. An age limit is set on these latter ones and are considered by most adults as a delectable expose of low European morals.

A great many of us are frightened by the scandalous lives that some of the Hollywood actors are known to lead. Whether this anxiety arises more over the innate repulsiveness of the continued divorces or more over the fear of what other nations might think of us, is difficult to say. But to the average European, especially the Frenchman, neither of these motives plays heavily on his reaction to American films. His main objection is that our films are either too infantile or too complicated, never attaining a good medium.

They are complaining now that the "Westerners" are becoming hackneyed. Admittedly, there is a good portion of the American public who have the same gripe. But here in France, where people do not have the means to attend the movies frequently, it is even more disagreeable to have to see practically the same scenario time after time. If it is not a "Westerner," it is a comedy of the Red Skeleton type. On the other side of the fence are the extremely complicated stories.

It is not so much that Hollywood is so weighted with intellectual genius that it cannot reach the average man. Rather the problem is that the European mind functions completely different that that of an American. It is hard to comprehend why a

314

spectacular success in the States, is a miserable fiasco in France. To answer that completely one would have to be both a European and an American, which would be obviously very difficult. Some of my foreign friends have tried to explain this phenomenon. Though I find it impossible to grasp the full meaning of both sides of the question, they were successful in showing me how—not why—love as understood by the Latins differs from our interpretation of the word.

When one begins to define the love of a particular people the etymological brackets in Webster's New International Dictionary (Unabridged) offer no help. One tries to put down on paper what the inner emotions are. But he is incapable. Perhaps he is successful in poetically describing what love means to him, only to find that there is another person to dispute him. Nothing could be more disagreeable than subjecting myself to the volleys of such an argument by trying to define both the love of the Latins and the love of the Americans. What can be shown is the difference that exists in the courting procedures and the outward manifestation of love.

At home the courting period can run the gamut all the way from a month to ten years (God have mercy on the poor girl who has to wait that long). It is a time when the couple revels in dreams of story-book happiness after marriage, make lavish promises, and explain to their parents how all will be a bed of roses. The parents are meanwhile trying to explain that roses also have thorns.

In France, the marriage comes as a sort of business contract. The wife will rear the children and the husband will bring in a living. Any reasonably attractive woman would do as a wife. And any reasonably responsible man would do as a husband. There is very seldom a mésalliance, or a marriage below the social status attained by either party at the time of the union. Generally, the men are less jealous of their wives, though that does not means that a high moral standard is not required. Of course, there is courting a period. But the couple generally do not see too much of each other and when they do it is in the presence of an adult. However, my French brother tells me that women are more savage than in the States. That is the French impression of American women. But even that varies with the individual.

With the Italian movie-making industry making rapid peace-time advance, the American films are gradually being replaced by ones with a Latin flavor. The Italian films are not only suitable for assimilation by the French mind, but they are also of a high quality, both in skill and in taste.

French productions themselves are not of an excellent quality, because of the low weekly attendance that the cinema draws. German productions are rare and American productions are losing popularity. But for the visitor it is always refreshing to be able to attend a movie from home, even if it is a story of cowboy and Indians or a nonsensical Bob Hope comedy.

ARTICLE #5

On July 14th all France celebrated its "Independence Day" in just about the same way it is annually enacted at home on the 4th. The masses from the cities and towns thronged the highways from Paris to the Riviera. The banks of the Rhone, the Seine, the Loire, and other rivers and streams were filled to overflowing with a jubilant crowd of bathers, fishers, and picnickers. At night the throngs flocked to the city squares, where they sang the Marseillaise and reflected on the joys of the waning day as the fireworks illuminated the skies.

Bastille Day is not what I wish to tell you about but rather the day before or the day after—the ordinary day that the French family lives from day to day. It is always astounding for a foreigner to learn that the people in another country are very nearly the same people with which he was reared. He tries to find something that will distinguish the new country. For the citizen of a nation known for a distinctive race, physical characteristics offer a splendid means to tell a foreigner from a non-foreigner. But for the American, who comes from the melting pot of all nations, physical characteristics are only passingly important. Apropos to this, my observation has been that most Frenchmen are rather dark-complected, are a little shorter than the average American, and have blue or brown eyes which invariably have a peculiar romantic brilliancy.

For me the greatest discovery which has offered the means to distinguish between the Frenchman and the American, has been the way in which the former spends his day as a part of the family unit. The family is a highly organized unit around which centers all recreational, intellectual, and social activities. This has been made even more feasible in recent years by the large families, which have resulted from the family allowances introduced by the government to solve the previously decreasing birth rate.

In the evening it is very seldom that the whole family does not assemble on the terrace or in the living room to discuss the happenings of the day and other such interesting topics that present themselves. Occasionally, the mother will knit. Perhaps somebody will read a book. But the thing that requires of the spectator a keen admiration is the unity. All that is needed for recreation or diversion is there in the family. This is not to say, however, that the children are fettered by selfish parents who prevent them from doing things that might be individually more pleasing.

One factor that largely regulates the activities of the family are the eating habits. In the morning the "petit déjeuner" consists of a cup of coffee and a slice of bread with some comfiture. At noon they partake of the big repast or the "grand déjeuner." Each item is served in a series. First a vegetable is served, the meat, followed by another vegetable. For dessert, cheese is served followed by fruit, pudding or ice cream. The family then retires to the living room, where coffee is imbibed. By this time it is 2:00. Everybody has eaten well, talked continuously, and are now ready to commence working again.

It is during this period following the "grand déjeuner" that the individual hobbies and pastimes are pursued. The light evening meal is not until late in the evening at about 7:00, thus giving everybody an abundant amount of time by themselves or together. The evening is then spent ensemble until all retire about 10:30. It is an inspiring experience to be a member of this unity. There are many miles yet to travel for this young scholar, but wherever the "yellow brick road" takes me, this will forever be a memory that will live and brighten what lies before me.

Sincerely,

R. Leland Johnson

Edwards Brothers Malloy
Thorofare, NJ USA
September 11, 2013